COMPLE
Stories with Cattitude

COMPLETELY
CATS

Produced by
Beth Haslam and Zoe Marr
In support of International Cat Care

Table of Contents

Foreword

In praise of stories...

International Cat Care is a charity that works for all cats everywhere. Our mission is to ensure that all cats – owned or unowned – are treated with compassion and respect. We work towards this goal by providing the best available education, training and advice for vets, vet nurses, welfare specialists and owners to help them better understand the cats in their care.

The focus of our work is often on veterinary science and data, but we never forget the amazing power of stories to move audiences in a way that simple facts rarely manage. We aim to help millions of cats, but we realise that millions of cats are made up individuals – each with their own story. Some of those stories have been beautifully captured here in the Completely Cats anthology.

Completely Cats shows how stories can create change. Despite the authors' very different locations and lifestyles, each tale reveals a genuine love for cats and a desire to understand and help those in need. These are stories of real lives and real cats. They reflect a world that is not always kind, is often unthinking and sometimes cruel, but at the same time they shine a light on special people who care, and whose compassion can drive them to extraordinary lengths on behalf of an animal. These are tales that can change the way people think about cats – and that's why these stories matter so much.

Claire Bessant
Chief Executive
International Cat Care
icatcare.org

About International Cat Care

In 1958, deep in the south west of England, a group of determined women formed a new charity for cats. They named it the Feline Advisory Bureau (FAB) and they knew they faced an uphill struggle. Back then, cats were largely considered unworthy of veterinary treatment and there was little interest in discovering more about them. However, led by the formidable Jean Judd, FAB's stated aim was to advance feline veterinary medicine and raise the quality of care. Despite the odds, they succeeded and built an internationally respected organisation that is now working for all cats everywhere.

We are now called International Cat Care, reflecting our expanding ambitions for cats worldwide, but we continue to be inspired by the passion and determination of our founders.

Charley at Hughes Hall: a Cambridge College Cat Extraordinaire
By International Cat Care

There are cats who love just one person in the home and there are cats who belong to the whole family. Some cats are comfortable with absolutely anyone – and of course others want nothing to do with humans at all.

Then there's Charley. Charley is a special cat because he has taken the bold and unusual step of creating an almost ideal feline existence for himself at the centre of his very own community of admirers and carers. Charley is the College Cat at Cambridge University's Hughes Hall.

Hughes Hall is a college for mature students, undergraduates and post graduates at Cambridge University in the UK. It was originally founded in 1885 as a teacher training college for women (it's always been very much at the forefront of egalitarian education). Nowadays it welcomes graduates of both sexes from all over the world studying subjects from law to business – and is still a beacon for those studying education. The College motto *Disce ut Servias* (Learn in order to serve) reflects the strong social calling that characterises the student body, academics and staff. It's also rather appropriate in Charley's case – we'll return to that a bit later.

It's not at all unusual for Cambridge Colleges to have their own cats. It's a tradition that probably dates back to the University's establishment in the thirteenth century. Colleges and cats seem to have jogged along in a more or less mutually agreeable fashion since the beginning. Most have at least one and they are all rather proud of them – you only have to wander into one of the many tourist shops that line King's Parade to find them featured in gift books and on calendars. But

7

Charley, a sprightly 12-year-old Maine Coon with gorgeous markings and an extra fluffy tail, is in a category apart. What's notable about Charley's story is that, while elsewhere it is the College that adopts the cat, seemingly it was Charley who adopted Hughes Hall.

Lorraine, Hughes Hall's Senior Library Assistant, is a great animal lover who has rescued a number of cats. Very much part of Charley's support network, Lorraine has a strong interest in feline behaviour and, since her arrival at the college, has been a key follower of Charley's unusual tale which she recounts here.

By all accounts Charley's early life wasn't out of the ordinary. As a kitten, he and two siblings were brought into the home of a kind owner who still lives near the college. When the three were old enough to explore, they started venturing into the grounds and began making friends as cats tend to do. Happily, they found a receptive audience among the students, the academics and the staff and so the college became a favourite calling point on their daily rounds. Charley must have found all the attention very much to his liking. Or maybe there was sibling conflict that pushed him out of the family home. Whatever the reason, little by little, he started to move out of the owner's house and into the college to start a new kind of life.

And little by little the college responded to his more regular appearances. People who liked to pause to fuss him started to feed him as well. The college offices would make sure he was fed and watered when he did his daily rounds. When winter rolled around, Paul from the Maintenance Department built him a little shelter. A stock of food and a little brush is kept in the shelter so, when staff and students have a few minutes to spare, they can spend some quality time with Charley and make sure his beautiful coat is kept in top condition. Students also signed onto a rota to keep an eye on him during the holidays. He definitely had his paws under the table, so to speak, along with a well-trained team of willing carers. But he wasn't yet a college cat – more a visitor with privileges. It took a medical emergency to change all that.

The medical crisis may have been the consequence of an accident or a fight, the upshot was a nasty infection requiring immediate emergency treatment. Since it was urgent, the Academic Office and Housekeeper swung into action and whisked poor Charley straight to the local vet practice. With the help of staff and students, who looked after him whilst he had to be kept indoors and administered his medication, he made a full recovery. The college then took the unusual step of formally acknowledging and adopting him with the owner's permission.

Cambridge colleges like to do things properly, so at a following meeting of the College's Governing Body, Charley appeared as an item on the agenda. After a full discussion and with the blessing of the President, Hughes Hall now pays for his health insurance and takes responsibility for his welfare.

His status as College Cat confirmed, Charley returns the favour in a multitude of ways. His is a far more modern role than the traditional College mouser and he's comfortably embraced 21st century innovations. He features regularly on the College's social media (where his posts are overwhelmingly popular). He has his own Facebook page, and the number of likes he receives vastly exceed the number on other posts: https://www.facebook.com/charleycat/ He's a well-loved Hughes Hall mascot, the star of college videos, May Ball invites and Christmas cards. He's a regular topic of conversation at mealtimes in Hall and other college functions. The Development Office recognise his celebrity status and keep Hughes' alumni updated on Charley's activities.

Maine Coons in general are known for their sociability, and Charley is no exception. He adores people, has a lovely temperament and enjoys all the attention, and has apparently never lashed out despite being constantly cuddled and fondled by all and sundry. He's often to be found in students' rooms or the centre of attention at College events, apparently he gets a little depressed during the holidays when he has fewer admirers around. He's good-natured and naturally gravitates towards those inclined to like him, and doesn't trouble those who don't. Mercifully, he seems to steer clear of students with cat hair allergies, which is just as well because he really is very fluffy indeed.

Interestingly, he also plays an informal pastoral role with many of the students, demonstrating the positive power of the human-animal bond. Karin from the Academic Office, one of his many fans, has noticed that Charley has a big impact on the social fabric of the college community. She feels that Charley has a unique character, and is a relaxing presence in the College which helps lower the blood pressure for staff and students, particularly during stressful times. She also believes he brings out the nurturing qualities in people, and helps those dealing with anxiety and mental health issues. Some students, often very far from home, miss their family and their pets terribly. Charley fills a gap in their lives and helps them to settle in.

Karin reveals that those students who struggle to communicate or who face challenges with their interpersonal skills find an ally in Charley, and they are often the first to offer to look after him during the holidays. That college motto, *Disce ut Servias*, is exemplified with a beautiful circularity. Charley has worked out how to serve the people in his community and in response, they have learned how to serve him. It's rather a good arrangement.

Comments from the students and alumni illustrate how very loved and important he is to the college community.

"Charley was a great source of comfort and companionship whilst I studied at Hughes. Studying at Cambridge can be very stressful at times and when everyone is tucked up in their books, Charley was often tucked up on my bed as he'd come in through the open window and then later leave at his leisure. I'm sure the plentiful supply of cat food I kept in my room helped! He's such a great character and is one of the biggest cats (both in size and in character!) that I've met. I'm really pleased to see that his popularity with students has continued and it's great to see the college looking after him in his advancing years. I know he'll be sorely missed when he finally does pass on."

"Charley is more than just our feline friend, he is the quintessential fixture of Hughes Hall. While the ivy-covered buildings stand as edifices to the college's distinguished past, Charley stands as the soul of its present. For a decade, this stray has become a friend to hundreds of students who have turned to him during times of academic and emotional stress. To many of the international students, separated from kith and kin by thousands of miles, Charley truly makes Hughes Hall 'home'. There was no greater feeling than to return on a drizzling night from class and hear Charley's meow piercing the night's thick air. And a corresponding response, along with the jingle of "Temptations", would coerce Charley to emerge from the garden bushes, spend a few hours cuddling on our bed, and sharing his love. Our experience at Hughes Hall will always be tied to Charley, the eternal college mascot and our best friend."

News of Charley's charm and exploits have reached beyond the college. It seems there is even some cat envy going on. One student from Hong Kong approached the Domestic Bursar to request a transfer to Hughes from her current college just so that she could be closer to him. She still sends regular deliveries of a pallet-load of cat food, and fieldwork absences haven't diminished her affection.

"Despite his size, Charley has a gentle heart. One day he got chased away from a tree by magpies. They were very noisy and kept biting his tail. Instead of fighting back, he simply walked away. Moreover, he is kind enough to share his food with them. Isn't he adorable? I was introduced to Charley on my very first day in Cambridge, by a visiting scholar who knows I am a cat person. Charley was not afraid of me at all. He was enjoying a sunbath with his tummy exposed, with his legs leaned on mine relaxedly while I was stroking him. I loved him at first sight! He has been my motivation to work since then. Nearly every day after I met my writing target, I visited him with his favourite meat in gravy pouches. It was a 45-minute walk from my college. Due to fieldwork, I've been away from Cambridge for half a year. I miss him so badly and plan to move closer to Hughes Hall when I am back. Hope he still remembers me."

Of course, there are downsides of being a College Cat with a high profile like Charley's. Not everyone is a fan and it's not easy to keep a free-roaming feline totally safe from ill-intentioned individuals. However, he does have the benefit of a many pairs of watchful eyes looking out for him and the college grounds and buildings offer lots of escape routes. On the upside, the risk from traffic, one of the biggest dangers for cats, is greatly reduced on a site where most of the students use bicycles and cars entering the car park are not generally moving too fast.

On the whole, Charley seems to have life pretty much sorted. He is a fascinating example of a cat who has found a balance that gives him freedom and flexibility while meeting his fundamental needs for food, territory, safety and contact. It's an uncommon arrangement to be sure, but there can be little doubt that it works admirably for all concerned.

At the time of writing Charley is twelve years old and as time goes on, he will need more care and different arrangements to support him. However, his community of carers is making plans to ensure that his old age will be a comfortable and contented one. There will certainly be no shortage of offers to take him in if he ever decides to give up his college cat status.

About Charley

Charley's Facebook page: www.facebook.com/charleycat/
Hughes Hall, Cambridge website: http://www.hughes.cam.ac.uk/

Emilio's Story
by Margit Völtz

Translated from the original German

You humans are very strange creatures. One of you hit me with your car and left me alone, completely unconcerned that I was lying by the roadside. I screamed for help so loudly and called for my mum and dad all night; I knew they would be looking for me. Why couldn't I get up? Why was my head so painful? My broken teeth had cut my mouth and everything hurt. Why did nobody help me?

I lay there for a long time and became stiff and sleepy. I thought if I just laid my head down, my suffering would soon be over. I was tired and I didn't have much hope, my voice was almost gone. I heard a noise far away. Was it a voice? Dazed, I lifted my head and listened to the soothing sound – I felt sure everything would be all right. A woman took me in her arms and I worried I'd get her dirty as I was such a mess. Obviously, she didn't mind because she spoke very kindly to me, which made me feel a little better. I listened to the promises of help and I found them calming. I was handed over to some other people who immediately began to treat me. Before long I could hear my mum and dad! Why did they sound so strange? Were they crying? I could smell their scent and then they came in to see me. Now I knew everything would be fine.

***

Emilio was born on the 17th January 2010. We got him from an excellent breeder and we knew at the time he was blind in his left eye. It never seemed to bother him and we certainly didn't mind. Thursday

13

20th November 2011 began completely normally. I fed Emilio as usual, and there was no hint of the drama that was about to send our lives into a spin.

Emilio, my little food monster, played his favourite game of 'How quickly can I empty the food bowls before the other cats get a look in?' He always ate his food with gusto, so I was immediately nervous when he didn't appear for his lunch. He didn't even come when he was called, which was very unusual as he always got a special treat. When he hadn't come home by the evening, our special bond made me feel sure that something awful had happened. Fear bore into the pit of my stomach. We searched for Emilio all evening and didn't sleep a wink that night.

The next day we received a call from Tasso, the microchip database in Germany. Emilio had been taken to a vet who had read his microchip and contacted the database. They left a message for me and when I heard it, a knot formed in my stomach. My husband didn't ask any questions, he just said, "I'll get the car. Take your cell phone, you can make the call on the way."

I rang the vet and they made it clear our cat was very seriously injured. He had obviously been hit by a car and the prognosis was not at all good – I should prepare for the worst. I felt light-headed and began to cry. I was desperate to know what injuries he had. I saw horrendous images in my head of cats with broken and bloodied limbs and heard words like paralysis, no pain reflexes, dehydration and hypothermia. I could think of nothing else.

A few minutes later we arrived at the vet. We were immediately led into a treatment room, despite the waiting room being overcrowded, so I knew what a bad state he was in. There he lay, a small heap of misery. I thought, *"That doesn't look so bad, no crushed limbs, where's the blood?"*

I approached him slowly and spoke to him. "Hey, my boy, what's happened to you?"

He raised his head with difficulty and only then did I see the extent of his terrible injuries. His mouth was deformed, his fur torn under his chin, his teeth broken. Dr Hellmann, the vet, looked at Emilio with such compassion it spoke volumes about his injuries and chances of survival. Emilio's hind legs and his left foreleg seemed to be paralysed, so to test his pain reflexes his injured legs were gently poked with a needle and pinched with forceps. He didn't seem to feel a thing.

I heard a familiar voice and I felt a caressing hand touch me gently, I'd recognise that hand anywhere. Finally, I could rest. I tried to sleep but couldn't. I heard approaching steps – what was happening now? Why was I being carried away and why didn't my mum come too? My heart was beating so fast. I didn't want to be left alone, I was so afraid. The dark room didn't smell good. I heard a buzzing and clicking, which sounded a bit like when my humans took pictures at home.

Someone said, "So, Emilio, we're done, you can go back to your mistress."

I was so excited, I hoped I wasn't dribbling. There they were! Normally, I would run so fast to go to my owners, but somehow I couldn't. I tried so hard but I couldn't move my legs, but the main thing was I was back with my mum and dad. Even the sting from the strange, long thing in my arm didn't bother me anymore. My owners were very close by.

As I gently stroked Emilio, his breathing calmed down and he purred, although I knew cats often purred when they were in pain. We took a long time deciding what we should do, Emilio looked at me as if to say *I know you'll make the right decision.* Perhaps it was his confidence in me that made me listen to my gut feeling, although I still had some doubts that it was the right thing to do. However, my decision was made.

I looked at my husband who said, "If you go through with this, I'll support you."

I told the vet to go ahead with the treatment plan he outlined, which began immediately with X-rays, a drip and putting Emilio onto a heat bed.

The vet discussed the next stage of treatment with us. First, Emilio needed to be seen by a spinal specialist so the vet contacted Dr Sylvia Kinzel in Aachen. It was a Friday so there were no consultations available, but we could take Emilio to see her anyway.

When we arrived in Aachen, we immediately felt we were in good hands. I only knew how Emilio reacted to our usual vet, Dr Martina

Schullenberg, and I didn't think other vets could be as gentle as her. However, we were really impressed by how Dr Kinzel and Dr Alexander Schumacher spoke to Emilio, how they examined him and treated him as one would a wounded child. Dr Kinzel demonstrated her incredible expertise straightaway when a brief examination of both eyes prompted her to stop further investigation immediately. Emilio had heavy cranial brain trauma.

"Your cat needs total rest now, with absolutely no stress, in darkness and under constant supervision. Hopefully, he'll survive the weekend, but it doesn't look good at all," she said, as she gave Emilio some medication. After Dr Kinzel had ensured that medical care was in place for the weekend, she said goodbye to us with hope and good wishes.

When we left the vet, I didn't think about the future. I decided to take everything step by step and would take each day as it came. I was just so happy to have my beloved Emilio in my arms. At home, I wondered where I should put him so he was comfortable and always close to me but without disturbing other family members. The living room seemed to be the best solution. It was centrally located and the heart of the action so Emilio would always have social contact with his humans. Complete isolation wouldn't help him recover as he has always been the centre of the family. I decided it would be best for him to stay on our sofa as the cushions could easily be arranged to create a large surface for him to lie on. The backrests ensured Emilio was confined and stopped him falling off. One side was for Emilio and the other for me.

I covered Emilio's bed with a washable incontinence pad to protect it, and put a layer of towels on top; we were well prepared for our first night. He lay in his cat carrier and looked completely unimpressed at what I was doing, although he was clearly relieved to be home. I turned the lights out, carefully lifted him out of the carrier and put him on his bed. He found his bearings, gave his bed a sniff, and fell into a deep, hopefully restful sleep. Only the occasional twitch of his upper body showed he was fighting as he slept. He woke up frequently during the night whimpering softly, asking whether his human was still nearby. As soon as I laid my hand on his body, he seemed to calm down and fell asleep again. After a troubled night, during which I kept waking to check if he was still breathing, I was relieved to see dawn break. One night down meant a further step towards survival. Emilio woke up, but his numerous injuries made it hard for him to lift his head. He looked me in the eye and seemed to ask *how is this going to work out?*

My motto, especially in difficult situations, is: patience, peace and confidence are the foundation upon which the world was built. There were no alternatives, and giving up was out of the question.

Emilio had passed urine overnight, although unfortunately not where he should have. He obviously could not control his bladder, which was a point I needed to bring up with Dr Schullenberg at our next appointment. Emilio made it clear he was uncomfortable so I changed the towels and wondered whether he would manage to eat anything. It was worth trying to see if he could as he hadn't eaten since before the accident.

I opened a tin of his favourite food and mixed it with two tablespoons of water, as Emilio hadn't drunk anything either. He couldn't drink from his bowl because it was too painful for him so I put the food and water mixture on a flat plate. He raised his head a little and turned his upper body toward the delicious scent. After a short pause, his hunger must have been greater than his pain, and the only sound was a satisfied chomping and sipping. He ate his food quickly, which was understandable considering how hungry he must have been. After the last crumb had disappeared from his plate, he lay back exhausted and fell fast asleep.

At 12 pm we took Emilio to his next appointment with Dr Schullenberg. After a warm welcome, 'Schulli' carefully examined Emilio. She pulled out two of his broken teeth because they were cutting the lining of his mouth. After giving him some painkillers, we agreed she'd see him again in the evening. Emilio slept for the rest of the day, and our other cats made no sound at all. Even though they usually charge around noisily, it seemed as though they were floating above the floor.

The phrase 'the body heals whilst asleep' certainly applied to Emilio. When Schulli spoke affectionately to him that evening, he was already much more receptive. She examined him very, very gently, and spoke softly to him with a tender voice. She was worried about his bulging bladder. Emilio could not urinate when he needed to, as his bladder had ceased to function properly. It now merely served as an overflow. Urine collected in the bladder, which could only empty when it was too full. Dr Schullenberg carefully picked up Emilio and took him to the sink. She pressed his bladder with quick, experienced hands and showed me how to do it too. The sight of his urine gave me a shock – there was lots of blood. It was no longer yellow or transparent, but deep red. Seeing our worried faces, Dr Schulli was quick to reassure us.

After a road accident such as Emilio's, it was perfectly normal for blood to accumulate in the urine, muscles and body tissues. According to the X-ray, the bladder was intact, so at least we didn't have to worry about that, rather his lack of control over his bladder was the problem. Dr Schullenberg showed me again how to empty his bladder. She demonstrated it several times, but I couldn't get the hang of it. Emilio grumbled every time I tried, and I wasn't sure if that was in response to his pain or my clumsy attempts. In the end I had to admit I couldn't manage it, and the vet said she'd come up with a solution by tomorrow.

The next day she gave Emilio a local anaesthetic and inserted a catheter. Guiding my hand, she showed me how to feel for a full bladder (if I had to describe it, I would say it was like a tennis ball at the back of the abdomen). The catheter was opened, the bladder supported from below and pressure applied from above to empty it. His urine was still discoloured.

Emilio calmly lay on the bench, letting everything happen around him. The vet listened to his lungs, which didn't sound good. In addition to normal breathing sounds, you could hear crackling or rattling, triggered by detached secretions, or swelling, causing a risk of pneumonia.

To avoid serious illness, it was necessary to move Emilio regularly, so both lungs could be ventilated. Dr Schullenberg gave him an antibiotic, cortisone and a pain reliever to make his night as comfortable as possible. We also had to think about his digestive system as, although the intestine was full, he hadn't been able to pass faeces since the accident. The vet expected to solve the problem the next day and I was so relieved to have got through that first week, although his life-threatening brain injury was always on my mind.

Overnight, Emilio pulled the catheter out and looked at me with a very self-satisfied expression. Also, despite constantly washing his bed, he didn't smell good at all. Emilio looked completely deflated and obviously did not feel well. What a dilemma. On one hand, I didn't dare stress him by washing him, but on the other, he was clearly uncomfortable. The middle road seemed to be the best plan. With a warm, damp washcloth, I cleaned the affected areas as best I could. I made it as pleasant as possible for him and afterwards gave him a piece of liver sausage as a reward. As I'd already made an appointment with Dr Kinzel for that week, I hoped she'd help find a solution to this problem.

On Monday evening Dr Schulli made a home visit after her regular consultations. She brought an enema for Emilio and introduced the fluid into the intestine with a thin tube. Emilio was not very enthusiastic and told us how he felt about the procedure. Dr Schullenberg wasn't deterred however, and talked to Emilio soothingly. He didn't make another sound. Brave little guy!

There was also another problem in that he didn't want to drink. He'd take liquid mixed with his food, but it wasn't enough, so the vet administered another drip.

Emilio has always been a very special cat. We deliberately chose him because he had a disability. He is blind in one eye, and it doesn't look very nice, but it's never bothered us. Emilio has an incredible charisma and wrapped us around his paw the first time we met him – from then on, I only wanted him. He was, and is, special, and perhaps because of his disability, he has developed a different relationship with people and is full of acceptance and serenity, which was extremely helpful during his recovery.

Dr Schullenberg is an exceptional vet who is always optimistic, even if a patient has a life-threatening illness. She always has a smile on her lips and a joke at the right time for moral support, when other vets would have given up or kept their distance. Without her, we wouldn't have survived this difficult time, and that's why we gave this cute nickname. She remains our Dr Schulli.

On Tuesday, with a knot in my stomach, we went along to the specialist clinic. Dr Kinzel had arranged a joint appointment with the resident vet, Dr Neumann, who was also a physiotherapist. Emilio was very calm during the examination and seemed to be saying *get on with it already!*

With a hint of hope, Dr Kinzel explained that pain reflexes had started to return and there was clear progress since the last examination. Only the left forearm didn't seem be regaining sensation. Emilio kept his left paw permanently bent inwards and the vet couldn't move it at all. It was clear Emilio could feel his hind legs during the pain reflex examination but there was no way he could support himself with them. Paralysis of the hind legs would be awful, but the patient could still get around using their forelegs. However, if three legs were paralysed, recovery would be very difficult. After his examinations, Dr Kinzel thought Emilio's hind legs had a chance of recovery, however, the front leg was still in a very serious condition. Dr Neumann disagreed, seeing the hind legs as still very serious but the front leg as having some hope.

What should I do now? How could I do what was best for a living creature I loved and had responsibility for? Responsibility also meant letting go at the right moment. What would Emilio want? Would he have a life worth living if he was paralysed? He was used to roaming free and playing with our other cats. Would he be able to cope without his freedom? These questions hit me simultaneously and decisions needed to be made. I remembered Dr Schullenberg's saying: Cats are incredible, and they can cope with far more than it might seem, trust them!

Taking some time to make the right decision seemed to be the best solution. I had nothing to lose and if I made the wrong decision Emilio could lose his life.

We went into Dr Neumann's consulting room, where she created an individual treatment plan for Emilio. She wrote it down, and showed me how to carry out the exercises Emilio needed. She discussed my questions thoroughly, and ironed out any difficulties. After an hour of practise, I felt well informed and confident I could do the exercises alone at home.

Dr Neumann noticed how unhygienic Emilio's rear end had become, so she told me about Luna. Luna was an incontinent cat, paralysed for most of her life, and had coped well with her disability for many years. Her owner had done lots of research on incontinence in cats and had found a good solution, using babies' nappies, and she posted the research on the internet. Dr Neumann gave us instructions on how to put a nappy on a cat and explicitly stated that we must avoid a constant urine flow to prevent further illness.

We left the clinic and went to buy nappies and disposable pads. Would Emilio, such a dignified cat, allow us to put a nappy on him?

If I said the process went smoothly, I'd be lying and, looking back, I must ask myself who had more patience with whom. Emilio seemed to pick up on my nerves and my initial awkwardness. It took a while before I got the hang of putting the nappy on him, but gradually we refined our process and, after several attempts, also found the best size to fit Emilio's body. At first, I wrapped him onto his bed to avoid unnecessary movement and stress.

The other cats completely ignored him, and I wasn't sure if this was because they understood his life hung in the balance. I think they did because their behaviour changed over time, but more about that later. As the healing process began, our routine changed. We still needed pads, but I no longer had to wash the towels four times a day. Emilio had about one square metre of space for his bed, and became more alert every day. The wound on his chin healed well and was already scabbing over.

At night, Emilio was still very restless and sought body contact. Fearful of hurting him, I'd built a barrier between the sofa cushions, so he could see me and I could put my hand on his body, but it kept him from coming to me. One morning I noticed that Emilio had dragged himself up the cushions during the night and had put his paw on the barrier. Although it was obviously difficult for him, the important thing was he could move.

We'd now settled into our routine. We got up at 5 am, I picked up Emilio, took him to the kitchen, washed him with warm water and cat shampoo. After a while, he adjusted so well he knew the sound of the running water meant it was time to go to the toilet, although he still needed some help. I wrapped him in a dry towel and took him into the living room, as it was warmer there. Now for the next, and supposedly most difficult part – the blow dry. I wasn't sure if he'd cope with the unfamiliar sound and the warm air, but there was no alternative. Letting him dry naturally would have been completely irresponsible.

I sat on the living room floor with Emilio on my lap, and the hairdryer, brush and nappy next to me. I switched on the hairdryer at the lowest level and, to begin with, Emilio wasn't sure about the noise at all. His confidence grew slowly, and he obviously enjoyed the warm air, as I could see him relaxing. Using a soft brush, I began to work the fur on his legs, lightly brushing the reflex points of his knees, and I was delighted to see his reflexes were triggered. I brushed along his back all the way to the base of his tail, first with the fur, then against it, and then with the fur again. I also stimulated the soles of his feet with the brush. Finally, I dried his tail, but using a comb rather than the brush, because he had no feeling in his tail and couldn't lift it, so it needed to be treated differently.

Now dry, I put the nappy on him. As he was already lying on one side, I fed his tail through the hole I'd made in the nappy, so that the sticky tabs ended up on his back. I pulled his hind legs onto his belly and so I could easily attach the adhesive strips at the back, fitting snuggly around his hips. *Voilà*, Emilio could go back to his bed.

The other cats showed increasing interest in him over the course of the week. The more alert and attentive Emilio became, the closer the other furries came. Fox, our six-month-old kitten, was the first to go to Emilio. Just for a cuddle of course, Emilio's special food wasn't the reason at all! Fox is sitting next to me as I write this and assures me again this wasn't the case.

At the end of the week I had an experience I'll always remember. I woke up and felt I was being watched. I opened my eyes and who was staring at me, sitting next to me? Emilio!

I closed my eyes, I thought I must be dreaming. I opened them again, and Emilio still stared at me, proud of himself. I couldn't contain my tears as I saw his left foreleg was bearing weight. He was sitting on the side of his butt, his hind legs out to the side. I have never grabbed my camera so fast and I photographed the special moment. That was the turnaround. Emilio steadily became more and more mobile.

Our next appointment was with Dr Kinzel and Dr Neumann, and I was looking forward to it, although I was anxious about how they'd react. Emilio was examined still in his cat carrier, which has a removable lid, and the nappy was taken off. Dr Neumann was delighted that Emilio almost looked like a real cat again and not like the pitiful creature she'd seen before. He also smelled much better.

The most special moment came next. The vets were delighted to see Emilio's progress as he put weight on his left front paw. If you didn't know that this leg had been paralysed, you wouldn't have noticed anything different about it.

"So now we know Emilio has a life worth living, even without his two hind legs," Dr Neumann said.

Both physicians were astonished that Emilio had made such important progress after so short a time, and now we were able to increase the physical therapy. His muscles needed to be built up because he needed to put more weight on his front and upper body. With a new appointment made, we left the practice and set out on our way home. Emilio would show us in the next few weeks what he was able to do.

The next morning Emilio's routine changed. Since he was now able to move both forelegs, I laid him down on the living room floor after the morning wash. I had prepared a cosy corner for him without any barriers; he would be part of our normal, everyday life again. At the first sudden noise, Emilio dragged himself under the sofa as fast as he could. The unfamiliar situation overwhelmed him, and I think he immediately remembered the accident. It would take a lot of patience to help him recover mentally. I could cope with that.

At lunchtime, I put his food near the sofa, as I knew exactly what my boy liked. I didn't have to wait long. He stretched out his furry head from under the couch.

"Do you still trust me?" I said. "Now come, my boy, nothing's happened to you."

Emilio peered out from under the sofa and looked at me guiltily. He had lost his diaper and urinated on the floor under the sofa.

"It's OK, it happens," I whispered to him as I stroked him.

He answered with a soft coo and stuck his nose into his lunch. He just needed some time to be able to trust this bigger environment. After a few days, Emilio could slide through the whole apartment on his backside and I swear my other fur-babies laughed as he did so. They were totally fascinated by him – a creature that looked like a cat, smelled like a cat, but had something on his butt and couldn't run. Emilio could slide by himself into the kitchen and eat with the other cats.

It was amazing how fast Emilio slid through the apartment. In fact, sometimes he was faster sliding on his bum than his four-legged friends could run. His upper body became visibly more muscular, and I began to place him on his hind legs more frequently. Mealtimes were useful for this as he was concentrating on his food and he didn't seem to know what I was doing with his hind legs. To start with he couldn't support himself at all and quickly fell on his backside, but soon he was able to support himself for a few seconds. Seconds turned into minutes – he was gaining his independence.

Emilio had forgotten how to walk naturally, especially as he'd had so little feeling in his rear end for so long, so I used a towel to help him remember. I put it under his stomach so his legs protruded at each end, and lifted him into the air. His hind legs now had no weight to carry so I could easily move them for him, although Emilio didn't understand what I expected of him. So, I put the towel down again and, with both hands, lifted his body and exerted a light forward pressure.

Now he'd got it! Awkwardly, he stumbled forward. He only managed a few metres before he was exhausted, but it was certainly progress and I knew he understood what I was trying to achieve. He worked hard and his expression told me he found it strange to feel his paws on the cold ground again. Working with the towel helped him remember natural movements, and before long he could move his hind legs independently. I took a video of the first time Emilio sat at his bowl, lifted his body all by himself, and stayed in that position for a few minutes. This cat was, and is, incredible. He had such strength to overcome his injuries.

Over the following days, Emilio showed us what he was made of. He overcame his pain and used his hind legs more and more. He walked with a very unsteady gait, but it was so beautiful to see, especially given his initial prognosis.

Emilio was brave, and as he became more mobile and increased his strength, I wondered if the time had come to remove the nappy. My cat trusted me, and now it was my turn to trust him. I put two litter trays in the living room, one near his bed and one near the scratching post. We added ramps to the litter trays to make access easier for him. The next few days were a bit like toilet training a toddler. During the day, Emilio didn't wear a nappy but he did during the night. Accidents happened every now and then, but he was making progress and the puddles became fewer every day.

My brave fur-baby showed me he didn't think he needed a nappy any more, as one morning I saw he'd removed it overnight. Wasn't he clever? I thought, *"What's the worst that can happen? Let's try it, and if it doesn't work out, he'll just need a little more time."* Ever since that evening, my beloved Emilio has not worn a nappy, sometimes you have to trust your four-legged friends. Emilio was once again a strong, independent part of the family.

Our other cats' reaction to Emilio is a topic in itself. We have seven other cats and it was noticeable that they gave him peace and quiet when it was appropriate and encouraged him to play when he might otherwise have become depressed. Has anyone ever thought that animals communicate with each other and know exactly, intuitively, what a group member needs?

One of our cats, Abby, reacted differently to Emilio as soon as he was no longer wearing the nappy, as if she wanted to say, "You look like a real cat again, now I'll treat you like one too!" From then on, she would carry in live food for Emilio, and the other cats. Emilio looked almost embarrassed the first time Abby dropped a mouse at his feet, as if he wanted to say, "What am I supposed to do with that? My teeth are destroyed!"

I can reveal that the mouse survived, completely soaked with saliva, but alive. Due to his broken teeth, Emilio is no longer able to do his job – mousing. He can drown the creatures with his saliva, but he can no longer bite them.

It was also Abby who encouraged Emilio to go out through the cat flap. When I saw where Emilio was I wasn't sure what to do. But what was likely to happen? He couldn't jump and the garden was fenced in. Emilio wasn't concerned about his limitations at all, and that's how it should be.

We left 2011 behind us; it had been an emotional and stressful year. For 2012, we set goals we knew were achievable based on the experiences and successes of the past year. Now it was time for Emilio to amaze the vets at the special clinic. They had only heard about his incredible improvements, now they would see for themselves. When Dr Kinzel entered the treatment room, I couldn't keep the news to myself.

"Guess what? Emilio can run on his own and has been managing without a nappy," I exclaimed.

Dr Kinzel was incredulous at such an enormous improvement within a short period of time.

I asked permission to film the examination and got my camera ready. When Dr Neumann entered the treatment room, Emilio showed what a small (or rather big!) miracle he'd accomplished.

Both doctors were amazed by his progress. They tested his pain reflexes, which were triggered quickly; his nerve endings had completely regenerated. They examined his left foreleg and there was no trace of the former paralysis.

Emilio could pull himself to the edge of the treatment table with both forelegs. His hind legs were still a little impaired, but that didn't prevent him from hobbling around the examination room. He made the vets speechless: a paralysed cat learned to walk again within three months, after a very serious car accident. His thoracic vertebra was still broken but it didn't seem to disturb him, he learned to walk with an altered gait. Dr Kinzel thought Emilio might be fully recovered within a few weeks.

Emilio received an anabolic injection at the beginning of February as his muscle development had slowed right down, and he will need more injections in the future. Today, Emilio almost acts as if nothing happened. He regularly goes out to the garden and does his business there. His behaviour has changed in that he is very attached to us and always wants body contact. He begs like a dog at the table because he knows I always give him a treat. He is no longer as easy going as he used to be and he wants to run away if he hears a sudden noise. His physical injuries are almost healed, but his mental trauma still needs some time. With lots of patience, Emilio will get there.

In memory of:
My mother 12.07.2001
My father 06.07.2011
Kira, my 13-year-old dog 05.11.2011

About the Author

Margit Völtz, Germany
Facebook: https://www.facebook.com/Emilio-701064913369715/

Brian's Story
By Emma Milne – BBC 'Vets in Practice'

"He's *not* the Messiah. He's a very naughty boy!" *Monty Python's 'Life of Brian'*

Since I qualified I've had five cats; two temporary, three permanent. They've all been waifs and strays with missing limbs or missing hair or missing brains! Gathering forlorn-looking, slightly damaged animals is as much an occupational hazard for vets as visiting brothels seems to be for premiership footballers who are married to beautiful, successful women. All my cats have had something about them that has made them who they are: something that has defined them as individuals. Charlie had his beautiful colour, his missing back leg and his incessant and sometimes *very* annoying yowling. If Nigel was a posh new hybrid he would be would be a Labrasloth. His combination of appetite and laziness has, over the years, strangely caused his head to shrink (admittedly this is an unforgivable way of saying that he is ever so slightly overweight) but it is Brian who takes the biscuit for quirkiness.

I know you're not allowed favourites but Brian is mine. He paddles in the water bowl before having a drink (I have no idea why), he likes to go for a walk with the dogs and has steadfastly tried to badger our dog Badger to be friends with him (Badger barely manages to tolerate his bread-making and winding around him and occasionally gently puts Brian's whole head in his mouth as warning that he's had enough) and recently, with the arrival of a mini human into a long standing animal-only household, Brian has been the only one to fully embrace this newest addition and attach himself to her side while she batters, pokes and 'tickles' him with all the finesse of a sledge-hammer.

When Brian was about a year old, my then-partner, Joe, and I moved from Exmoor to Cheltenham. We both fancied a change of scenery and I'd found what looked like a great job with a better salary and a much better rota than where I had been. The fact that the man who owned the practice was the devil incarnate is neither here nor there and is probably a story best left for a book about terrible decisions I've made over the years! We moved into a rented bungalow, imaginatively called 'The Bungalow' in a fairly upmarket part of town near the surgery. It had a slightly odd location in that it sat in a kind of open space which formed access to the rear of some lovely regency houses but didn't really have any obvious neighbours. We'd really struggled to find somewhere to rent that allowed animals and were very grateful when we found this lovely place. We'd even been allowed to put a cat flap in the back door.

Joe was working part time and so he was often home when I got in from work. One evening I arrived back and wandered into the kitchen to get the obligatory post-work glass of wine. On the kitchen floor was a very beautifully-made glove puppet of the children's character Sooty. I could hear Joe was in the bath and I called out, "Where did the Sooty puppet come from?" assuming a client had given it to us for the dogs or Joe had picked it up at the pet shop for them.

After a couple of seconds' delay he murmured from deep in a surf magazine, "What puppet?" with all the interest of the dead.

I shrugged to myself and thought nothing more of it, although in hindsight, you'd wonder why I didn't question more strongly how it came to be in the house. Maybe another day working in my living hell had sapped my ability or desire to ponder such things!

The next day when I went into the kitchen there was a plush, expensive-looking owl puppet laid tenderly on the kitchen floor. Now my interest was piqued. I leaned against the worktop and stared inquisitively at the latest arrival. Where had they come from? Was Joe turning into a weird kleptomaniac or breaking into houses in some somnabulatory trance? I picked up the toy and put it next to Sooty on the worktop. Things got very surreal on the third day when I found Sweep. Going to the kitchen was starting to be like Christmas. I couldn't wait to see what had arrived overnight. I'd just picked Sweep up and was pondering doing my own puppet show when I heard the distinctive clatter of the cat flap. I instinctively turned at the noise and that was when all became clear. Brian was halfway through the flap

28

with a brilliant sock puppet, the type my mum used to make when we were kids when even she had to admit the life of one of our socks had come to an end.

Brian saw me the minute he got his head through with his special prize. He froze instantly, one foot in and one foot out and stared intently at a spot in his middle distance. I had subconsciously frozen too and so there we were, locked in a bizarre Mexican standoff. It was evident that Brian believed that if he stayed completely still I couldn't possibly see him. The fact that he is bright ginger, quite large and was dragging a bright blue sock with gaudy yellow eyes stitched onto it seemed to have escaped him. After what seemed like an eternity, but was actually about two seconds, he obviously got bored, realised it was a fair cop and hauled the rest of the sock into the kitchen, dumped it unceremoniously on the floor and sauntered off as if it was the most natural thing in the world for one of the planet's most finely honed hunters to bring toys made out of underwear proudly home.

The next few days brought two more puppets and a large pair of blue, men's slippers. The most impressive thing about the latter was that he had obviously had to make two trips to make sure he brought the pair. By now we were in a bit of a quandary. Somewhere nearby a small child was almost certainly being beaten not only for losing so many lovely toys but for lying about it too. But we had the fear. We'd left it too long. How could we own up that our cat was a cat-burglar? What if the owners of the toys wanted us to get rid of him or make monetary reparations for the awful slippers? Added to which we had no real neighbours so how far afield and in what direction should we go? I confess, after all these years, that we never tried to find out. If, about fifteen years ago, you were about six and living near The Park in Cheltenham and you've been horribly mentally scarred by the gradual disappearance of your favourite toys and your dad's slippers, I apologise unreservedly. It wasn't me, it was the cat!

So it was that eventually the time came that, having survived living together in rented accommodation, Joe and I decided it was time to get ourselves on the property ladder. Not long after we started looking we were extremely lucky to have an offer accepted on a gorgeous end terrace house with lots of stripped floorboards and a beautiful big stone fireplace to keep the pyromaniac in me happy. I think we've always been really lucky with how our animals have coped with moving house and adapted, and they didn't let us down this time either. Our happy little band seemed to be content as long as we were all together and it didn't seem to matter where that was. We had virtually no furniture but our first night in the new house was full of excitement and the fact that we had to sleep on a futon mattress on the floor just made it all the more romantic somehow.

We gradually started to accumulate things to sleep on and sit on and did bits and pieces of DIY to put our stamp on the place. We'd been there about a month when the next pair of slippers arrived. I was pretty used to getting up to find a multitude of elastic bands in the house, kindly and lovingly brought home by Brian, the catcher of all things inanimate. It had taken me a while to figure out why he found so many, but then I realised that they were discarded by postmen once they'd unwrapped bundles of banded mail. Not very environmentally friendly if you ask me but luckily I had a cat who was on the case of tidying up the planet single-pawedly. Elastic bands and a few half-desiccated frogs were all we'd had since the puppet fiasco of the previous year so I wasn't expecting to see the slippers and almost did Brian the injustice of thinking he'd got sloppy and only brought one. The one I'd seen was in the kitchen near the cat flap. This time it was another large man's slipper but not furry, this one was your classic Marks and Spencer quilted tartan. Brian was sitting nearby, lazily inspecting one of his paws and glanced up at me with a smug and self-satisfied look on his face as I gingerly picked up the slipper by as small a corner as I could to avoid some unknown contamination from a stranger's foot. I was about to mockingly berate Brian for losing his edge and not bringing a pair when I noticed the other one just outside the cat flap in the garden. Maybe he was just catching his breath from the effort of heaving them into the house.

Our newish neighbours were a lovely couple who we'd got to know as well as any neighbours do through odd pleasantries exchanged over the fence. The man of the house certainly seemed like the type who might own this type of slipper so I made an effort to look out for him later that day. I finally spotted him in the garden and put on my best apologetic face and took Brian's hard-won bounty with me outside.

'Hello, how are you?' I asked by way of warming him up.

'Fine thanks.' The obligatory polite answer.

'Erm, I don't suppose you've recently lost a pair of slippers have you? I'm afraid our cat, Brian, might have stolen them from your house.'

'No I haven't but when we got up this morning our budgie cage was tipped over on its side.' Uh oh.

Thankfully the bird was fine but it made up my mind once and for all that I would never investigate where Brian was going on his late night foraging trips. It seemed he might be doing more than just stealing toys and foot wear. But his exploits didn't end there. He teamed up with Badger for one spectacular assault, possibly to get me back for throwing his new hard-won slippers away.

The house we'd moved into was in an area of Cheltenham which was near a warren of small roads of little terraced houses. Joe's surfing friend, Pete, lived a few hundred yards away through a maze of interconnecting, quiet streets. By this time we'd got into a neat routine of walking the dogs round our block last thing at night before bed and the intrepid Brian loved to come too. He was half stealth cat and half wannabe dog. We'd set off on our walks and sure enough about thirty seconds after we left we'd hear the cat flap bang at the back of the house and then out of the shadows we'd start to catch glimpses of the ghostly shape of Brian. He'd catch us up and spend some of his time adoringly trying to be just like his god, Badger. For some reason he would never break into a canter, possibly through some cat pride issues or because the dogs always trotted and he wanted to be a dog so he would trot too. The problem for him was that the dogs are leggy collie crosses so in order to keep up he would have to do a ridiculous super-trot that looked like a sped up film clip and made us laugh every single time we saw him. He always held his tail ramrod straight, pointing straight up with an inch-long section at the tip flicking this way and that as he steadfastly super-trotted right along the kerb stones, hardly ever on the pavement or on the road. At random intervals he would veer towards Badger, give him a chirpy meow and try to stay glued to his side if he could. Badger would carry on oblivious to the attention and Brian would keep trying until some unseen or imagined danger made him dart into the shadows of a parked car only to reappear ahead of us after a short cut. This was all fine and very humorous until we wanted to walk to our friend's house one night for a few drinks.

We didn't even think about Brian as we set off to Pete's one evening. But as we heard the distinctive clatter of the cat flap we looked at each other and groaned to see Brian skipping along to catch us up. We thought he'd realise we were going somewhere new and get scared and go home so we just ignored him and waited for him to scarper. But he just kept coming. I don't know if he just got so far and then was too scared to go back by himself or whether he just fancied a night out with his boys but we got to Pete's door and Brian waited patiently while we knocked.

We thought he'd get bored and go if we went in without him so that's what we did. After about five minutes of very uncharacteristic mewing we opened the door and he trotted in. He was distinctly uncomfortable in his new surroundings and was clearly torn between being a petrified cat in new surroundings and a dedicated follower of Badger. Eventually I couldn't bear his uneasiness anymore and said I'd walk the boys and him home and try to come back without him. I got to the house and opened the front door and we all trooped in. I waited for Brian to disappear into the depths of the house and then I ushered the confused dogs back out of the front door, slammed it shut and legged it before Brian could get out the flap and round the house. It isn't really normal, evening behaviour for twenty-somethings to run like a headless chicken and the immediate effect was to make the dogs think this was a bloody brilliant game. They started leaping and barking and trying to nip me as I sprinted down the street. This was, at best, a bit annoying but then Badger decided to try and have a go at it from the front. In so doing what actually happened was that he just got in front of my legs and stopped dead, broadside to me. I'm by no means fleet of foot but going from full tilt to zero miles an hour with a thigh high dog being the cause of the stop resulted in me being spectacularly catapulted about three metres through the air and landing like a schoolchild in the playground, palms and knees down, scuffing through the gravel on the pavement.

Not being a pliable schoolchild and not having actually fallen over for well over a decade I crashed to the ground, with my dignity as shredded as my hands. I jumped up, cursed Badger as lividly but quietly as I could in case anyone was watching, pretended my hands didn't hurt like mad with a stinging sensation I'd not experienced since primary school, looked round to see if anyone had seen me and tried to walk off as if nothing had happened. Bloody animals!

After the initial stealing, everything went quiet for a while. Years later I moved to York to be with my new partner. One day the window cleaners came to the door for their payment and asked if we had cats. I said yes and he said, "because there's a big dead hamster in the garden". I smiled condescendingly at him and said I'd be sure to check into it. He had to be mistaken. How stupid I thought to myself. He doesn't even know the difference between a hamster and a field mouse. I went into the garden and spied with horror the huge, black hamster dead on the lawn. It was at that point we decided that yes, silence is golden.

Extract taken from *Tales from the Tail End* by Emma Milne.
Copyright © Emma Milne, 2012.
Published by arrangement with Summersdale Publishers Ltd.

About the Author

Emma Milne BVSc MRCVS, UK
Website: www.emmathevet.co.uk
Facebook: Facebook.com/emmamilnevet
Twitter: @emmamilnethevet
I'm a vet, author and animal welfare enthusiast. This story about our brilliant cat, Brian, comes from my second book, *Tales from the Tail End*. Brian was a great character, loved our dog, Badger, with a passion that few men know, and is greatly missed. Enjoy.

Mitten the Minder
By Val Poore

Given that shaggy dog stories are more my stock-in-trade than mangy mog anecdotes, it's wonderful to be given the opportunity to tell the tale of Mitten the Minder, the cat-who-thought-she-was-a-dog, thereby creating yet another shaggy dog story in feline form. I would like therefore to profusely thank the editors of this collection in advance for indulging me in my natural tendency to, shall we say, ramble on a bit, because ramble I do, complete with a plethora of hyperbole, not to mention a generous smattering of totally unnecessary but colourful adverbs. I should mention before I start that absence and time have refined (and some might say embellished) this story, but they have not detracted from my fondness of the moggy in question as she really was a one-off. And in fact, the story is totally true. Really. But let me not digress any further.

It all started when I moved from the UK to a remote mountain farm in South Africa.

By spring of our first year, which was September 1982, we felt as if we belonged there. We had already experienced the hottest days of summer in January and February, the magnificence of a Natal Midlands autumn in May, and the parched dryness of winter in July and August. In addition, we had survived the sometimes nerve-shattering drama of African weather changes from violent electrical storms to crippling drought, neither of which we had ever experienced in Europe. There were days when we were shrouded in cloud at the top of our mountain, enduring soaking drizzle. Then again, there were the weeks of blistering heat with searing blue skies and endless horizons.

I loved it. I had never been happier. England, with its economic hardships made indescribably wretched by cold miserable winters, seemed like another lifetime – a distant memory. Even better, we had found truly wonderful surrogate grandparents for our young children in our landlords, who were very dear friends to us older 'children' as well. We also had the best near neighbour we could wish for in Gwen, who had been our mentor and guide since we first moved in.

Gwen had been a staunch stalwart from the first. I called on her repeatedly during the early days, and her advice was invaluable, especially when interacting with the local Zulus, as she spoke their language fluently and understood their customs and habits in a way that was both sympathetic and realistic. She showed me many useful skills as well, ranging from how to use the farm phone – a wonderfully archaic wind-up affair – to how to remove the menace of blood sucking ticks from the skin with a red-hot match tip or cigarette butt.

Generally speaking, Gwen stood no nonsense and was immensely practical. In contrast, though, she operated at a deeply intuitive level, her knowledge of what we now term alternative remedies was extensive, and she had an awareness of plant and bird life that seemed almost mystical to me. I was intrigued, influenced, charmed and drawn to this slim, almost boyish looking grandmother who seemed to breathe the life of Africa.

The cottage Gwen shared with her husband, Edward, formerly belonged to our landlords, and was a pretty, white-painted chalet that perched on the side of the mountain where it sloped down to meet the road. They had a gorgeous garden filled with bougainvillea, plumbago and climbing geraniums. It also had a lusciously green lawn, but because of its steep angle, its only apparent use was for the children (both her offspring and mine) to roll down it in interminable tumbling games – a pastime which seemed to carry an obligation to scream and giggle hysterically, all of which Gwen took in her cool, collected stride.

She adored all young things, which was of course reciprocated enthusiastically, and my daughters, Jojo and Mo, loved the afternoons we spent at the cottage. 'Gork', as her grandchildren called her, always had interesting things to look at and play with, and seemed to have a limitless fund of patience to tell stories about her precious collections. There were shells and stones, as well as African bead work and little models, and everything had its own story. With a child on each knee, Gwen told fables of Zulu legend and myth that had my two usually hyperactive infants both enthralled and blissfully quiet for hours at a time.

To add to their delight, especially Mo's, Gwen also had a cat. Our landlords had three large dogs, Danny, Suzie and Brutus; all delightful animals, very friendly and good natured. But when you are very small yourself, cats are relatively more interesting in terms of cuddle value. Result: Mo was obsessed by Gwen's motley-coloured moggy, a female of great character and apparently prolific breeding, for during the first weeks of each spring, she produced a large crop of healthy kittens providing Gwen with the perennial problem of what to do with them.

Following the first birthing of our residence, I was aware that hints were being dropped with the subtlety of a ten-ton cannon ball, but I remained determinedly obtuse and blithely ignored Gwen's loaded remarks about my daughter's affection for her feline nursery. I told her firmly and repeatedly that I didn't want to be saddled with any pets until Mo herself was less dependent on me.

During the first spring, this ploy succeeded, despite several assaults on my emotional fortitude. I suppose this was because at that stage, Mo was too young to be vocal about it, and as a result, unable to practise her manipulative skills on either Gwen or me. However, in the second spring, my defence system failed me. Gwen's cat again produced her regulation litter of kittens and naturally, we were called upon to pay our respects to mum and babies alike.

Granted, they were adorable. There were six of them, and they were mostly all tabby, with the exception of one that was tortoiseshell and white. They looked like six little wriggling sausages lined up in a neat row as they suckled their proudly purring mother, and I found that even my stubborn determination was vulnerable, although I adamantly refused to admit it – even to myself.

For Mo, it was love at first sight. Now she had found her voice, she pestered me tirelessly and cajoled me unremittingly, but I was not to be moved. What I didn't know, however, was that she was simultaneously working on Gwen, convincing her with all the wiles available to a scheming two-year-old that we needed a cat of our own, and that it was something I really wanted, even when I said I didn't. I might have guessed that resistance was pointless, but I suppose I was reluctant to acknowledge that I could be over-ruled by a daughter who had only recently learnt to speak. Such an admission wouldn't really bode well for my future role as a guiding influence in her life, so it was safer for my self-esteem to pretend otherwise.

Given the odds that were stacked against me, though, I shouldn't have been as surprised as I was one morning when Gwen's husband, Edward, appeared at my door carrying a tiny tortoiseshell and white handful of fluff with a bunch of claws at each corner. This diminutive creature was yelling with loud indignation from what seemed to be to be disproportionately strong lungs. Handing the resentful bundle into the suspiciously ready arms of my youngest child, Edward guilelessly informed me that he had brought me my kitten.

It took me a moment to realise he wasn't joking and was not going to be taking this bundle of fur-coated flick-knives home. I was utterly speechless. It appeared to be a fait accompli. Or a brilliant stroke of genius. How could I now be so rude as to blatantly repudiate what clearly seemed to him to be a pre-arranged delivery? I couldn't of course, and I was left with not just the kitten, but the uncomfortable realisation I had been trounced in the first of many battles of will with my little Mo.

Gwen was conspicuous by her absence on this occasion, and I was more than ever convinced that she was fully aware of my ideas on the matter. She knew perfectly well I didn't want another addition to my household. What's more, I couldn't help feeling that it was a well-planned manoeuvre on her part to send an ignorant envoy in her place. Her husband's innocence was my undoing, but as it turned out, Gwen was right in the end.

The kitten quickly endeared herself to us all, and in place of the exotic African name she arrived with, soon answered to the simple call of Mitten. The girls were only too happy to take care of her and their diligence at house training the poor animal was comical. Never has a cat been shown the garden more frequently and with such enthusiastic instruction to do its duty than that tiny, bewildered creature.

Over the weeks following her arrival, and about once an hour during the day, I got used to seeing one or other small person dashing through the kitchen with Mitten clutched unceremoniously under an arm or stretched out in front like the blunt end of a battering ram. The next moment, there followed a peremptory command of "wee, Mitten, wee!", with much disgusted sighing and tutting if the poor thing failed to perform. Nonetheless, the rigorous training was a success. Mitten was probably the cleanest, most reliable cat I have ever had, and would have passed muster with the strictest sergeant major.

I should add here that she was even more prolific than her mother and within the next two years, she produced five litters of kittens, falling pregnant on each occasion within six weeks of her previous confinement. The strange thing was that I never saw a candidate for her affections in the area, and none of our immediate neighbours owned up to having a Tom. All the same, she must have been shamefully promiscuous to have found so many suitors, because her litters were marked by their variety and she hardly ever had two babies the same.

Most of our neighbours accepted that cats had unwanted kittens, and were unsentimental about disposing of them by drowning immediately after birth. We were too lily-livered for this, and couldn't bring ourselves to such a level of detachment. We loved cats too much. So, like Gwen, we resorted to fair means and foul to secure homes for our furry burdens. To both my amusement and guilt, I found myself practising flagrant acts of emotional blackmail not only on the children's friends, but also on my own, or their house staff, or anyone I could persuade into giving a home to one of my poor 'orphans'. I am both ashamed and proud to say that it worked without fail. Who says you can't teach old dogs new tricks? Or cats, for that matter.

Eventually, though, I did manage to have her spayed before she could 'grow' a new crop of babies, but after that, I think she felt deprived of her maternal role and as a result, adapted her mothering skills to a different and grander purpose. Mitten decided to take control of the dogs and become their minder. It became a daily and hilarious sight to witness the way she bossed them around. When we arrived home, there would now be four greeters at the gate: Danny, Suzie, Brutus and, of course, Mitten, who would mostly be leading the pack. There she would stand, tail vertical and ramrod straight, barring the curled over tip that made it look like a question mark. The three dogs would be bouncing around behind her, barking furiously but not daring to step in front of Mitten the Minder.

She also made it her business to decide who slept where and if she had a fancy for one of the dogs' baskets, she would get in, stretch out and make herself very comfortable, leaving the poor mutt concerned looking balefully at us as if to say: 'Can't you do something?' Large and boisterous the dogs might have been, but they were no match for

Mitten, whose flick-knife claws were kept well sharpened. She was most definitely The Boss.

However, the most memorable of her exploits was the day she saved us all from The Snake.

In South Africa, there are real snakes. They are big, bad and villainously venomous. The worst are tree snakes and if you get bitten by one of those, you might well be looking at the curtains drawing inexorably closed on your life. Mitten was terrifyingly brave when it came to snakes. I would usually be in the kitchen in the morning when she brought her latest catch in to present to me. For some reason, she seemed to think I needed to view her booty before tucking into it. Perhaps she was trying to tell me something about her diet, but when it involved reptiles of any kind, I simply could not get the message. Luckily, the snakes would mostly be headless when she carted them in, tails still twitching, but even so, she was very miffed and clearly didn't understand when, wielding a mop like a crazed jouster, I chased her back into the garden with her 'gifts'. But my squawks of horror had nothing on her disgruntled hissing at my ingratitude, and she would slink off growling with the snake still squirming in her jaws. However, there was one day when I was inordinately grateful that she was so fearless when it came to creatures of a serpentine nature.

During the winter, I found South Africa, or more specifically Kwazulu Natal, beautiful both scenically and climatically. The nights could be freezing, but the days were nearly always sunny, cloudless and warm. It was nothing for the temperature to range between zero and twenty-five degrees during a twenty-four-hour period. Nevertheless, the houses were poorly insulated and heating was minimal, which always struck me as odd because it really was bitterly cold at night for a good three months of the year. There was no such thing as central heating, and we only had a wood fire in the evenings. As a result, the house became like an ice box overnight. It also took until well into the afternoon to warm up inside before the temperature plummeted again in the evening. This meant that on most days, my small daughters and I used to go for a walk along the sunny open sand roads to catch some warmth. What I didn't know early in my life there was that snakes like to do the same thing. In fact, as time went on, I realised it is quite common in winter to encounter large snakes curled up in the middle of the road enjoying the warmth of the sandy surface, but no one thought to tell me this at first. Well, you wouldn't, would you? Not if it's normal, that is.

On one particular day, which must have been during our third or fourth winter because I know Mitten was fully grown, I took the girls for our customary walk along the road. There was very little traffic along this side of the hill and the road itself was dry with deep sandy ruts.

All three dogs were bouncing along snuffling in the grassy verges, and Mitten was trotting beside us with her tail straight up in full alert mode. I, on the other hand, was in dream mode. I was gazing up at the trees and pointing things out to the girls, waxing poetic and lyrical about the light, the sun, the shape of the branches; in fact, anything that was above us, not on the ground where I should have been looking. Luckily, one of my offspring wasn't listening because I was rudely woken from my dream state by an ear-splitting scream. At the same moment, I felt my arms being yanked back out of their sockets.

"Maaaaaaam!!"

I froze in mid-step. Which was just as well.

Looking down, I watched in fascination as my foot hovered above the biggest, most monstrous of pythons. I'd like to say the biggest I'd ever seen, but the truth is I'd never seen one before at all, not like this; in person and in front of me. By this time, both infants were cowering behind me, which was also just as well. The snake raised its head and regarded my foot with a chilling glare.

I now had something of a problem. If I just moved my leg, the snake might well strike out at me. I'd been told they do not have very good sight and follow movement. But if I jumped back, I'd fall over the girls and we might all get bitten. The dogs were completely useless; they were still snuffling about in the verges oblivious to their pack leader's dilemma. But then the other pack leader, the real one, saved the day. Mitten drew herself up till she was twice her normal height, doubled herself in size with a flick of some invisible switch, snapped her claws for good measure and sprang, hissing like an out of control steam engine.

I don't know which of us was more surprised: the snake or me. I could at least see what was happening but the poor snake probably thought it was being attacked by a swarm of angry bees. Mitten's claws couldn't inflict much damage to its skin, but the sheer number of her extended weaponry might cause severe and stinging discomfort. The

41

snake clearly decided that discretion was the better part of valour, and maybe even that this spot was a less than ideal sunbed. Anyway, to my immense relief, it started slithering rapidly away into the undergrowth, followed by a still growling, hissing, spitting Mitten. Only after it had disappeared out of sight did she stop, shake her paws off, lick her chest and weave her way back to us, her upright but waving tail expressing all her satisfaction at a successful mission accomplished. The dogs remained oblivious.

At the time of this episode, Mitten would have been around two years old. She went on to live until she was fifteen during which time she became the absolute matriarch of our household and trained several more dogs to accept her leadership. I have a sneaking suspicion she actually thought she was a dog as she certainly preferred their company to those of our other cats, and in later life, shared the dogs' beds with them. But Mitten the Minder showed her mettle from day one. I absolutely adored her and soon forgave Gwen for landing her on us. Our wonderful neighbour had a way of knowing things, so maybe she sensed that Mitten was the kitten I had to have – whether I wanted it or not.

About the Author

Val Poore, South Africa
Website: https://vallypee.blogspot.nl/
Twitter: https://twitter.com/vallypee

The first half of this story was adapted from my memoir, *African Ways*, a collection of memories about my life on an African Farm. By day, I'm an Academic and Business Writing lecturer, living in the Netherlands. Writing has been both my work and hobby since the early 1980s when at twenty something, I moved from the UK to South Africa, where I lived until 2001. I loved Africa and its people dearly, and it was this affection that inspired me to write *African Ways*.

44

Brutus
By Beth Haslam

It seems like a lifetime ago, but actually, it wasn't. This story tells the tale of how my husband, Jack, and I came to share our lives with a feral cat.

One evening during the renovations of our tumbledown country property in France, we were sitting outside on an old section of broken wall. Worn out after another session of floorboard sanding, we chatted about the latest construction disasters we'd encountered that day. I was in mid-sentence when our post-mortem was interrupted by a strange sound coming from the nearby bushes. We both stared intently, but couldn't see a thing. Then we heard what seemed like a meow. We peered again – nothing. It sounded like a cat, but with no neighbours for miles around, we assumed we were imagining things. The problem was we couldn't be sure.

That evening, as an experiment, and much to our dogs' disgust, we left some of their food outside in a dish. I rushed out the next day and was excited to find there wasn't a scrap left. Jack told me it had probably been eaten by a fox, or other wild animal, and not to fuss too much. He may have been right, but I still had a hunch we had a cat somewhere nearby. Each evening we banished the dogs to a safe distance and began a very pleasant beer-drinking-on-a-boulder vigil. Our patience eventually paid off.

About a week passed before we spotted her – a small face peeking timidly through the undergrowth. No wonder we hadn't seen her before, her tortoiseshell markings blended perfectly with the foliage. Sitting absolutely still, we watched and talked to her, hoping she'd have the confidence to venture out. It took a number of days, but when she

45

finally emerged we were treated to the sight of a beautiful, petite cat who was obviously stuffed full of kittens.

Over the following week or so her confidence grew. She'd creep closer and closer each time, purring tensely as she approached. We were eventually allowed to stroke her whiskers, the sides of her face and body, but never her ears – these were her radars, always pricked and alert for the sounds of danger. Amazingly, despite appearing to be completely wild, she was incredibly mild-mannered and trusting. After a while, she even let me brush her. This was evidently a blissful new experience which caused her to purr ecstatically like an outboard motor. The little cat had no collar and there was no explanation for her appearance, so we concluded she must be a feral who lived in our woods. If she was going to stay around I decided that she needed a name. Sadly lacking in inspiration, we ended up calling the poor animal Pusskins.

A couple of weeks later her evening routine changed and she became even more furtive than usual. Showing a massively distended belly, Pusskins roamed restlessly around the barns, mewing anxiously. We assumed she was ready to give birth and needed somewhere safe and dry to have her kittens. Then, quite suddenly, she disappeared. I was utterly distraught and hunted high and low, worrying she might be in distress but it was no good, there was no sign of her anywhere. At this stage I had all but given up hope. Jack, once again, told me not to fuss. She was a feral cat, he said, and therefore likely to be tough and resourceful. He was probably right but it didn't stop me from being terribly worried.

Some days later I was passing the tractor shed and was distracted by a scuffling sound coming from behind one of the old crates. I stared vainly into the gloom. At first all I could see were dusty pieces of old farm equipment, but then there was a movement. I looked harder and a smile gradually crept across my face. Gazing dreamily back at me was our little feral cat surrounded by several balls of fur. Pusskins had given birth. At that stage I had no idea how many there were, but I could certainly see tabbies, a ginger, and a cream coloured kitten. I couldn't believe my eyes. They were absolutely gorgeous. I rushed back to the house to break the news to Jack. He came back out with me and we carefully uncovered the full litter, confirming the arrival of six new kittens into our home.

Now we had a difficult decision to make. One of the projects we had started was raising pheasants and partridges to re-populate our woods. At the time, we had around 300 chicks in brooder sheds close by. Our worry was that with several hungry mouths to feed, our new mum would be very likely to use these fledglings to teach her youngsters some early hunting skills. This would be perfectly natural behaviour but definitely unwelcome.

Unsure of what we should do we asked our French vet for advice. Doctor Arnaud told us there was a serious feral cat problem in the area. Interbreeding and disease were rife amongst the feline colonies, and we should do everything we could to prevent them contributing to the already burgeoning population. The writing was on the wall – have the litter put down, or take them in. Decision made – we took mum and her kittens in.

It was a great idea in theory but not so simple in practice. First things first, we had to catch the kittens. This was very tricky because they were brilliant at skittering behind and under the machinery, and then squishing themselves into the tiniest spaces imaginable. Luckily, Jack had been a pretty nifty cricketer in his day so he had the job of fielding the most slippery fugitives. After much clambering around, cussing and falling over oily bits of machines, we finally managed it. We took them into the house and made a nest out of an old puppy bed, and put them in a large dog cage for safety.

Our next worry was how we would feed them. Fortunately this was where Pusskins came into her own. Her terror of entering a building was overcome by the instinctive need to feed her young, so mealtimes quickly became a team activity. Once our dogs had been removed, she would pluck up courage, creep stealthily into the house, and pop into the cage to nurse her hungry mob. We'd close the cage door to give her complete privacy, and she'd lie there until the job was done. She would become restive until we re-opened the door, which allowed her to speed back to the freedom of her outdoor domain. She repeated this twice a day, but it wasn't enough.

As we all know, kittens need several feeds a day so, under instruction from our vet, we supplemented her efforts by bottle feeding. This, by the way, is not an easy task because kittens are very wriggly little suckers! Jack was elected as midwife because his safe cricketing hands were large enough to hold each one securely whilst administering the bottle. He was a natural.

Four weeks later, and our next task needed to be performed. We'd been told that cats were ready to mate very soon after giving birth so, if we were going to save Pusskins from a life of constant pregnancies, we had to act. We hated to put her through the trauma of being trapped but there was no option. We waited until she had completed a feeding session then unceremoniously bundled her into a cat box and took her to the vet to be sterilised. It was the least we could do to help maintain her health.

It must have been a terrifying ordeal for her, but she coped fantastically well during the pre-op examination and after, and never growled or fought once. Meanwhile, we continued to bottle feed the kittens and gradually introduced them to solid food.

Pusskins made a perfect recovery from her surgery, and after about six weeks of constant feeding she instinctively seemed to know her job was done. She took less and less interest in her kittens and, eventually, she rarely ventured into the house, preferring to dine al fresco. So, there we were – six fluffy beauties who ate, played and generally caused havoc. Well nearly. There was one who was different from the others. Although it was very big, it was always much more reserved, and very nervous of us humans. I was instantly drawn to this timid creature.

Much as I wanted to, there was no doubt about it, we couldn't keep the whole litter. But I'd been brought up with lots of cats so I was desperate to keep at least one. Jack agreed, so we decided to invite animal-loving friends of ours to come round and see if they could give homes to the others. This was a great arrangement, although I would later realise how hard it was to see our kits being examined by prospective new families. I was under strict instructions to let them choose whichever kitten they wanted, which was agony because I always knew which one I wanted to keep.

Prior to the first visit we had tried to establish what sex they were. Most of our friends said they wanted to have females so, after consulting the internet for technical information on the subject, we unceremoniously turned each kitten bottom-up to try and work out their gender. Fairly sure of our findings, we named them because it was easier for identification purposes when we were picking each out for feeding sessions. Unfortunately for the little critters, I'd been reading a Roman history thriller at the time so they mostly got saddled with names almost as awful as Pusskins.

We wanted to do everything properly for the kittens, so we arranged for them to be picked up by their new families after their first vaccination. Our trip to the vet to have this done also involved a confirmation of each animal's gender. As it turned out we weren't world-class experts in the cat-sexing department, so some rapid re-naming had to be done. Caesar became Cleo, Maximus became Maxine, but Ginger remained Ginger although she was a girl. Then there were three boys. Hercule, so named because he was incredibly nosy, Tigger who was on springs and completely hyperactive, and finally the huge, but terribly timid, Brutus.

Our first groups of friends came to examine and coo at the kittens. After much playing and cuddling the girls were selected, but the boys were left. I was terrified that Brutus would be next, but I needn't have worried. Hercule was big and bold and Tigger was the litter comic so they stole the show. But Brutus hung back, resisting all attempts at being handled – he was rejected. Everyone decided that he was the true feral, and would never make a house pet so left him to hide in a corner. How wrong they were.

One day I returned from a dog walk in the woods; it had been a hot day so I'd left the doors wide open to let some air into the house. As I walked in I was idly thanking my lucky stars that Brutus had not been chosen when I noticed what looked like a ball of fur sitting on one of the kitchen chairs at the far end of the room. I stared in horror. *Oh no*, I thought, *I must have left the cage door open, the kittens could be anywhere by now!*

I quickly looked over to check the cage, but happily it was closed with six snoozy kittens inside. That was a relief! Still not sure what it was on the chair, I put the dogs in the utility room and cautiously approached the furry bundle.

To my surprise, I found it was Pusskins. This was strange, we thought she had returned to her wild habitat. I was just trying to work out what had caused her to be brave enough to come into the house when I spotted her left eye. It was closed, horribly swollen and seeping thick pus. It looked so dreadful that I wondered if she had lost the eye – it was too inflamed to tell. The poor cat was hunched up, bedraggled and had lost lots of weight. Stoically, she allowed me to gently manipulate the rest of her body for signs of other injuries, but there was nothing obvious. I was just finishing when Jack appeared.

"Oh my God!" he uttered under his breath. "What on earth's happened to Pusskins? She's in a terrible mess."

"I know, I've no idea, I just found her like this when I got back from my dog walk."

We decided to try and bathe the eyelid with a saltwater solution. Thankfully she let us handle her, but gently cleaning up the affected area with cotton wool pads made no useful difference at all. Fresh pus immediately oozed out of the tightly closed eye, matting her fur as it coagulated on the side of her face. It was no good, we had to get her to the vet.

I made an appointment for that afternoon. Jack collected the cat box and we spent a few minutes working out the best way to place her in without harming her eye even more. After all, the last trip she'd taken in it had resulted in a very stressful experience, so we naturally imagined that she'd associate the carrier with the vets and put up a fight. Not a bit of it.

I gingerly wrapped my arms around her skinny body and slid her into the box. I couldn't believe how easy she was to manage – she didn't resist at all.

We still had lots of jobs to be done that day so Jack stayed back while I took her. On her last trip to the vet, Pusskins had mewed softly all the way, but this time it was different. There wasn't a peep out of her. I was beginning to worry that she might be critically ill, that she might have internal injuries of some kind in addition to the eye problem. I'd soon find out.

Fortunately, it was our usual vet, Doctor Arnaud, on duty. I explained the situation, and reminded him that since she was a feral cat and unused to being handled, he might want to use gloves. I'd seen the ligament damage done by a domestic cat to another vet so I felt it was the responsible thing to do. To his credit, Doctor Arnaud said he'd prefer not to because he didn't want to be rough.

I gingerly drew our panting little bundle out of the box and placed her onto the examination table. She immediately pushed into my tummy, shying away from the bright lights of the surgery and trembling violently.

Doctor Arnaud made an initial appraisal, sucked in his breath and said, "*Alors*. Extremely painful this is for her, *bien sûr*. I think I know it now. Not just an infection by itself, I am sure in the eye she has a *corps foreign*." (That would be his version of a foreign body).

He explained he needed to treat it immediately. If it was left too long the eye could become damaged and she was liable to lose the sight in it. He would try to remove it using a local anaesthetic, but if this didn't work she would have to have another general anaesthetic. I couldn't possibly imagine how she could cope with the vet poking around in her eye while she was conscious, but agreed it was better to make the examination and try to sort it out as soon as possible. Doctor Arnaud called in a veterinary nurse and we got to work.

I held Pusskins firmly against me while the nurse held her head. At no point so far had she tried to escape or fight us, but she continued to tremble terribly, her open eye filled with fear and pain.

Doctor Arnaud prised open the damaged eyelid and applied a solution. Still no battling, still no claws – Pusskins was rigid against me. To my horror, he produced a blunt ended pair of forceps.

"Surely you're not going to use those on her eye?" I whispered tensely.

"Don't worry, they are especially designed for this. There will no pain be, *pas du tout*," he replied.

The peeled-back, swollen eyelid immediately revealed the cause of her suffering. Even I knew what it was. The sharp end of a large ear of corn was embedded in the bottom part of her lower eyelid and the upper lid had closed over the top of it. Pusskins must have been in agony.

"Oh *no*, how terrible!" I gasped under my breath.

"*Oui*," the vet replied, "this, it will have been very, very painful."

Using a different instrument, Doctor Arnaud deftly removed the foreign body. Pusskins winced, but remained steady as a rock. He held it up for me to see. To all intents and purposes, it looked like a half centimetre long spike. I was dismayed at the thought of how she had suffered. Doctor Arnaud explained that it was common at this time of year for dogs and cats to get seeds and other particles stuck in their eyes, and prompt action was always required to avoid the animal suffering permanent damage to their sight. He added that he thought it had become lodged perhaps two or three days earlier. If it had stayed in the eye for much longer, he'd added, it would have been a very different matter.

The vet thoroughly cleaned the affected area and gave Pusskins an antibiotic shot to protect her from infection. He also supplied me with eye drops to administer for the next three days. That was easier said than done and would mean incarcerating her in the house again. There was nothing for it though, she needed the treatment.

Pusskins slipped silently back into her cat box, still looking battered and bruised, but undoubtedly without the searing pain that must have plagued her for so many hours.

I was preparing to leave the clinic when Doctor Arnaud said, "She is a cat very gentle. *Pas du tout* seeming like a cat from the wild."

"Yes, I know, she has a lovely, kind temperament. I still can't believe she came to the house like that though."

"Oh, I think I know why," he replied, smiling. "She came to you for help."

We kept Pusskins in a Labrador-sized dog cage for the next two days, duly applying her eye drops as prescribed. By the beginning of day three her eye was wide open and looked perfectly healthy, but she was becoming increasingly fractious and nervous in her cage. So much so that we decided it was better for her general welfare to release her. We gave her one more meal and managed to apply one last splodge of lotion as she wriggled and squiggled but never scratched. We then opened the cage door and without even a glance in the direction of the kittens she pelted out of the house to the safety of the woods. Our brave Pusskins was back where she belonged.

By the time they were 10 weeks old, all the kittens had gone apart from Brutus. Pusskins had reverted to her ghost-like character and now even spurned some of our suppers. But I was happy. She was content in her own habitat, and we still had our beloved Brutus.

A richly-coloured tabby, to my eyes he was an extraordinarily beautiful boy, filled with feline grace and poise. As the months passed he gained more confidence in himself and us, and purred like mad when stroked and cuddled.

However, whilst he was loving and tactile with my husband and I, his expression would turn to one of pure terror if someone else came into the house. He was the same with machines, the very sound of which would cause him to run for cover underneath our bed.

Today, seven years later, Brutus is exactly the same. He has grown into a fine, big cat who is the gentlest animal we have ever had the privilege to share our lives with. His exquisite face and gentle, sensitive, temperament closely resemble that of his mum, as does his natural nervousness. But with us he plays and wrestles and snuggles, and does all those things his siblings did – but only with us. We adore our feral cat.

About the Author

Beth Haslam, France
Website: www.bethhaslam.com
Facebook:
https://www.facebook.com/profile.php?id=100005130648927
Twitter: @fatdogsfrance
Blog: http://bethhaslam.blogspot.fr/
Instagram: fatdogsandfrenchestates

I'm crazy about animals and have been for as long as I can remember. My husband and I moved to rural France a few years ago. It was an incredible adventure and still is. Nowadays, I juggle my time between writing about our epic experiences in my Fat Dogs and French Estates series, and nurturing our ever-growing menagerie of animals. Zoe Marr and I share a deep love for cats. We decided to use our combined skills to help cats in need and through this Completely Cats was born.

Orion and Cassiopeia
By Rohvannyn Shaw

It all started with a crab enchilada.

I was visiting my parents in Eastern Washington at the time. I was a college student but getting close to finishing. We were in sage country, near the town of Moses Lake. My mom and I went on a walk one sunny afternoon in a wilderness area. It was a beautiful day. The red-winged blackbirds were warbling in the cattails surrounding a little stream. We'd eaten at a restaurant before the walk, celebrating my birthday, and I still had a crab enchilada, packed in Styrofoam, in the back of her car.

We came back from our walk, and at first everything seemed normal. Somehow, I sensed we weren't alone. Then I saw something furry and black in the back of the car, apparently trying to get into the take-out container. It turned out to be a long leggedy, black kitten. His big, golden eyes blinked at me as I tried to figure out where he'd come from. He had no collar, and he was half-grown and obviously hungry. With no idea where he came from, the only thing we could do was take him back to town, both of us secretly hoping the animal shelter was closed. It was, since it was a Saturday.

We couldn't bear to leave this bright-eyed little guy at the shelter anyway. My mom bought litter, a carrier, and food for him; she's always a soft touch when it comes to cats. He ended up traveling back over the mountains with me although it was summer time so I didn't have a permanent dwelling. I was temporarily living in a house near Sorority Row, but I had the basement to myself so I kept him secretly for a few days. He made a small, ebony ball in the blankets of my pallet on the floor. I was terrified he'd be discovered.

55

A friend of mine agreed to board him, since he had an apartment in a city about eighty miles to the south. When summer was over, I moved in with my friend and his other two cats. Before long my furry little spider had climbed into my heart. He had a funny, serious meow that sounded like 'raaaa'. I had a hard time naming him. There were too many good options and I still wasn't sure if he was a boy or not. The strange thing was, we bonded from the start. No matter how many times I had to be away from him, he always knew he was mine and I was his.

Eventually, after we figured out he was a male, and around the time he was fixed, he earned a name. We called him Orion, because of his black coat with few white hairs sprinkled through, and his hunting ability. Although, I usually called him Rat because of the way his voice sounded and the fact that he liked to chew cardboard. He didn't seem to mind, he'd just smile at me with his slightly overlong fangs.

He was a funny boy. He used to sneak up on me and tap me on the shoulder to startle me, accompanied by a 'brrt' that sounded suspiciously like 'boo'. He also learned to give hugs and he'd walk on a leash. Once, my mom visited me and we took him on a trail walk together. He made it nearly a mile before asking to be carried. When it was a little more possible to do, Orion liked car rides too. When I went to work, he always knew when I was going to come home. My friend told me that Orion would be looking in the correct direction. If I was east of the mountains, for example, he'd be looking for me in the east.

Orion behaved as if he'd always be safe if I was near. When I took him to the vet for the first time, he lay in my arms, calm and quiet, and I could give him to the vet tech without any fuss. He was always like that for me, even with the dreaded vet. Once I took him to PetSmart, and he walked on his leash, or rode in my arms, all through the store. He didn't freak out. He had to be one of the most mellow cats I've ever known, though he could be stubborn with other people.

Time passed, and circumstance forced us to live apart. I had to move out of my friend's place with very little notice, and I hadn't even been looking at apartments. With the help of a good friend, I took my things and looked for a place to stay. Since I was taking flying lessons at the time, the owner of the aircraft rental place agreed to let me stay there. It was a weight off my mind, but what to do with Orion? I couldn't even think of giving him up.

At the time, I was working in home health care and I was lucky enough to be able to board Orion with an understanding client, who already had a cat. I didn't have any other options and I fervently hoped he wouldn't run way. Oddly, he stayed where I told him – I came back every day and he was always there, ready for me to feed him and pet him. He always trusted I'd come back.

Eventually I bought a little house in a nearby town and we were reunited. It was so good to be with him again. He seemed happy too, and he loved having new windows to lie beside. My partner moved in with me too, and Orion befriended her also. Sometimes, after they became close, he'd worm his way under her arm as she slept on the couch.

Orion was my Halloween kitty, my miniature panther, enforcer to the other cats who sometimes lived there, and my 'little husband' because he'd tell me when to go to bed every night, then escort me up the stairs. I'd wake up in the morning with him stretched out next to me, his head on my pillow, golden eyes looking into mine. He was very good at nudging me in my sleep so I'd move to the edge of the queen-sized mattress, leaving him, a little ball of black fur, in the very middle.

He learned to jump into my arms on command. Then he'd hug me by wrapping his paws around my neck. He'd also lie in my arms, utterly limp, and let me do anything with him. I could play with his toes and he'd always just smile at me. My partner would marvel at how boneless Orion could be.

Everything changed for the better one warm summer evening. I was sitting in the living room with my partner. She'd just returned from a trip and we were enjoying our reunion. Our conversation stopped when we heard a distinctive sound, a kitten crying piteously.

I'm not sure who was faster to go outside, myself or my partner. We tracked down the high-pitched meows. Out there in the dark was a tiny kitten, yowling pitifully, calling to us for help but obstinately not letting us near. We tried for quite some time to capture her but she retreated every time we got close, at the same time calling to us. All we could see was a little ball of fluff. Loud fluff. The yowling continued. Eventually we had to give up but she stayed near, mewing all night under my partner's window.

First thing next morning, I went out and looked for her. Eventually I found the kitten hiding under our overgrown jungle of tea roses. She was way in the back, protected from paws or hands. I went off and

57

found the garden loppers and worked my way in, snipping branches until I freed her. She was skinny and her fur was matted and thin. Later we found deep bite marks on her that looked like they had come from a cat. What fur she had was long, and she had patches of black and orange on a white base. Quite honestly, she was rather homely at that time, with a funny mark on her mouth that looked like half a moustache. Still, her big greenish yellow eyes looked into mine, and she quieted her squeaking when I held her.

There was something wrong with her back leg. Later we realized it was broken, and she was having trouble walking. It would be a long time before she could walk well or jump. There was only one thing to be done. I took the box the TV had just come in, put bedding and a water dish in the bottom, and waited for my partner to get home so I could go buy kitten chow. I was reminded of when I'd found Orion years ago. I was instinctively responding to need and a cat's request for help.

We figured out this flea-infested little waif had left her mother and litter-mates, or possibly been driven away by a neighborhood tom. The place where she'd come from was a crack house, and we knew her mother was also neglected, but had recently birthed a litter. Our kitten, for she'd certainly chosen us to be her family, had left her brothers and sisters and crossed two yards with mean dogs in them, all to reach the one house in the neighborhood that might help her. It was as if she knew she'd be safe in our territory, if nowhere else. She'd been right. We marvelled at her bravery.

As our foundling grew stronger, we held her and carried her practically around the clock until she could maintain her own body temperature. One of us would get home from work, take the kitten and hold her while we gave the one who'd been at home a welcome break. We rid her of the fleas, fed her soft food and kitten chow, cared for her leg till it healed. We named her Cassiopeia, though we usually called her Mouse because of the improbable squeaks she made.

Orion didn't accept her at first. It was odd because I was used to him being fairly gentle. He hissed at her when she was on HIS petting station, and was jealous of her time with me. I showed him he was still loved, and petted him every time I petted Cassiopeia. No matter how much he hissed, he never really harmed her. Gradually he warmed, beginning to like her, even love her, and they were friends within two weeks.

Once again, I was impressed by Orion's character. I'd always been told that male cats wouldn't tolerate a foreign kitten in their territory, much less raise them, but my boy had always been different. He might have been tough but he had a gentle soul. After the first week or so, he helped raise her as if she was his own kitten. He washed her fur, looked out for her, slept curled up in the sun, right beside her. He taught her everything he knew, even some of his tussling skills. Even so, she never would be a fighter.

Cassiopeia grew up, becoming a beautiful long-haired calico girl with lime-gold eyes and an incredibly photogenic face. She wasn't homely at all anymore, and was instead one of the most beautiful cats I've ever known. Her coat grew thick and luxurious, her tail long and plumy. She revealed she was a curly-tailed cat – she often held her tail in a spiral to avoid brushing it against things. She would reach out and touch things with it, and sometimes flick it against people as a greeting.

Eventually we adopted another cat, this one we named Parker for his short grey fur, which looked like it was parker-ized. He was another one who adopted us, asking my partner for a place to stay. He was well mannered, yet somewhat timid. Cassiopeia tolerated him. Orion mentored him. This involved training in household rules and the occasional swat when he needed it. I found it a little odd because Parker was an unaltered male, but Orion knew who was truly master of the house, and his lack of fuzzy pompoms meant nothing. He still had muscles of steel when he needed them, and he beat Parker at wrestling every time.

Once, Orion caught Parker sitting in a window he wasn't supposed to be in. With a single smooth motion, he grabbed Parker with his paws and threw him bodily out of the window seat. It was the most amazing display of kitty-judo I've ever seen. Even though he became a little enforcer, Orion was still gentle when he needed to be. I often saw him washing Parker, gently tussling with him, or sleeping with him in a ball.

Life was good between the three cats. They cuddled and played, often washing each other and had 'licking wars' where the winner would have the privilege of washing the loser's neck. They loved thundering up and down the stairs, chasing each other. They sounded like a herd of elephants when they were upstairs!

One day, though, our cats had cause to worry. Parker had come to us with worms, so they all needed to be treated. My partner and I both anticipated trouble. Orion would probably deal with it fine, but Parker and Cassiopeia were growler-yowlers when it came to pills. Yet, the pills needed to be administered no matter what, so we came up with a plan. We'd use a towel and a syringe of water so that ever-popular pill would go down. First, we tried it the nice way, holding the cats on our laps and talking to them gently, explaining why we needed to give them the odious pill, and telling them they wouldn't be hurt. Parker was first, and he didn't listen at all. Instead he tried to scratch us. With no choice left, out came the Towel of Doom. Now he really acted like he was being murdered.

As Parker was struggling and yowling, I saw Orion come up behind him. I was surprised by what Orion did next. Instead of sympathy, he delivered a hearty whack to Parker's towel-wrapped rear end! It was as if he was saying *calm down, you idiot!* We pilled Parker, and then wrapped Cassiopeia up. She started howling and doing the same things Parker had. Orion gave her a whack too, but not as hard.

Now it was Orion's turn for the pill. I looked at him, standing there, not running away or hiding.

I asked him, "Are you going to take your pill like a good boy?"

He still didn't run, so I took him onto my lap and gave him his pill with a minimum of fuss, without even the need for a syringe of water. No scratching, no biting, not even one yowl. He still trusted me. I petted him and told him he was a good boy.

We had several good years together. When we discovered Lolcats and the Cheeseburger Network (amusing websites featuring animals) we decided that Orion must really be Basement Cat. He didn't seem to disagree, but only gave us the Evil Kitty stare that he'd perfected, as if to prove our point.

Things went well for a while as I worked tech support. We liked being solid members of our small town's community, in a place where the chamber of commerce shared space with the power company office and a flower shop, and even the postmistress knew us by name.

Eventually hard times came. My job was outsourced to India after I'd had the privilege of training my replacements, and I was suddenly without work in a bad economy. Armed with two weeks' pay as my severance package, I went looking for another job. That took a while, and for a time I couldn't make my mortgage payments. It left a financial hole my replacement job, and my partner's job, couldn't fill.

Eventually, we were forced to sell the house, and we re-homed Parker. He was the nervous type and wouldn't do well on the road. A friend had promised to let us work on her ranch in Nevada, so that looked like the best prospect. We put some things in storage and left home with a futon and a collapsible greenhouse strapped to the roof of my Elantra, along with clothes, supplies, and many pounds of beans and rice. Both cats rode along too. We let them out for walks and such during the trip and eventually made it to Nevada.

Unfortunately, the ranch deal fell through. We looked for work and a place to live, but there was nothing to find. Time went by and we were still stuck, living in that tent in Nevada, bailing our water out of a river and running it through a filter, boiling beans and rice over a fire every night. Winter was rapidly coming on. It had been a month and a half and we were tired of living this way. It was also getting cold enough that we were waking up with frost on our faces. The cats stayed warm in a nest we made in a carrier, padded and insulated with blankets, but we were tired of being cold. So we decided to head farther south, where it would be warmer and easier to find work in my field.

Arizona was lovely. We found someone who let us camp in their yard while I was waiting for my first pay check from a job I found almost immediately. Cassiopeia was doing all right, but Orion fell ill. He'd probably gotten a case of Valley Fever, most likely from when he had his first ecstatic roll in Arizona dust. Valley Fever lives in dust, and it's a fungal infection that can be difficult to treat, even with veterinary care. My boy would have needed strong antifungals. No vet would talk to us, however, and with my recent history I couldn't qualify for Carecredit. We grew desperate. Orion stopped eating and lost weight no matter what we did. Despite our best efforts, and my partner's attempts at CPR at the end, Orion passed from this world at about 2 am one December morning, cradled in our arms.

His loss tore me up inside. I sobbed all night, inconsolable. In the morning, we laid him in the ground, digging through the hard Arizona soil, laboriously making a hole large enough and deep enough for his body to be protected. My partner wrapped him in her favorite sweater, that he'd so often liked to sleep on, and we said a few words over his grave. We put him under a tree where birds lived, bred and chattered, where he'd loved to watch them. I told my mother and she donated to a cat charity, putting the gift in his name. A big part of my life was gone; now I'd lost my home, and my best friend.

We both mourned him for a long time. We missed him so much, he had been such a vibrant presence in our lives. Gradually, as the pain faded, we realized he wasn't truly lost. His body might have been in the ground, but his spirit was still with us. We felt him curled up at our feet at night, or stropping against our legs during the day. With his physical form gone, he was set free to follow us where he willed. Cassiopeia mourned him just as much as we did, but we've caught her playing with his spirit too, late at night. Every once in a while, they'll still have one of their chase-games.

We found an apartment, moved in, settled down. I got used to my new job and realized it was better working in this town than where I'd come from, and the pay was improved with a lower cost of living. We started to see there was hope. At the same time, we discovered more things about our Cassiopeia when she embraced her role as Only Cat.

For one, we noticed that her skull was highly domed, with plenty of room for brains in there. As she grew older and wiser, she began showing her intelligence. We learned that she liked the sound of Japanese better than English, so her name morphed into Nezumi, which means Mouse in Japanese, because she liked that better than either Cassiopeia or Mouse. We learned she could throw her toys, sometimes quite high. We also learned how well she understood us, and how much she missed Orion. We heard her imitate his meow, and sometimes she woke up late at night, calling for him.

Nezumi took over Orion's old duties, putting us to bed when it was time, and watching for me when I was due to come home from work. Later, she learned her own tricks, like patting us on the knee or cheek when she wanted something, or wrapping her tail around one of our wrists to hold hands. She discovered lettuce, which she loves to eat, and she is an inveterate hunter of moths. At one point, she even learned the command to lie down. It's not a trick, but rather her understanding of our request and complying with it. She can even tell time. We say, "Nezumi-chan, one more hour. Bother me then." She understands.

Now she's our artists' cat. She oversees all writing and drawing in the house, watches over our computer use, monitors my blogging. She's also happy to pose for photographs.

We moved to a better place with tile floors and wonderful light, and now our girl has a big front window she can see me come home and watch the birds through. Her legs, once so weak, are strong and staying that way with the help of her daily dose of Cosequin. She's getting a little older now but is still very full of life. It's plain she remembers Orion and what he taught her...

... because she still puts us to bed at night, and wakes us in the morning.

About the Author

Rohvannyn Shaw, USA
Website: http://mind-flight.org
Twitter: @rohvannyn
I feel privileged to know the cats I wrote about. Because of them, I have learned about myself and what it truly means to share a bond of trust with a being as different from me as an alien would be. Inter-species communication is not only possible, it's common, and to be treasured! Cats are some of my favorite people.

Socks
By Ray Marr

It was during my second posting as a junior officer in Her Majesty's Royal Air Force, that I succumbed to owning a cat. This is not a requirement of the service, far from it. It's more usual to obtain a dog, whose breed and pedigree are appropriate to one's rank, and who sits in one's office during the day generally chewing things, jumping up and slobbering on airmen and trying not to fart when the Station Commander invites himself in for coffee. The sequence of events of obtaining the cat was not straightforward, rather it was a series of incidents where if any single one had not occurred, there would be no cat. Somewhat similar to a major disaster in many respects, but little was I to know that it would lead to a minor crisis of my own.

I was stationed at RAF Wyton in Cambridgeshire, a former Pathfinder Squadron station for Bomber Command during the Second World War, where the young, brave aircrew were tasked with marking targets, at night, for the main strike force to attack deep into Nazi Germany. Now it was home to many logistical support integrated project teams, and the only flying was done in small propeller aircraft by the newly-graduated young officers from RAF College Cranwell, undertaking their Elementary Flying Training. I had a small bedroom in the Officers' Mess, but after a few months I had managed to get to the top of the waiting list and obtained a suite to stay in. It sounds rather grand, and in comparison to the other rooms, it was positively palatial. It consisted of a comfortable living room, separate bedroom and a bathroom shared with the occupant of the neighbouring suite. Unfortunately, there was no room service for my lowly rank of Flight Lieutenant, apart from a basic cleaning service we knew as batting.

65

As comfortable as this upgrade in accommodation was, it wasn't suitable for all my requirements. What I needed was more space to allow my two young daughters from my previous marriage to visit me, ideally, a married quarter. This is a house owned by the Ministry of Defence and rented to service personnel at a very favourable rate, compared to the civilian world. To this end off I went, cap in hand, to the Officer Commanding Personnel Services Flight, to see if my having children entitled me to move into a quarter. Her title always seemed to be rather unfortunate as it made the poor incumbent sound like she ran the station bordello! To my great surprise and delight, she informed me that I was eligible, although if a married service person arrived and there were no quarters available, I would potentially be given 30 days to relocate to the Mess. I thought this was fair enough, and besides I'd noticed many of the houses were being sold off, so there could hardly be a shortage. Two weeks later I got the keys to a rather nice three-bedroom detached house with a large garden, complete with apple and pear trees. As it turned out, this house was for higher ranked officers than me, but as the others were being sold off, this was what was available and I wasn't about to complain.

During one Christmas, my wife, Zoe, and I were in our favourite room, the kitchen, when we heard a strange squeaky noise outside the door. Upon opening it, we were greeted by a sad looking little calico cat. It didn't appear to be injured, just clearly hungry. Now, as I said, this was before we owned our own cat, so our options for cat sustenance were limited to say the least. We had plenty of mince pies, Christmas cake and wine, but I suspected this wasn't going to go down too well with the cat, and I wasn't about to share! In desperation, we opened a can of hot-dog sausages, you know – the kind kids love for some unknown reason, never for one moment expecting the sausage to be met with the approval of the cat. To our utter amazement, the little cat pounced on it as if it were a mouse sent by the gods themselves and demolished it. This was quite a feat seeing as the sausage was as long as its leg.

"There's another one!" Zoe exclaimed.

"I know, there's a whole can of them!" I said sarcastically.

"No, you idiot! Look!"

I followed the direction of Zoe's outstretched hand, and there on the kitchen windowsill was a carbon-copy second calico cat. We let this one in too, and more hot-dogs were consumed. It was particularly cold that winter and there was no way we could leave them outside, not knowing if they were homeless. We didn't have anything resembling a litter tray, so a quick trip to the 24-hour supermarket was in order. Despite the size of the shop, we couldn't find any litter trays, so some creative thinking was in order. As it was Christmastime, there was a wide selection of disposable turkey roasting trays for sale. We chose the largest tray we could find, a bag of cat litter, some tins of cat food and a couple of plastic bowls. The cats had certainly found the right house to call on in their hour of need; they already had us wrapped around their paws. These little friends became known as Cat One and Cat Two, catchy, eh? They became regular visitors, often appearing after I returned from work for a free feed.

We noticed that when the cats left us after eating they went to a house across the road from us. Concerned that we saw no movement there, and knowing it was normally occupied, we went to investigate. Looking in the side window, through which the cats were jumping into the house, we could see it was a utility room with several tins of cat food lined up on the side. None of them had been opened. The door to the rest of the house was closed so we could see no more. Whist walking home, we were approached by a lady asking us if there was a problem – she'd seen us peering in the window. We explained how the cats had turned up on our back door step, starving hungry, and we'd been feeding them for a few days now. The lady told us the owners were away on holiday for two weeks, and she was scheduled to feed the cats during the second week. It quickly became apparent that whoever was asked to do week one hadn't done so. I hope nothing serious had occurred to prevent the unknown friend from carrying out their duties, but we never did find out the reason, and at least the cats were being cared for by us.

Once their owners had returned from holiday, the cats still came to visit us regularly. Our new friends would often stay the night with us, claiming the area under our bed and the spot under the radiator on the landing, but I would ensure they were out before I left for work as we didn't have a cat-flap fitted.

A couple of months went by, and the owners of Cat One and Cat Two, also a military family, were posted away, and so we had to say goodbye to our little friends. Their owners had written us a note explaining that they were moving and knew the cats often visited us. They asked if we would mind keeping them in if they came round on moving day so they wouldn't have to go searching when the time to go arrived. They also offered to reimburse us for any expense incurred for entertaining the furry guys, which was very nice of them, but unnecessary – we loved having them around. We got to learn their actual names as we handed them over, Suzuki and Gixter – clearly the owners were motorbike fans.

As the experience of having cats around had been quite favourable, I moved on to the next stage of the procurement process and suggested to Zoe that we get our own cat. It seemed logical to buy food for our own rather than feeding everyone else's, and we still had quite a bit left over from Cats One and Two (I still prefer our names for them). I blame my decision on a certain Mr Tallisker, whose delightful beverage I was enjoying during a phone call to Zoe who was also a junior officer in the RAF, but was stationed at RAF Brize Norton in Oxfordshire at the time. Normally, drunken suggestions are not taken seriously by Zoe, but on this occasion, she leapt at the chance, and went to visit the local animal shelter as soon as possible.

It's often said that your pets choose you, and it was certainly true in this instance. After looking at all the cats in the shelter, Zoe drew up a list of four cats to view more closely. The first two were sweet enough cats but there was no real connection. Socks was number three. As soon as the shelter staff opened the door to her enclosure, Socks leapt out and straight into Zoe's arms. There she stayed, purring contentedly and snuggling into Zoe's neck. The fourth cat on the list didn't get a look in; it was obvious that Socks was going to become our cat.

The shelter staff asked that I drop by to see the cat before we took her home. I suspect they wanted to check me out and make sure I wasn't some sort of psycho cat hater. I duly went by after work, still in uniform, and this seemed to satisfy their needs as not one of them asked me anything. I met Socks and found her to be very affectionate, just as Zoe had described – exactly the sort of cat we had wanted. We left for home with our new cat, a little under four days since my telephoned suggestion.

Socks was, and still is, a lovely little affectionate tuxedo cat with quite a timid demeanour, despite her initial show of affection. She is literally a scaredy cat, but she took to her new home with vigour and was constantly at Zoe's or my side. We were advised to keep her in for three weeks to allow her to bond with us and learn where her home was, but after two weeks we gave her some closely-observed freedom, and she enjoyed exploring her new surroundings. The trees in the garden were particular favourites of hers however, we had to stop putting bird seed in the feeders otherwise it would have just been bait for Socks to use in her hunting exploits.

Now, life in the armed forces requires you to move locations on a regular basis, be it a posting to a new job or a deployment overseas. This, for officers in the RAF, is usually every 18 months to two years – if you are lucky. Many of our colleagues have had much quicker turn-arounds than this and it can be a huge strain on a relationship. My next posting was to RAF Wittering, also in Cambridgeshire. Wittering is only about a half hour drive from Wyton, so I was given the option to retain my current quarter, which I readily took to avoid the hassle of moving again, and I'm sure Socks would have approved. The house in Wyton also had the distinct advantage of not being right beside the busy A1 road, which Wittering is, so there was less likelihood of any accidents involving the cat. As it turned out, this was a wise move as a few months later I was on my travels again, this time to Headquarters Air Command at RAF High Wycombe in Buckinghamshire.

Usually a move comes with a Posting Order, which informs the administrative staff at your current and subsequent station of your move. This allows them to sort out new quarters for the individual. This situation was somewhat different. I had not changed my job, rather my office had relocated. As I had not been posted, no Posting Order was issued, and hence no house had been allocated for me.

I visited Personnel Management Squadron at High Wycombe to try and get a house without a Posting Order. Whilst trying to explain my situation to the young airman administrator and convince him to accept my application, his squadron leader appeared, who happened to be a friend of mine. One signature from him and I was allocated a new home with a move-in date in of a month's time.

This house was more befitting my rank with a very small garden, but loads of storage space – just what you need in the military. The rear border of the garden was a row of garages, and there was a small tree next to them. Once we'd settled in, this was used to great effect by Socks as access to the garage roof, where she would often be found surveying her domain. High Wycombe is known for its population of red kites, a beautiful bird of prey a little larger than a buzzard. I was quite worried one of these might view cats as a food source and make off with Socks, but my fears were, thankfully, never realised.

In the meantime, I still needed somewhere to live, as the commute from Cambridgeshire to Buckinghamshire was not an option. I therefore requested temporary accommodation in the Officers' Mess, and since I had a cat to tend to, I was obliged to ask permission to keep her in my room. This is usually a formality, but it is the correct thing to do. I found the relevant contact details and emailed the Mess. I received a very nice reply from the President of the Mess Committee (PMC) saying that as I had asked 'very nicely', I could bring the cat. So far, so good. The actual Mess building was full, so I was given a room in an excess married quarter. This was a simple two up two down house, shared with another officer. I never met my housemate, but it looked like the place was a temporary solution for him too, as there were no home comforts on show. The house was basically furnished, no TV (you provide that yourself), but the kitchen amenities were amusing. As a cost saving measure, someone had worked out how many white goods were needed per person in mess accommodation. This resulted in our house having a cooker, but next door had the fridge. Military logic – priceless! Thank God it was only temporary.

My accommodation was sorted till the quarter was ready. I just had to transport Socks each weekend from home to work. Sounds simple, right? Put the cat in the cat carrier, strap into passenger seat, put the tunes on the radio and drive off – job done! Unfortunately, Socks doesn't travel well. She doesn't wail or jump around, no; she's a very quiet traveller. She just decides to express her annoyance at car travel by emptying her bowels at some point during the journey. This either happens at the beginning when you are just too far from home to run in and get a wad of kitchen towel or, more often, right at the end of the trip, never halfway. You know, just when you think you've survived, just when you think you can get in and relax, she then pulls the rug from under your feet as if to say 'Thought I had forgotten, eh human? Have a whiff of this!'

It was just this latter scenario that played out one Sunday night. I was a mere 200 metres from my destination when the smell stealthily filled my nostrils and sent the signal to my brain to despair. "Oh, for heaven's sake!" was my natural response, although the actual words may have been a bit more colourful. Sadly, as I've mentioned, Socks is a bit timid, so this outburst only served to relax her sphincter even more and the floodgates opened in the cat carrier. *Oh no*, I thought, *how am I going to clean this up?* The carrier wasn't going to be an issue, it's an inanimate object and the mess was contained, but the smell was getting to me and I thought I might be saying hello to my dinner on the dashboard at any second. The real problem was the cat. Cleaning her was going to be a different matter altogether.

I got her into the house and made straight for the bathroom. I closed the door behind me, both to prevent her escape and to contain the mayhem I was sure was about to follow. I put her in the tub where she stood passively. This was unexpected; surely it was going to be harder than this? OK, no problem, just her hind legs were a lovely shade of brown and I hadn't turned on the water yet. Thinking naively that I might succeed where many before me had gallantly failed, I held her gently but firmly at her shoulders, and proceeded to turn on the shower head. I quickly discovered that my definition of firmly wasn't the same as hers, and at the sound of rushing water all hell broke loose.

Socks was trying to clamber up the side of the bath as I desperately tried to keep her in, all the time looking for any purchase her claws could find. The sides of the bath offered no traction and the first thing she could grip was my upper arm. With searing pain, water splashing around and her mess flying over the walls as if we were inside a ghastly snow globe, I tried in vain to restrain and clean the now demonically-possessed feline. No chance! It wasn't going to happen. I made one more attempt in the forlorn hope that she would understand I was trying to help, but no dice. She was completely unsympathetic to my potential plight of having to explain to the PMC that the cat had taken offence to the décor in the bathroom and had changed it to a nice new colour called 'Guess what I had for dinner'. I decided to abandon Operation CATWASH and throw myself at her mercy. I dried her off and observed where she went around the house, cleaning up afterward as and when necessary. I had no right to expect any leniency after all that had just transpired, but this solution appeared to appease Socks. I tended my wounds and gave my shirt a last farewell into the bin with full military honours.

Thinking my problems were over for the night, and the cat appearing to be beginning to forgive me as she was now rubbing against my legs, I decided to do what any British serviceman would to regain calm – brew up and have a cup of tea. Besides, there was no beer in the house. Whilst doing this I noticed the kitchen door was ajar. Odd, I thought, and was immediately hit by a wave of panic as there was now the possibility of someone else in the house. Arming myself with the nearest thing I could find, the mop, I cleared the lower floor. This was a very quick task, seeing as downstairs was just the kitchen and living room, so sparsely furnished that it would be difficult for a mouse to find a hiding place. Certain now of my solitude, excepting the soggy moggy, I returned to inspect the kitchen door. The door latch seemed to be faulty, it just wasn't engaging. As a Chartered Engineer, I thought I was more than qualified to fix this, so I set about it with gusto. There was no way I was going to bed with an unsecure house. So focused was I on the task in hand, that I neglected to realise I had now provided the perfect temptation and opportunity for my irritated and damp captive to escape.

Socks didn't need to be given this chance twice – a black and white flash shot by my legs and out into the night. NOOO! How the hell am I going explain this to Zoe? "Sorry but the cat has run away because I left the door wide open"? I think not!

Right, genius, think. How do you get a cat that thinks you're the devil incarnate back into the house? Where is she? OK, she's on the garden path, easy now, no quick moves. Try to beckon her in.

So, there I was, cooing to the cat, making an utter fool of myself and getting the look of *you've got to be joking, human! You just tried to drown me!* I backed off into the kitchen and looked around for anything I could use to coax her in, and settled on the obvious – food. I went outside with some cat biscuits, offering them up to her, but she wouldn't come close. I decided to leave a trail of them up the path and into the kitchen, in true Scooby Doo style. This seemed to be doing the trick, and she started to come back up the path towards the door. *Great, it's working*, I thought, as I really didn't want to lose her but no, she had other ideas. She ignored the trail into the house and shot straight past the door and through the fence onto the base where I couldn't easily follow. Aaargh! Better start thinking up a bloody good excuse now. There was no way I was going to be able to find a similar looking cat and pass it off to Zoe as Socks – it's not the same as replacing a goldfish or a hamster. Anyway, I didn't want a replacement, I wanted my cat back too, safe and sound.

I searched around the back of the house, looking under bushes and peering through the perimeter fence. I caught occasional glimpses of movement but she was perfectly camouflaged for the night and severely annoyed with me, so I couldn't be sure if it was her. She could have been anywhere. I honestly thought she wasn't going to come back, and I had that sinking feeling in the pit of my stomach when you feel totally helpless. On top of this I still had the door problem to fix, so I resigned myself to this task and had it accomplished in relatively quick time.

Just then I heard a rustling outside, Socks was back! She was still unreceptive to my beckoning, which was hardly surprising, but it was encouraging to see she was willing to return. I felt so relieved and happy. OK, Plan B. Let's use this new development and see if she'll come in of her own accord. So, with the kitchen door wide open and me standing behind it, I waited, coiled like a spring, cup of tea in hand. Well, I wasn't going to waste my tea was I? It was the only thing going to plan right now. About five minutes passed, and then a tentative white paw crossed the threshold with a cautious face scanning for danger. *Stand by...* A second paw followed. *Stand by...* The rest of the cat came in, each small step accompanied by the same sweeping look. Slowly she moved into the kitchen, looking for her enemy – me. *Where was he, that soaker of cats, that traitor?*

Stand by...

Finally, after what seemed like an age, she advanced far enough into the room and was almost in the centre of the floor. Still unaware of my presence and position I received the mental command... *GO!* I released the potential energy of my pseudo-spring and slammed the door shut. For a moment, I thought I'd overdone it as the glass rattled loudly in the frame but thankfully it didn't break. Socks, meanwhile, shot out of the room and up the stairs like the proverbial scalded cat, but I was successful, she was in!

I returned to the kitchen, finished my now-cold tea and did a quick poo patrol around the house but found nothing, and even my slamming of the door hadn't had any adverse effect on the poor thing. It appeared my earlier fears of cat mess all over the house were unfounded, but time would tell. The cat herself was hiding underneath my bed, confused but safe. Later she would emerge and curl up by my feet, ultimately settling by my head and purring contentedly. Now that all was as it should be, with my marriage, and my life, no longer in danger, I decided to bravely call Zoe and tell her of the evening's escapades. That man Tallisker has a lot to answer for!

About the Author

Ray Marr, UK
Ray never intended to own a cat, and now he is owned by three.

Athena's Rescue Story
by Marie Symeou

Sometimes I dream about how I used to live.

As very young kittens, my sister, Lily, and I were left out in the cold and had to fend for ourselves. Lily was a black cat and I am a brown tabby. After the death of our mother we found ourselves totally lost and alone in the world. Soon we became very hungry and we couldn't stop ourselves shivering from the cold.

There were scary times ahead as we searched for food without our mother to guide us and without her protection. At night, there was lots of noise and I couldn't sleep. Nestled up close to my sister, I was scared to close my eyes because I feared we'd get eaten alive by a big fox or dog. Perhaps I would die just like my mum.

But we got lucky. Big hands came out of the sky and took us to the cat shelter. Here nice people with caring hands and gentle light around them took care of us. I was happy we had somewhere nice and warm to sleep and food to eat, but I soon began to worry about the future. You see, I'd noticed some of the cats being carried out and they never returned.

I was deep in thought when I heard a woman with dark hair in a ponytail and an older lady with brown curly hair, come in with the human who took care of us. They both smiled and each had the glow you only see around nice people.

This was my new mum. I could sense it. She came forward and her eyes lit up as she gazed at me. I couldn't wait any longer so I jumped up to greet her, claws clinging to the mesh door. I had dreamt of this lady, dreamt I lay happy and content in her arms, licking her ears and neck.

She spoke to our human, looking at the other cats as she did so. The older lady walked off to stare at the other cats and kittens. My mum stuck her finger in the door again and I licked it. I hoped she had some food for me but she didn't. But I liked the way she smelled and the loving light around her calmed me.

But then she walked off to look at the other cats.

"Please don't like them better," I meowed, sending her messages from my mind I knew she would pick up.

She had that kind of aura about her. Anyway, even if she had been looking at the other kittens, I could tell I had already found my way into her big heart. The older woman, her mother, hesitated. She liked another cat better than me and I panicked as I thought my new mummy might like him too.

She came back to me, but she seemed to want to look at my sister now, touching Lily's nose just like she'd done mine. She felt sorry for her and wished she could take us both home. "Do you only home them in pairs or can I just take the one?" she asked the human that took care of us.

"You can take one cat only if you prefer," he said. "We understand it's not always practical to re-home our cats in pairs for some people."

I pounced up and down. "Look at me! Take me!"

Mummy laughed, touching my nose again.

"Me! Me! Take me!" I climbed up the door.

"I'll take her," Mum said.

And then she left and I was still there.

"It's not fair," Lily said sadly. "You've found a new home. What about me?"

***

A few days later I found myself being carried in a cat basket out of the pen. I thought Lily was coming too but no. I was very sad I had no time to say goodbye to my sis and I could hear her meowing as I was being carried out.

I panicked in the carrier, trying to keep upright. "Mind how you carry me!" I meowed loudly. I was rolling around and banging my tiny head in there. But I realised I could smell Mum's scent on the towel in the carrier. I liked that smell. Immediately picturing her kind eyes, I snuggled down all comfy.

My new mum was here. Standing at the desk writing something down. She turned and our eyes met, her beaming smile lighting up my world. Our human put me down on the floor and Mum bent down to say hello and picked me up, placing me on the seat next to my new granny. Granny spoke to me as Mum was still busy at the desk. Other humans who worked here looked at me, oohing and ahhing and saying how cute I was.

When Mum finished writing at the desk she came over and picked up the carrier. I heard everyone say "Bye" and "Good luck!" as we headed for the door. Then it opened, I smelled the outside and was immediately struck by how loud everything was. It hurt my ears! I'd forgotten how loud the outside world could be. I tried not to panic but I couldn't help but feel scared.

***

I was now inside the house from my dream. Mum opened the carrier and I slowly crawled out, sniffing the carpet and air.

"There, there, sweetie," she said, stroking under my chin. "You're home now."

She was so big and tall, and I felt the urge to jump. I did and I found myself hanging from her dress, my claws clinging onto her.

She laughed. "Oh, Athena, baby, get down!"

Lifting me in her arms, she looked at me as I lay back and gazed up at her. She had such a nice way about her. When she put me down, I devoured the food she placed in front of me all in one go. Later I sat on Mum's lap. She soothed and stroked my fur and I purred with delight. I felt so warm and safe. I gazed up at her again.

"Mummy loves you," she said, smiling as she stroked me under the chin. "What a pretty little girl you are."

I felt so happy.

Mummy gave me water too but I didn't like it in the bowl, so I followed her upstairs when she went to have a bath and waited for the water to drip from the tap. Mum worried about me not drinking and so she ran her finger under the running water and gave me a bit to taste. I liked it very much. I couldn't believe how thirsty I was!

Mummy picked me up, placed me outside the bathroom door and locked it. I meowed like crazy. Why did she do that? Why could I not go in there too? What was she doing in there? I didn't like the loud noise the water made. What if she hurt herself? I meowed some more and started scratching at the bathroom door.

"It's alright, Athena, baby," she called out from behind the door. "Mummy's having a bath. Don't worry."

"Meow!" I cried. "Meow!" It was Mummy in kitty language. I wasn't happy with her leaving me out here on the landing. I was scared something had happened to her. I laid down, pressing my ear against the door to hear if she was still in there and alive. I hoped she wasn't going to leave me here for a long time. Maybe she wouldn't come out again. Maybe she'd left me all alone.

It seemed like ages, but I heard her move about and the water splashed. Then I heard water going down the drain and Mummy moving about again. The door finally opened and lots of warm smells came out. They were nice smells. Mum came out and I jumped on her immediately. I was so happy to see her again! She lifted me to her face and kissed my forehead.

She put me back down on the floor and I slipped past her into the bathroom. It was warm in there and very steamy. The flowery smell was strong. I jumped on the side of the bath and then into it, and skidded around in the left-over water.

Mum laughed again. She picked me up and took me downstairs where we played with some of my new toys.

I loved playing with Mum. She knew exactly what I liked. Both Mum and Granny bought me many toys and some catnip too, which made me go crazy when I first sniffed it. Mummy won't give it to me a lot now because back then I was so naughty on it. It made me feel happy and cheerful, all warm and loving inside. It made me run like mad and chase the ball that Mummy threw across the room. I liked to bat the ball towards Mum with my paw and she would hit it back to me.

Sleeping on Mummy's bed was something I looked forward to the most, and still do. The first night we spent together was so special to both of us and we bonded forever. Being such a hungry little kitten, I thought she, being my new Mummy, would feed me the way my real Mummy had once fed me. But I couldn't find what I was supposed to drink my milk from and searched hungrily until I found her earlobe, which I made all wet trying to find some milk. I felt the warmest, most beautiful love envelope me then as Mummy cuddled me close. I nibbled on her long fur too, which I know now is called hair on humans.

It was all fun and games in my new home that I soon forgot the sadness of my early life. But sometimes, in my quiet moments, I did think of Lily. I missed her a lot. I hoped she had found a lovely new home and family too.

I wondered why Mum couldn't rescue both of us together. But I accepted that my sister was meant to live her own life with her own human family. I gave it some more thought and concluded that, had we both come to live with my mum, then Lily would have been even more jealous of me because, let's face it, how could my mum love us both equally?

I know she has a big loving heart, but I think Lily would have been jealous every time Mum cuddled me. And Mum's lap would not have been able to accommodate us both. Not when we grew big.

We could have taken it in turns, I suppose. But then what about at night? You see, I loved cuddling with Mum at night. Sleeping on my mum's bed was a real highlight for me. That's when I was at my most content – and still am. Mum loves it too.

Like I said, the fun and games I enjoyed with my new mum were endless. Really, we had such fun. She would throw some small, spongy balls for me to chase and catch with my paws, or she would dangle fishing rod-type toys in front of me. I loved to jump up high to catch the toy or feather at the end of it.

I made her and Granny laugh with my crazy antics as I sped across the room, skidded across the floor and caught the ball in my mouth. Sometimes, when Mummy was upstairs working at the computer I liked to carry the ball in my mouth up to her and place it in front of her as a gift. She deserved it for everything she'd done for me. If she had not come to see me that day, I would have been so unhappy. I know it. In fact, I dread to think what would have happened to me. Oh, I sure hope nothing nasty has happened to my sister.

It was funny when I launched myself onto the wall and clung on with my claws, scratching at the wallpaper. I needed to mark my territory, but Mum and Granny didn't think this was important.

"My wallpaper!" Gran shouted as I shot out the room and up the stairs.

I would shoot past her legs and leap up the curtains and swing from them, turning my head sideways for extra cuteness. I could tell that

Mum's heart melted because the light around her grew pink and big. But Granny shouted again. Why do humans always worry about material things? Life is about fun and love. Good times to enjoy. Why does everything have to be perfect?

For me, perfection lies in the love we all share.

***

A few weeks after she got me, Mum placed me in my carrier again "It's alright, sweetie. Don't worry," she said in her soothing voice. I could listen to that voice forever. It was a special voice only for me. She didn't speak to anyone else like that.

But I hated the carrier and I panicked and started to roll and scratch inside it. I meowed loudly. "Mum, please! Don't leave me!"

"It's OK, Athena. Mummy's here. Nothing to worry about," she said as she peeped into the carrier with her warm eyes.

We went into a building and the smell of dog attacked my senses. I was freaking out but decided to keep quiet. I tried to stay calm and sat huddled up right at the back of my carrier. The dogs barked loudly now, I hated that sound. Most dogs have large mouths and they could easily swallow me whole if they caught me. One almost ate me and Lily when we were abandoned in that garden as kittens.

Mum put me on the floor and spoke to a woman behind a glass wall with a desk attached to it. The dogs were still barking and I could smell some other nervous cats too. It smelled a lot like the place Mummy got me from but this was a different place. She could tell I was terrified and kept speaking to me in a calm voice. The voice I had always trusted. I wasn't so sure now. She was probably like all the other humans.

We waited for a while as more and more dogs and some cats came in with their humans. Then the door opposite opened and a human, the vet, called a name and a dog and his human went in. This happened a few more times before it was our turn. I wasn't that scared now because I noticed the other animals before me had gone in but had come out with their humans again and had gone out the front door, which could only mean they were going home together. Safe and sound. But what happened behind the door with that vet? That's what I wanted to know.

I didn't have to wait long to find out. When I went in with my mum she put my basket on the table and opened it, but I wouldn't come out. Then the vet pulled me out. I didn't like the smell on his hands. It

80

reminded me of when I was small and big hands had done things to me. Oh no! It was happening again. Same thing but different hands, although they smelled the same.

Mum was still close-by at least. How could she let him do this to me? I felt something go into my neck. It hurt a bit. Another needle. It was done and I was put back in the carrier.

Mummy spoke with the vet, and she took me to the glass window and desk where I saw her pay the woman behind it. Then Mum carried me outside. We then walked up the road and waited a bit for what I presumed was the bus home. Cars whizzed by and made a lot of noise. I huddled in the back of my carrier. The bus came and we were home in no time.

Mum hugged me when she took me out of the carrier and gave me some food.

***

All was fine for a few weeks and I could tell I was growing up fast and putting on weight because I was being fed the most wonderful food ever. I felt loved and pampered. I slept with Mum on her bed and sat on her lap and purred. We played. She took me out in the garden but she made me wear a harness to keep me close to her.

Being out was fun. But there was a nasty tom cat in the garden. He kept appearing and teasing me. He was a ginger tabby, and liked to make fun of me when I was indoors looking out of the big glass door in the living room. I was happy and content in the cosy house, my home, when he kept appearing, staring in through the glass at me. I rushed up to the door, angry. I stood up and pounded my front paws against the door. I wanted to get at him. He had no place here, he had his own garden and home to go to. How dare he trespass on my territory and make fun of me too in the process. Silly male cat!

"Haha, look at you," he said. "You can't go out. Scaredy cat! Your mum won't let you out like mine does."

"Go away!" I meowed. "At least my mummy loves me. Yours doesn't because she lets you out all the time."

Soon this stupid cat, who was called Mister, a silly name for a silly cat, brought other cats to taunt me. They were bullies and they made me angry. Because I was still a kitten they thought it was fun to poke fun at me. I'd show them, I thought.

81

I had to watch them go to the toilet in our garden too. My garden. How dare they! I jumped onto the glass door and stood and pounded my paws with anger and frustration. Why was Mum letting them do that? She was in the kitchen and I meowed loudly for her to hear me.

She came into the room and looked out at Mister trying to poo in the flower bed. She closed the living room door so I couldn't get out, and went through the kitchen door instead and shooed him away. She didn't seem angry at him though. Mum liked all cats. Even Mister Nasty Tom. I hoped she wouldn't like him more than me. Anyway, why did he have to come here to do his smelly business?

There were many fun things to do with Mum, which made me forget those bullies for a while. I was so happy and I realised those other cats were simply jealous of me. Not just of my good looks, but of my lovely mum. She cared about me and would never let anything happen to me.

We played a lot so I could never get bored. I liked to invent games with Mum. That was the real fun. She thought she was the one inventing them, but really, it's been me all along. I was the one who gave her ideas, even as a small kitten, usually through my mind. I learned to picture what I would like her to do and she soon picked it up in her own mind. The bond of love is what keeps us telepathically linked, though Mum does have quite a gift for knowing instinctively what I want.

Another of my favourite games was playing hide and seek with Mum. I hid behind the sofa or the bed and when I heard her calling my name I'd stay in hiding, letting her search the house for me. But when I heard the panic in her voice, I realised I had to show myself because I couldn't bear to see her upset. That's when I knew it was time to stop the teasing and show her some love instead.

I think she worried, and still does, that I might have sneaked out through an open window. She does worry a lot, my mum. It is my job to keep her safe, loved and happy. Just like it's her job as my human mum. Everything was just great. I was content.

And then it happened again.

I struggled to break out of Mum's grasp as she tried to gently push me into the carrier. But it was too late. She locked the door and there I crouched unhappily, looking out at her with my sad eyes. I hoped she would feel sorry for me, but it didn't work. She ignored me.

I watched nervously from inside my prison as she put on her jacket. We were going out. It was obvious. She hadn't just put me in the carrier so we could stay home and play.

I couldn't believe it. I was back at the shelter! Oh no! I scratched frantically at the carrier door, meowing loudly.

"It's OK, baby. Don't worry." Her soothing voice calmed me down a bit but could I trust her now?

We went in and waited in the reception area. I remembered so well that this was where she picked me up that day and how happy I'd been. I remembered her loving glow as she smiled into my carrier and said hello. If I could cry like a human right now, I would. It was so upsetting to know that maybe our time was up. Maybe the good times were gone.

I could smell other animals. Dogs, not just cats. It made me more nervous. The vet called our name and Mum carried me in the carrier to the vet's room. Oh, yes. I'd been to this one before. I knew it well, and I panicked more and more when the vet, a young woman, smiled down at me as she helped drag me out of the carrier. Mum was hesitant to bring me out. I sensed she didn't want to do what she was meant to be doing. I had already realised that this time she would be leaving me there and going home. She had sent me pictures with her mind that she was going to pick me up again later, but I could no longer trust her. She'd betrayed me. And, even if she was coming back for me, why had she brought me here in the first place? And what was going to happen to me?

The vet took my temperature and checked me over. I hated it and leaned up against my mum as she bent down to hold me. I nestled my face into her neck and drew in her comforting scent. My mum's loving scent that I thought would be mine forever, but now it seemed she was slipping out of my life. Maybe forever. I clung on with my claws. "Please don't leave me, Mummy!"

I could tell she couldn't let me go. She didn't want to. I felt her love envelope me as she hugged me. Then I started to feel woozy, as I closed my eyes and drifted…

***

Whatever they did to me, I didn't feel it. I had fallen asleep and couldn't feel a thing. I was very woozy as I started to come round. I had no idea how long I'd been asleep. I didn't care anymore. Not without Mum and Granny. Just then I thought I could hear their voices in the distance, though I couldn't be sure. I felt so weird and out of it.

Someone picked up my box and I felt myself being carried out of the room. I was put down on the floor somewhere. Dog, cat and rabbit scents greeted me, awakening my senses. And then, oh, it couldn't be, could it? I heard Mum's soothing voice. I knew it was her. I crept slowly forward to the front of my carrier and I saw her black boots. And Granny's too. They both looked down at me and smiled.

"Athena, baby, Mummy's here."

Did this mean we were going home? It did. At home I felt sleepy and dizzy as I slowly crawled out of my carrier. I still felt scared and wanted to hide behind the sofa.

"Oh, sweetie," Mum said as she stroked me. Wondering whether to trust her, I turned my gaze to hers and felt the most brilliant love beaming from her heart to mine. I sent her the same love back, as well as blinking at her, and she bent down and picked me up. She held me on her lap and stroked and kissed the top of my head.

I wasn't happy that the vet had shaved the side of my belly though. It looked ugly and there was a scar there too. Mummy looked at it. "It's going to be alright, my darling. Your fur will grow back in no time."

I picked up her thoughts that told me why this had been done to me. I was getting good at reading her mind now. I was growing up, after all. It was to stop me having babies. Humans did that to cats. They believed it was for the best to make sure there were less starving kittens in the world desperately needing homes. Apparently, not everyone loved cats, or animals for that matter. These humans had black smoke or fog around them, though sometimes they managed to fool others. Animals could sense their evil souls and see that their hearts were black.

But Mum and Gran didn't have that. They had lots of loving, beaming light around them and hearts full of pink light and love. I knew I would always be safe with them.

So, there you are. That's my story about how I found my forever home. I hope you enjoyed reading it. I also hope, as does my mum, that by sharing our story we have raised awareness of animal adoption. There are many kittens, and cats, as well as dogs and other animals that need loving forever homes too. Lots of abandoned animals would love a home in which to feel safe, loved and cared for.

I do feel lucky and blessed to have found such a lovely family to love and take care of me. My home is the best forever home any cat could wish for. My humans are perfect in every way and we were meant to be together. They don't only take care of me. I take care of them.

Mum is stroking me under my chin now. I gaze up at her, give her a long loving look and blink my eyes to show how much she means to me.

I love her. And she loves me.

Abridged version of the book *A Forever Home for Athena.*

About the Author

Marie Symeou
Email: mariesym6@gmail.com
Website: http://www.athenacatgoddess.com
Twitter: @athenawisekitty
Twitter: @mariesymeou

The Kiss of the Vampire
By Maggie Raynor

In the late 1960s, I began a three-year MA course in printmaking at the Royal College of Art in London. Then, as now, it was incredibly difficult to find anywhere affordable to live; most students ended up paying a small fortune for a cramped bed-sit.

There were four of us looking for accommodation: myself, my boyfriend, Dave, and Maggie and Rita who were close friends from art college in Sheffield. Dave was a sculpture student from the RCA, Maggie and Rita were both studying painting at the Slade. (Rita was actually a bloke. His proper name was Peter Reeve but he'd been called Rita Peeve since time immemorial.)

After weeks of searching, we finally struck gold in the shape of a self-contained basement flat in Earls Court. The flat had two rooms and a kitchen. The front room was the biggest but, as the flat was located on Finborough Road, one of the main trunk roads out of London, sleeping here meant you had articulated lorries thundering along approximately six feet away from your head. The back room was bijoux in the extreme, just room for a bed, a small desk and a chest of drawers, but it looked out onto what we fondly called the 'garden'. Dave and I went for this option whilst Maggie and Rita were happy to settle for more space.

I haven't mentioned a bathroom, mainly because there wasn't one. We had to clean our teeth and wash in the kitchen sink (a great incentive to keep on top of the washing up) or have a shower at the college. There was a toilet in the back-yard just outside the kitchen door – not very handy on a freezing winter's night but, as three of us were Northerners, we were well used to this particular arrangement.

Central heating? No chance! A two-bar electric fire in each room did the job – sort of.

'There you go,' I think I hear you say, 'those pesky baby-boomers, already living off the fat of the land!'

And, indeed, it seemed we were at the time. Our dark, noisy, damp and cold flat was the envy of many of our fellow students. We had our own front door, a garden...and, it was cheap!

Our landlord, an affable Asian, lived in the three stories above our basement, along with his wife and numerous children. Two or three times a week, the wife would open our front door and trudge down the hall carrying a large basket of damp washing, that she would hang out to dry in the garden. One day, she appeared carrying a spade and a bag of onion sets. She then dug up most of the 'lawn' and planted the onions. Her command of spoken English was on a par with my command of spoken Urdu – so any attempt to inform her we had a doorbell and it was the custom of the country to use it, was met with nods of the head and a happy smile.

The landlady was not our only intruder. At this point in time, Earls Court was not one of the most salubrious districts of London. The inhabitants were mainly a) Australians b) inmates of a large, nearby hostel for the homeless or c) both. In other words, many of the locals were drunk most of the time. Our flat had a wrought iron gate and railings in front of a steep flight of stairs leading to a small yard where the dustbins were housed. This secluded area seemed to draw those in 'an advanced state of liquid refreshment' like a magnet, mainly to do a spot of cider recycling...or, worse. Mission accomplished, they invariably found it impossible to negotiate the steps back up to Finborough Road and either rang the doorbell for help or just slept it off amongst the bins.

Late one night, there was a frantic banging on the front door. As everyone else was already in bed, I went to open up, expecting to find yet another helpless heap of humanity imprisoned in our yard. As I unlocked the door, it was pushed violently open and a wild-eyed bloke rushed past me, ran down the hall, through the kitchen and out the back door into the garden, presumably heading for Brompton Cemetery, which lay on the other side of our garden wall. Half expecting a troupe of whistle-blowing, truncheon-waving police – *a la* Keystone Cops – to follow him through the house, I held the door open for a minute before locking up again. I shrugged, put on football socks, gloves and a balaclava...and so to bed.

But, hey! This was London in the Swinging Sixties, and we were right there. The RCA – still basking in David Hockney's reflected glory – was arguably the coolest place in the whole universe. We didn't exactly swing, but we twitched gently along with the prevailing zeitgeist. We were as happy as pigs in blankets, and about to become even happier.

At the local newsagent, I saw an ad offering 'adorable kittens' for sale. Hoping this wasn't a front for the neighbourhood brothel, I went along and picked up a tiny scrap of silver-tabby fur, with large, pale-green eyes – love at first sight! We called him Murphy, as his origins were definitely Irish. His name went on the door-bell, and he quickly became an indispensable part of the establishment.

As a small kitten, he must have led a boring life as we were out all day, working until college closed at 9.30 pm. However, he soon found ways to pass the lonely hours. Free-style weeing was his first diversion. Ignoring his litter-tray, he weed wherever the fancy took him; no pair of shoes or pile of discarded clothing was safe from his attentions.

His other significant hobby was wool-sucking. The minute one collapsed on the bed of an evening, Murphy would be there, dribbling in anticipation, drawn irresistibly to the smell of warm woollie like a blowfly to roadkill. He'd plant himself on your chest and suck away at whatever clothing you happened to be wearing, kneading with his paws and purring ecstatically. Eventually, all my sweaters and T-shirts looked as if they'd been tie-dyed; pock-marked with little white patches where Murph had sucked out all the dye. Fortunately, this was a fashionable look in the '60s.

When Murph was around about six months old, we decided it was time to fit a cat-flap. He needed to broaden his horizons and we needed the luxury of wee-free clothing. The landlady looked enquiringly at this addition to the kitchen door. We told her it was now a legal requirement in all rental properties, enabling fire-fighters to push a hose through into the kitchen in the event of conflagration. She nodded, smiled happily and went out to tend to her onions.

The next few weeks were filled with anxiety, as we were deeply concerned for Murph's safety. It wasn't the usual worry of traffic – there was no way out onto the road – it was the problem of the neighbourhood cats. We'd seen them strutting their stuff through the garden, a motley crew of mangy, tatty-eared, ferocious-looking feral creatures who lived wild in the cemetery, the Brompton Massive no less. Expecting Murphy to get along with these dudes would be like throwing a pre-pubescent William Rees-Mogg into a gang of Brixton heavies and leaving him to get on with it.

As things turned out, we needn't have worried. One afternoon, I came home earlier than usual from college. As I opened the front door I heard a sudden scurrying, followed by a huge kerfuffle (what a lovely word, always a pleasure to use it!) in the kitchen. On going to investigate, I discovered two members of the Brompton Massive fused together in the cat-flap – presumably the result of a badly judged synchronised exit. I opened the door to let them out and saw another couple legging it up the garden path. Murphy was having 'At Homes!'

This seemed to be quite a sensible arrangement. The Massive had an operations HQ, complete with snacks and clean drinking-water, and Murphy finally had a social life. Did it have a beneficial effect on our urinary problems? Not a bit. Every cat entering our premises seemed to regard spraying the walls/soft furnishings/lino as a form of clocking-in, so we were worse off than we were before.

Although weeing may have been *de rigeur* amongst his bad-ass mates, I'm fairly sure wool-sucking wasn't. Nevertheless, Murph continued to pursue this rather unmanly hobby with his usual enthusiasm despite his new-found gangsta status.

One day I was contacted by a friend who lived in Paris. She'd met a talented flamenco guitarist from Marseilles, Gilbert, who was coming to London to play a series of gigs. Could we put him up as he didn't know anyone in the city? We agreed we could. Despite having no guest bedroom, we did occasionally offer accommodation to fellow-students who'd either missed the last tube home or temporarily lost the use of their legs. We had a hall and a single mattress that was stored pushed up against one of the walls. It was used as the backdrop for 'who-can-pee-the-highest' games at Murphy's more rowdy *soirées* but, as long as you remembered to put it damp side down, it was reputed to be fairly comfortable.

We arranged to meet Gilbert at the club, listen to his set and bring him home. He was the guitar part of a flamenco ensemble who were good, if rather loud. Physically, he was a bit of a disappointment. A flamenco guitarist from Marseilles? In my imagination, he was a sort of Gallic Heathcliffe, swarthy, wild of eye and hairdo, wearing washed-out Levi's and those cowboy boots with high heels and slightly turned-up toes. In reality, he turned out to be small and dapper. His hair was dark and curly, but it was short and perfectly coiffed. His jeans were new and had a crease ironed down the front. He wore a black velvet jacket, a white polo-neck and dainty little black, patent loafers. His one concession to the '60s was a luxurious pair of auburn side-whiskers. He strutted around a bit; he obviously found himself attractive and I suppose he was in a Post-Napoleonic kind of way.

He seemed dismayed when we introduced him to his quarters. This was unfortunate, as I'd been to some trouble to make him comfortable. There were clean sheets and pillow-cases, there was my nan's old eiderdown and even a chair to put his clothes on. (We couldn't find a coat-hanger as none of us wore the sort of clothes you had to hang up, and anyway, there wasn't a wardrobe. For obvious reasons, all our clothes were safely stowed away in drawers, apart from Dave's jeans, which were so stiff with plaster-of-Paris and fibre glass resin that they were unfoldable and had to stand up by themselves in a corner.)

I'd scoured the sink and given him a tin mug to put his toothbrush in. He had a little torch so he could navigate his way from the light switch at one end of the hall to his mattress at the other without becoming entangled in the ironing-board. Even the roll of scratchy Bronco toilet-paper (other papers were available, but not affordable on a daily basis) had been replaced with a luxurious roll of Andrex...what's not to like?

Eventually, after much Gallic puffing and pouting, he settled down for the night and, for a while, all was peaceful. Then, early in the morning, came a piercing scream followed by a crash from the hall. This was no kerfuffle. This sounded more like a major incident. Dave leapt out of bed. I was more circumspect, letting him make the initial recce as I'm not good with blood.

"What's wrong?" I asked as he came back into the bedroom, smirking.

"Someone 'ave sucked 'is face!" he said, doing his best, but still rather poor, Maurice Chevalier impression. (Dave's from Cornwall.)

Intrigued, I got up. Rita was already there, comforting Gilbert by telling him he'd probably been visited by one of the unquiet, long-dead inhabitants of the cemetery at the bottom of the garden. Then I noticed that one of the luxurious, auburn side-whiskers was glistening with what could only be cat-spit.

"It was Murph!" I cried delightedly, and explained we'd got a cat with bizarre behavioural problems – but the thought of having been snogged by a cat seemed to upset Gilbert more than the thought of being snogged by one of the un-dead.

Reader, I pitied him. There he was, small, frightened and alone, a stranger in a strange land. He was blue with cold, shivering in his little white singlet and Y-fronts, whilst the three of us, warmly cocooned in Polar sleepwear, were sniggering at his plight. I released him from the embrace of the ironing-board and made him a cup of tea. I helped him back into his bed and put a rug over the eiderdown for extra warmth.

Once back in my own bed, I remembered the French, shunted as they are up their own evolutionary siding, don't take milk in their tea. Probably, they don't take the three large spoonfuls of sugar I'd added for the shock, either. Sure enough, in the morning all that remained of Gilbert was a stone-cold cup of tea beside an empty mattress. There was also a pool of yellow liquid by the wall and a trail of wet footprints leading to the front door.

"Do you think he'll be back tonight?" Maggie asked. She wore earplugs and would have happily slept through the last Trump (different times, different Trump – but probably the same end result), so she'd missed the night's entertainment.

"I very much doubt it!" I said.

And I was right.

About the Author

Maggie Raynor, UK
Website: http://equestrianprints.co.uk/

I studied Sculpture and Printmaking at Sheffield College of Art, then post-grad Printmaking at the Royal College of Art. I work as an illustrator and cartoonist – mainly equestrian but I also do cats and dogs when the opportunity arises.
I have written a children's pony book, (*Finders Keepers* published by Forelock Books) and am currently working on my second.
I live in Sheffield, where I have the privilege of looking after two cats, a whippet and a large, skewbald horse.

The Cat That Changed My Life
By Lucinda E Clarke

I suppose, looking back on it now, it's not fair to blame the cat. We all make our own decisions in life, don't we? We are responsible for the path we follow and the choices we make. Or, are we simply victims of fate that gives us a push, or on occasion a huge shove, in the right direction? Either way, in this case it's a lot easier to blame the cat than blame myself, especially on those days when I look back and ask, 'What was I thinking?'

Let me start at the beginning or what follows won't make any sense at all. Although, come to think of it, I'm not sure it makes sense to me even now.

I had a rather torrid upbringing so I couldn't wait to leave home. Having been an avid reader, I'd learned that if you were going to survive successfully on your own, you needed to be qualified for a job or profession that would support you. Life with my poor mother may have been miserable, but it was better than living in a cardboard box on the streets.

I escaped for three years while attending college a few hundred miles from my local town, but then the pressure to live close to home descended. I found a teaching post about thirty miles distant, which gave me space during the week, but come the weekend, back home I would go to keep Mother company. As you can imagine, this had a dampening effect on my social life – always away for the weekend parties and festivities.

But somewhere along the line, fate took a hand and one weekday night found me in a night club, my first ever visit of that kind, with a couple of girlfriends. I was approached and asked to dance. Three times

I refused, being particularly shy, nursing my soft drink, deserted by my friends and wondering how I'd got myself into this predicament.

Eventually, an acquaintance wandered in and I rushed over to talk to him, introductions were made and reluctantly I agreed to grace the dance floor with a man I didn't know. Up to this moment, the cat had not made an appearance in my life, so I can't blame anything on her at this point.

I accepted a few dates with this charismatic, blond-haired, blue-eyed man, despite the alarm bells jangling loud and clear inside my head. He was fascinating, witty, fun to be with and very intelligent. It was difficult to put a finger on exactly why the chimes were deafening.

For several months, every time I left my car I had to park it at the top of a hill – luckily the city where I lived had lots of hills. The reason? The battery was flat and I didn't have a spare penny to buy a new one. The car was also talking to me loud and clear; several knocking noises emanated from under the bonnet, which did not bode well.

"No problem," said my new friend. "I'm a fully-trained mechanic, I can repair cars. Just leave it with me, no charge, I'll have it as good as new in no time."

There was one problem. It was the end of term and I was due to return home for the holidays. I went home, left my car behind and settled down to a few weeks of misery until I heard from a girlfriend who'd seen my car exceeding the speed limit in the main street.

I made some foolish excuse, hitchhiked back to the city and staked out my new friend's lodgings. I'll cut the story short here – we've still not got to the cat. I decided to stay in my flat in the city, while he also replaced the seats in my car and un-supercharged it so it was possible for me to drive again.

The first couple of days I mooched around the flat, but on the third I rather reluctantly agreed to accompany him to work. He was driving one of those huge cement mixers, you know, the kind with the large, revolving drum on the back.

It was a totally new experience for me, perched up on the passenger seat, speeding past the English countryside, delivering cement to all kinds of places. It was the day we visited the farm that the die was cast.

I hopped out of the truck as it backed into position, preparing to pour out the cement for the new pig sties. I was admiring the cats and dogs as they frolicked or dozed in the farmyard, and noticed the farmer walking past carrying a plastic bag, which was heaving, moving and mewling. I had to ask him what was inside.

"Them's kittens," he told me. "**** cat's 'ad another **** litter afore I could catch 'er and had her done."

"How many kittens are in the bag?" I asked, thinking it was a rather uncomfortable way to transport them.

"Dunno," he replied. "Four or five. Soon be none."

There came an extra loud squeal from the bag and I was undone the moment I went to peep inside. I saw a mass of black and white fur, small limbs fighting for space, clambering one over another. It was impossible to count them but I could see at least four heads. However many there were, they were all in deep distress.

"What are you going to do with them?" I asked naively. "They look far too young to go to new homes."

The farmer stared at me with a pitying expression on his face.

"They ain't gonna go to no good 'omes," he replied with a deal of satisfaction in his voice. Them's gonna go to the water tank."

A rush of comprehension as I realised he was going to drown them. I was appalled. I thought of my own cat back home: fat, contented, cuddling up on my lap, purring while she curled herself round my legs every time I returned to nursemaid my mother.

"I'll take one," I blurted before I could stop and think. "Let me have one. Please."

"Sure if'n you want one, take yer pick."

I thrust my hand into the bag, grabbed the closest kitten and pulled it out. It was small enough to fit in my palm and its eyes were barely open. It can't have been more than a couple of weeks old at most.

"She's so small!" I gasped while investigating the furry ball to see if it was male or female.

"Tha's cos their mum was sneaky and 'id them well away. Knew what would 'appen if I found 'em."

I shuddered. If only he'd had the cat sterilised before this tragedy occurred, I wouldn't have to watch him stride off on his way to commit murder in the water tank.

I looked down at the scrap of fur in my hands and wondered what I'd done. How could I keep a kitten? I went home every weekend, there was already a cat in residence and there was no way my mother would agree to an extra mouth to feed. Even if I transported it back and forth, during the week I was out teaching all day and there was no garden to the flat. I couldn't bear the thought of locking it up inside all day.

My charismatic hero walked round the side of the cement mixer. "What have you got there?"

"Um. A kitten, I've just saved its life. The farmer was going to drown it." I burst into tears.

It didn't faze him at all. He smiled as he tickled the ball of fur with his finger and told me to hop up in the truck. Have you ever tried that with a kitten in one hand?

The only place to put it was the glove compartment and make for the nearest pharmacy to purchase an eye dropper and some milk. How I wish they'd sold baby wipes in those days.

The next priority was to procure a suitable bed and luckily an empty shoe box fitted nicely into the front of the truck. Armed with some nice soft bedding, we were good to go.

"A name, we must give it a name."

"Boy or girl?"

"Girl, I think, and I'll get her done as soon as she's old enough, six months if I remember correctly."

We spent the rest of the day throwing one name out after another but couldn't decide on anything we liked that didn't sound too twee. It wasn't until I crawled out of the cab at the end of the day and glanced upwards that it came to me. Premix was the perfect name for our kitten. It was unlikely we would ever forget the day we got her.

Now, you may have noticed I'm using the 'we' word. It all started that day – 'we' were now an item, bonded by the smallest bundle of fur which ever attacked an eye dropper with unbridled enthusiasm.

At this point fate took another turn. As I walked up the steps to my flat that night, who should I meet coming down them but my landlord. He eyed the box in my hand and barked, "No pets! You know the rules."

"Goodness no...of course not...wouldn't dream... just popping in to collect something and taking it round to my boyfriend's place. It's his kitten. His landlord doesn't mind one small kitten." I hoped he recognised the sarcasm in my voice.

As I continued towards the front door, I was hoping and praying the landlord would disappear, but no such luck. He leaned against the wall watching and waiting for me to go back out.

I was relieved to see my new boyfriend's car parked close by and as I tumbled into the front seat I blurted out the whole sorry tale. I could still see my landlord in the wing mirror, he was still watching and still waiting for us to drive away. So we did.

We had more luck as we successfully smuggled Premix into the other flat. For the next couple of weeks, we sneaked in and out, morning and night, with the cat under a coat, or in a pocket. The rest of the time she grew up in the glove compartment and played out on the grass while the cement dispersed its contents at various venues.

I worried about what I was going to do when the school term started again, but in the meantime, we got caught.

For once Premix mewled a little too loudly and gave her and us away. We were given three days to vacate my boyfriend's flat.

Always the optimist, my friend suggested we rent a cottage together, somewhere out in the country saying, "Premix is a little older now and needs a garden to play in." This decision was hastened by my hero getting fired, my first experience in a long line of downsizing, redundancies and outright letting go.

Off we trekked and were lucky to find a cottage with a huge garden just perfect for a cat or five. It was far away from any other dwelling so unlikely to be part of an area claimed by any other felines. We could safely leave her here while we were at work and, to make matters perfect, there was even a cat flap in the back door.

Life was uneventful for a few months, if you don't count the wedding, a one day honeymoon, and two more jobs gained and lost by my other half. I thought life for Premix was uneventful as well, but I was wrong.

I was certain that you couldn't have a cat spayed until they were six months old. I was thankful, as it gave me the opportunity to save up for what I assumed would be a rather large vet bill. Premix had other ideas. By her fifth-month birthday, her tummy was already swelling out of all proportion to her tiny frame and as the magic sixth month approached there was absolutely no doubt – she was pregnant.

I groaned. Feeding one extra kitten we could manage, but a whole lot more? In those days teachers were not paid a fortune and with the breaks between jobs for the other half of our relationship, the only regular income was mine. What could I do but let nature take its course? I vowed that the moment she gave birth she was off to the vet.

A few months later found me bullying the children in the classroom into taking a kitten home with them. I took one to school on the excuse it was for a natural history lesson, but in reality it was a sales exercise. To my enormous relief, I managed to foist five squalling kittens onto my pupils, promising them excellent marks for the rest of the year. I'm normally a law-abiding citizen, but there are times that call for desperate measures.

I stuffed Premix into a handy pillow case and headed off to the vets, only to return home to greet my other half holding yet another severance cheque in one hand and a half-starved kitten in the other.

Leaping forward several months saw us heading off for Scotland to begin a new life crofting. My charismatic husband (now my ex) could sell ice cubes to Eskimos and by comparison, I was a total push-over.

By now, our family had expanded. Besides my teaching job I had also begun to breed small animals. I won't go into how all that started – it's a long story.

We loaded them up into the self-drive removals van. Four cats and six dogs in the cab with us and various furries in the back. We'd travelled less than twenty miles when Premix had an accident through sheer fright, which resulted in my transferring her into the back of the van. I changed my clothes since the cat had chosen my lap in which to relieve herself. You'd think spending the first few weeks of her life in the glove compartment of a Premix cement truck would have made her immune from travel sickness but no.

At the motorway service station, I gingerly lifted the back door and slid inside to replenish water bottles on the cages and check on our travelling companions. All were well. None of the cages' occupants appeared fazed by the cat, while Premix glared at me balefully.

Just as I was inching forward to try and pacify her, the sliding door descended on my back leaving me pinned, half in and half out of the van and there I stayed for what seemed like an eternity, until my ex came to rescue me.

On the road again, we arrived at the small croft we'd mortgaged in the far north of Scotland. While I arranged the cages in the outbuilding, Premix and the other four cats sniffed around with guarded expressions on their faces.

In the house, I had two baskets in front of the Aga stove containing Muddle, Trouble and Tempest, proud mummy Cairns to the most adorable puppies. And I too was in process of re-populating the world.

They were so stoic about bringing new life into the world that I was shamed into silence as my body ached and creaked as I grew larger and larger and my gait became more cumbersome.

By this time, we'd also taken in a Pyrenean Mountain dog, which pinned me against the wall on numerous occasions refusing to let me go until I'd scratched her head and tummy to her complete satisfaction.

Now I can't say our crofting adventures were going well. No, our efforts were a complete disaster. The animals were happy, the air was fresh and clean, the ex had a good job and all was well. Until the lurgy struck.

It began slowly, one morning I found one of our rabbits dead in the outhouse. Premix, who seldom left my side, came in with me to investigate and then fled, tail erect, fur splayed out, and ears flattened. I should have realised her instincts were more finely tuned than mine.

The following morning there was another death, this time one of the gerbils. For the first time, Premix had not accompanied me into the shed, she kept her distance and sat outside waiting and watching.

We dug holes and buried the bodies. In desperation, I took a couple of the sad little carcasses to the vet and through a veil of tears sobbed about our losses.

He sent the samples, as he referred to them as, to the veterinary department in Aberdeen and the answer came back in a matter of days. It was pseudotuberculosis, if I remember correctly. There was no cure, and we were told that in time, every animal would go to the pet menagerie in the sky.

"But where did it come from?" I asked in despair. Our little croft was miles from any other dwelling and while the cats might wander off occasionally, and the dogs run on the nearby fields, they were all healthy.

Apparently we had a carrier, but who? The dogs were fine, so too were the cats. Did we wait for all of them to die to see who remained?

By now, Premix was refusing to go out on the side of the house closest to the outbuilding. She was as cuddly as always and followed me everywhere else, but never there. She still crawled up onto the lap I once had every evening, and purred while she gently kneaded my huge tummy with her claws. She seemed to sense the new life inside me, with the same perception she knew the death lurking in the shed the other side of the wall.

To my great relief, we were told it was unlikely the new baby would be affected by the pseudotuberculosis, which was rampaging through our breeding business. We debated loud and long about what to do. The decision was taken from us as in one final night, the last of these animals went to the great menagerie in the sky. All that is, except the misnamed Rebecca, the buck rabbit we'd rescued from the home that didn't want him.

"There's your carrier," said the vet pointing to the only remaining animal. "He will have to be put down."

"How soon can we start again?" I asked, devastated. "I've scrubbed everything with cleaning fluid and sterilised all the bottles and..."

He interrupted me. "Never, I'm afraid. The risk is too high. You've got wooden cages, you'll have to burn them."

With me not working due to being so pregnant, and the ex currently hunting for work, life looked bleak. Then my other half bounced through the door one evening and announced we were off to Africa.

"But what about our animals? We can't leave them behind!"

"The McMaddons over by Banff are happy to take the Cairns and the Cars on the far farm have made friends with the cats. They'll be fine." In my ex's book, if he said everything was going to be fine that was the end of it – they would be fine.

"I'm taking Premix, and that's final." I found the courage to stand firm. "She was the beginning of all of this, I'm not leaving her."

He said nothing, but walked away while I hugged Premix so tightly she squawked. I was in despair and she seemed to sense my mood, for she didn't leave my side for the next few days.

There followed the trip into hospital, returning with a bouncing, healthy girl. As soon as I walked into the house, I was greeted with a loud meow as a black and white bundle of fur flung herself at me.

"Aren't you worried the cat might smother the baby?" people asked.

"No, I trust her completely, she's got an instinct I can't fathom. She does sleep in the carry cot but always at the bottom. I feel she's watching over my daughter. We're still working out how to get her to Africa, but she's coming with us." Such comments were met with disdainful expressions and raised eyebrows.

Time moved on. We began to pack, and I brought home a cat basket. Premix eyed it with suspicion. I remembered the accident in the last removal van during the journey north, and hoped for the best.

Four days to go. The house was looking bare, the clothes for storage in one pile, everything we were placing into the suitcases in another. I was feeding the baby when there was a knock at the door. A neighbour from the fishing village at the bottom of the hill stood there in tears. "I think I've run over your cat," she sobbed.

It couldn't be Premix. Not Premix, the cat who seldom strayed out of the house, and never, ever strayed out onto the quiet country road that ran past the house.

But it was. Whatever possessed her to venture so far in those last few days I shall never know. She had been a constant companion, a loving friend and behaved more like a dog than a cat. She slept on my bed, weaved round my legs and purred like a steam train, and now she would never purr again, never cuddle on my lap.

She was not quite three and a half years old when she died. My only consolation, as we locked up the house before driving away, was to look at the small memorial above her grave, remember she had escaped the water tank, and while part of our family, she'd had a happy, if short, life.

Premix July 1971 – November 1974

About the Author

Lucinda E Clarke, UK
Website: http://lucindaeclarkeauthor.com
Blog: http://lucindaeclarke.wordpress.com
Amazon: http://www.amazon.co.uk/Lucinda-E-Clarke/e/B00FDWB914/
Twitter: @LucindaEClarke https://twitter.com/LucindaEClarke

Lucinda fell into writing after an appalling radio drama audition at the South African Broadcasting Corporation – she was told to 'go home and write'. After that there was no stopping her and she scribbled from morning till night for radio, TV, magazines, newspapers, mayoral speeches, even advertisements. If it needed words, she wrote them. Now retired, Lucinda is writing what she wants to write and to date has published eight books in three genres: memoirs, comedy and action adventure. She's won three international awards, hit the number one spot in genre on Amazon, and says she just can't stop writing.

Cat Naps with Cattitude
By Johanna Tarkela

About the Illustrator

Johanna Tarkela, UK
Website: www.johannatarkela.com
Facebook: https://www.facebook.com/JohannaTarkelaART/

I'm a Finnish illustrator with a big love for animals of all kind (but possibly a slight preference for cats :)). I graduated in 2015 with a degree in illustration and have been making a living with art since. I work mainly digitally at the moment, but I have roots in traditional art and love to get back to making it occasionally!

Father Dougal
By George Mahood

We had a cat called Father Dougal. He was named after the character from the sitcom *Father Ted*. Like his namesake, he had a slightly bemused expression when he was a kitten. He was also black with a white bib and so looked like a clergyman.

Rachel and I moved into our first house together in 2002. Our first encounter with Doug, our neighbour, was a conversation over the garden wall. It was December. He was wearing a vest and whistling a tune I didn't recognise. Doug was particularly chatty and friendly, with a warm smile and he was eager to learn lots about his new neighbours. He was in his early sixties but had taken early retirement to be a full-time carer for his wife Christine (Chris).

We became extremely close to Doug and Chris over the following ten years. Rachel and I moved into our house unmarried, with no children. Doug and Chris watched us grow into a family and met each of our three children – Layla, Leo and Kitty – when they were only hours old. Doug and Chris were pretty much perfect neighbours; always there to keep an eye on our house, lend us things, or just discuss the troubles of Northampton Town Football Club over the garden wall.

They also became particularly fond of Father Dougal. They used to have an elderly cat called Lucy (who names a cat Lucy?) and Father Dougal would sneak through their cat flap, beat the crap out of Lucy, eat her food, and then leave. To begin with, Doug would shout at Father Dougal and chase him out. He then started falling for Father Dougal's charm and affection. He began to allow him to come and eat Lucy's food, and soon he was actively encouraging it. After Lucy died, Doug continued to buy cat food and feed Father Dougal. We gradually grew to accept the arrangement as it was nice that Father Dougal was getting so much attention. It also reduced our cat food bill significantly.

Doug and Chris then gave Father Dougal a new name. They called him Basil, which we found a little weird to begin with. I'm not sure whether they just thought the name suited him better, or whether, as Christians, they considered it insulting to name a cat after a man of the cloth. Either way, he became known as Basil at their house and Father Dougal at ours.

"Have you seen Basil this morning? Sorry, I mean Father Dougal," asked Doug over the garden wall one morning.

"No, I don't think I have. He popped in early evening yesterday but I haven't seen him since. Have you not?"

"No, I haven't seen him since yesterday. I think he's gone missing again. I've got a bad feeling," he said.

"He'll be OK. You know what he's like. He's probably just gone for a wander or maybe he's been shut inside someone's house. I'm sure he'll be back soon."

"I hope you're right, George. I hope you're right. We miss him already."

Father Dougal had gone missing once before. He disappeared just before Christmas a few years ago. There were no sightings of him for several weeks and we had almost given up hope of seeing him again, when he was found wandering the streets about half a mile away. It's unclear how or why he went missing. Our house is a mid-terrace and there are no access points into the back gardens other than through the houses. Father Dougal has a habit of nosing through neighbours' back doors to see if there is any food on offer, because being fed at two houses is clearly not enough.

The couple that used to be our neighbours on the other side to Doug also had a cat. It was called Nigel (who names a cat Nigel?). This cat was very old and Father Dougal used to take full advantage and sneak through the cat flap and eat his food, knowing full well that poor old Nigel would not be able to retaliate. Our neighbours quite rightly hated Father Dougal. I was sitting outside in the garden one morning, drinking a cup of tea, when I heard shouting from next door.

"YOU BLOODY CAT!" and then a blur of black fur leapt over the wall as Father Dougal made a dash for it. Then Andy, our neighbour, reached the doorway still shouting and swearing at the cat, and threw a pint glass full of water towards Father Dougal. Andy didn't have time to notice me sitting by our back door as the water skimmed inches away from my face.

"Oh my gosh, I'm so sorry," he said, completely mortified. "I didn't know you were there. It was just...your cat...and Nigel...you know...sorry!"

"Don't worry at all. It sounds like he deserved it. I'm sorry that he keeps coming into your house," I said.

So, the problem with living in a mid-terrace house, and having a cat that likes to visit other people's houses, was that you had to rely on him coming back out the same way that he went in. If he went into a house through the back door, and was then chased out the front door onto the street, there would be no way for him to get back around to the garden.

On the way back from dropping Layla at school the following day, I passed Doug on his doorstep.

"Any sign of Basil?" he asked.

"No, not yet, I'm afraid. I walked around the streets late last night but no luck. He'll come back soon."

"Remember last time, he was gone for over a month."

"Was it really that long?"

"Yes, it was. Four weeks to the day. It felt like forever, though. I don't know what we would do if he didn't come back. Chris and I didn't sleep a wink last night."

I could empathise with how Doug felt. The previous time Father Dougal had gone missing was before we had children. The cats were very important to us. Then children came along and our priorities changed slightly, and although he was still an important part of our lives, Father Dougal had slipped further down the order of precedence. It also felt as though Father Dougal was choosing to distance himself from us. He was spending more and more time at Doug and Chris's house and exploring further and further afield. It was no wonder he had got himself lost.

It was incredibly important for me to try and get Father Dougal back, though. If anything, I felt an even greater sense of duty and responsibility because now it was no longer just Rachel and I that would miss him, but Layla, Leo and Kitty, and almost more importantly, Doug and Chris.

He still hadn't returned the following day. I had phoned all the local vets and animal shelters without success, so made a MISSING poster and printed off 30 copies. The five of us walked around the neighbourhood with Doug, attaching the posters to lamp posts and telegraph poles.

I received a phone call later that afternoon.

"I've found a cat wandering the street outside our house. I think it might be yours."

"Really?" I said, squealing slightly.

"Yes, although it looks a bit different to the one on the poster."

"Ah, OK. Well, it's not a very good photo."

"This one has a blue collar."

"Oh, right. Our cat's was definitely red. But maybe someone put a different collar on him. Does he look like the picture?"

"No. Your picture and description said your cat was black and white. This one is ginger."

"Oh," I said. "Thanks anyway."

As the days turned into weeks, with still no news, we knew it was more and more unlikely that Father Dougal would return. Because he had gone missing for a month before, we were still clinging on to a shred of hope that he would be found. I still looked for him whenever I went out for a run or bike ride, but I had started getting used to the fact that we may never see him again. Doug asked on a daily basis whether we had heard any news. It had clearly affected him and Chris very badly. I was used to seeing Father Dougal sprawled on their sofa whenever I called around to visit, and their house felt noticeably emptier without him.

A month passed without any news. Then, one Sunday night at 9 pm, the phone rang. We initially planned to ignore it but I then decided to answer it before it woke up Kitty.

"Hello, have you lost a cat?" said the well-spoken lady on the other end.

"Yes, we have. Father Dougal. He's a big black one."

"I've found him."

I grabbed the car keys and headed straight over. The lady lived a few streets away and she had noticed a cat sneaking through her cat flap for a couple of weeks to eat her cat's food. She had not been able to get close enough to read his collar but had managed to lock the cat flap on the most recent occasion. Father Dougal was in quite a bad way. He had lost a lot of weight, and had somehow got one of his front legs through his collar so that he was now wearing it across his body like a beauty sash. Maybe that's how all the cool cats wear them on the street these days. The collar had cut deep into his skin and the wound was dirty, matted and severely infected. It was so amazing to see him, and he seemed very pleased to see me, too. The lady refused her cash reward so I dropped around a bottle of wine and box of chocolates the following day.

Rachel had knocked on Doug's door to tell him the good news and he was at our house waiting when I returned home with Father Dougal.

"Oh, Basil! We're so pleased to have you back. We didn't think we would see you again. You had us all properly worried this time, you little tinker," he said, rubbing the top of his head. The cat's head, that is. Not his own.

"Poor little fella, he looks like he's in a bad way. He needs to see a vet urgently," said Rachel.

"I know, but it's 10 pm on Sunday. They will all be shut," I said.

"I'm sure there will be an emergency out-of-hours place," said Doug. "Don't worry about the cost. I'll pay for it."

"That's very kind of you, Doug, but you don't need to do that. Do you not think we should just wait until the morning?"

"Doug's right. It might be too late tomorrow. How would you feel if he didn't make it until morning?" said Rachel.

"OK, you're right. I'll go and call them."

"I'll come with you," said Doug eagerly.

"Thanks Doug, but it might take a long time. You'd better stay and look after Chris. We'll be OK."

"OK, if you're sure. I'll be over first thing tomorrow morning."

After finding an out-of-hours vet, I put Father Dougal back into the cat carrier and drove the three miles to the practice.

The vet was one of the most beautiful women I have ever seen in my life. I, on the other hand, looked like one of the roughest human beings ever to grace this planet. I had not slept at all the night before, and had not had time for a shower before spending the day shepherding three young children around a zoo.

"So, he's been missing for tree months?" she asked in her lovely Irish accent.

"Yes. We didn't think we'd see him again. He's quite smelly as well since he got back," I said, trying to transfer any suspicions she may have had for my hygiene problems over onto Father Dougal.

"Yes, he does whiff a bit," she said, seemingly convinced. "I tink what I'm going to do is try and clean up dis here wound and hope that the wee fella then…" she continued, but I wasn't listening to a word she said. I was completely transfixed by her eyes and sexy hypnotic voice. I nodded, and said *yep* and *uh huh,* occasionally, to show I was listening. The strangest thing was that she was staring right back at me throughout, with a cheeky smile. Her name was Wendy, which was a name so at odds with her appearance that it almost tainted her beauty, but she somehow managed to pull it off. "We'll keep him in overnight, but don't worry, he'll be grand," she said.

"What was that?" I said, being woken from my hypnosis. "IT'S GOING TO COST US A GRAND?"

"Ach, no. I said he'll be grand. He's going to be OK. He's a lovely wee fella, isn't he? I've got a cat that looks just like him."

I left the surgery feeling relieved Father Dougal was going to be OK. I got back in the car and caught a glimpse of myself in the rear-view mirror. It was at this point I noticed a huge smear of chocolate cake icing across my upper lip and another on my chin. It was no wonder Wendy had been smiling at me. The cow.

I was fresh, clean and cake-icing-free when I returned to pick up Father Dougal the following morning. The receptionist handed him to me in the carry basket, and I didn't even get a chance to show Wendy how well I scrubbed up.

"Wendy wants to see you next week," said the receptionist.

"Really? Does she? What does she want to see *ME* for?" I blushed.

"She wants to check Father Dougal's stitches and make sure the wound is not re-infected. It's standard procedure."

"Ah, Father Dougal! Oh, yes of course."

It was great to have Father Dougal home, and needless to say, Doug was delighted.

"The vet has asked that we monitor what he eats over the next few days, just to check he's recovering," I said to Doug. "Would you mind not feeding Basil for a few days just so we can keep track of what he's eating?"

"Of course, absolutely," he said.

During breakfast, I could hear Doug whistling for Father Dougal. Father Dougal had not eaten much at our house since coming home, so I decided to politely mention it again.

"Doug, would it be OK if you didn't feed Basil for a couple of days?" I said, when I saw him out in the garden later.

"Yes, that's fine. I'm not feeding him at all. Just the odd snack here and there."

"Please could you not feed him any snacks either? It's just for a couple of days. We need to check he's eating enough and we can't do that if he's eating at your house too."

"Oh, OK. Fair enough," he said.

Later in the day I heard him whistling again, and again I saw Father Dougal emerging from Doug's cat flap a while later licking his lips. Again, I had another chat with Doug.

"I haven't been feeding him," he said. "I've only been giving him cat biscuits. That doesn't count, does it?"

"Yes!" I said, getting slightly frustrated, before a feeling of guilt hit me. If Doug didn't feed Father Dougal, there was a chance that he might not go into their house. This would be a huge loss to him and Chris – even if only for a few days. Did I really want Doug to stop feeding him because of what the vet had said, or was I just getting excited about the idea that Father Dougal would be exclusively our cat again, albeit temporarily? As important as the instructions from the vet were, I realised that it was more important for Doug and Chris to see Father Dougal/Basil, and it was clearly obvious that Father Dougal was eating properly, that was for sure.

"No, you're right," I said. "Biscuits are fine. In fact, he's looking a lot better now. Carry on as you were."

"OK then. If you insist."

Over recent years, Father Dougal had started regularly spraying urine in our house. He tends to favour things made of plastic: the vacuum cleaner, plastic bags, and, unfortunately, buggies and children's toys. The smell and the clean-up was truly disgusting.

He first started doing it the year before our eldest daughter, Layla, was born, when I was away from home on a three-week bike ride. Before that, he was a happy, loving, affectionate cat who never sprayed at all. Whilst I was away for three weeks, Rachel noticed he'd started to mark his territory in the house. She said he was more agitated and nervy than before I left. She was convinced it was because of the change in dynamics in the household, with him becoming the alpha male in my absence. I maintain – secretly – that it was probably more likely a reaction to spending three weeks alone with Rachel. After living with Rachel for so long, I'm surprised I haven't started urinating everywhere because of the stress. It's only a matter of time.

I finally decided to look into the issue properly and see if there was anything that could be done.

There are various spray deterrents, tablets and soothing music CDs available to buy, all of which I had dismissed in the past because they had lots of negative reviews and hefty price tags. One product that did sound hopeful was a plug-in pheromone diffuser. I have to confess it sounded like a load of rubbish to me, but I was happy to give it a go. It was basically a Glade Plug-in (an air freshener brand) that releases a cat pheromone, which calms and de-stresses the cat, therefore stopping it from urinating. It stops the cat urinating INSIDE the house, obviously. I didn't want it to stop urinating completely. That would be unhealthy and he would likely explode.

I bought one of these diffusers and plugged it into a socket near to where we feed the cats, turned it on, and hoped for the best.

Despite my cynicism, the pheromone diffuser worked wonders. It was a truly remarkable purchase. It felt like he was a new cat. Not only had he stopped urinating in the house, but he also became a very affectionate cat again. In the evenings, he would now come and sit on our laps, allowing us to stroke and cuddle him like he used to in the 'good old days'.

"It's so lovely having the old Father Dougal back," said Rachel.

"It's amazing," I said, tickling him under the chin as he purred on my lap.

"I didn't think that Glade Plug-in thing that you bought would be anywhere near as effective."

"I know. Neither did I."

"Who would have thought a simple thing like that could calm him down so much and stop him being so stressed out and agitated all the time?" she said.

"Do you think they do them for humans?" I asked.

"What do you mean?"

"Perhaps they do human pheromone diffusers too. I would order one immediately and plug one next to your side of the bed. It might have the same effect on you as it has on Father Dougal."

"You're such a dick," she said.

Rachel and I had decided we were going to move to Devon. With our children too, obviously. It sounds completely crazy and irrational, but the main reason I had been reluctant to put the house on the market was not because I didn't want to move, not because I was scared or apprehensive about the prospect of relocating, and not because I had been too busy with other things. It was because I was terrified about breaking the news to Doug and Chris. I felt awful telling them that we were going to be moving away. And what about Father Dougal? The prospect of Doug and Chris losing another cat – albeit one that wasn't actually theirs – would be unbearable for them. Losing Basil would mean taking a huge part of their life away from them, and the thought made me feel physically sick.

But the feelings of a neighbour couldn't shape the way we made decisions as a family. As much as I didn't want to upset Doug and Chris, I knew that I couldn't let the uncomfortable feeling inside delay me telling them. I hated the idea that they would find out first from a 'For Sale' sign going up outside our house. We had to tell them.

It was going to be hard, but I needed to be the one to break the news. Doug would prefer it to come from me.

"Rachel?" I said, wimping out. "Would you be happy to tell Doug today about us putting the house on the market?"

"Sure," she said.

Either Rachel was a lot braver than me, or she didn't have the same level of compassion about the situation.

An hour later I could hear her in the garden. Doug had come outside to hang the washing.

"Hi, Doug."

"Hi, Rachel. Bit warmer today, isn't it?"

"Yes, it's lovely. Doug, we've decided to put our house on the market," she said, quite bluntly.

There was a slight pause.

"OK, well good luck," he said, which was followed swiftly by the sound of his backdoor closing.

"That didn't go too well," said Rachel in the kitchen.

"I know, I heard. It sounded very awkward. Poor Doug. Don't worry, I'll talk to him."

I saw Doug outside the front of his house later in the day and so nipped out to have a chat with him. We had a long conversation about the move, and he told me how he and Chris had been in tears when he had told her. But he understood that we had outgrown our house, and he knew that we couldn't live there forever.

"We will both just miss you all so much if you moved," he said. "You're like family to us."

"We will miss you both too. But we'll still keep in contact, and come and visit."

"Will you really visit?"

"Of course we will. I will have to come back to Northampton regularly for work, so I'll always call in to see you both when I'm up here."

"We'd love that. You're welcome to come and stay any time. There's always a bed for you here, kiddo," he said, putting his arms around me and squeezing me tightly. "Don't you forget about us, will you?"

"There's no chance we'll ever forget about you. This is certainly not goodbye, that's for sure."

The issue of Father Dougal and our impending move had been playing heavily on my mind. It would be hard for Doug and Chris when we moved, but losing Basil would be even harder for them. I had been toying with the idea of leaving Basil in Northampton with Doug and Chris. But Rachel wasn't so keen on the idea.

"He's our cat," she argued.

"I know. But he spends most of his time next door. We hardly see him anymore."

"But if we moved house then he would be just our cat again."

"Do you really think he wants to move house? He is very happy here. He has almost an entire house to himself next door with nobody to bother him. If you were a cat, would you choose a house with three loud children that chase you around all day and try and pick you up, or a nice warm house in which you have a choice of rooms and nobody disturbs you?"

"I'd choose Doug's house. But it just doesn't seem right."

"What about Doug and Chris? It's going to be horrible for them when we leave, but what happens when they lose Basil too?"

"Maybe you're right. But imagine not having Father Dougal anymore."

"But imagine Doug and Chris not having Basil anymore. At least we can come and visit him when we are back in Northampton. Doug and Chris would never see Basil again if he came with us to Devon."

"That's true," she said, pausing. "OK, I think you're right. It's probably for the best to leave him here. But what happens if Doug doesn't want to keep him?"

"I don't think there is any danger of that."

"Morning, Doug," I said to him over the garden wall the following day.

"Morning, George. It's 68 degrees today," he said, looking at the thermometer that hangs in his garden like he did several times a day.

"Is it? Wow," I said, never quite sure whether that is considered cold, hot or average for the time of year. I don't understand the Fahrenheit scale at all, so it meant very little to me.

"I think I'll take a risk putting the washing out," he said.

"Doug, Rachel and I were wondering if you would like to keep Father Dougal, sorry I mean Basil, when we move to Devon?"

"But he's your cat. Surely you'll be taking him with you, won't you?"

"Well we've had a talk about it and we think he would be much happier staying here with you."

"I don't know about that, George," he said, his eyes watering slightly.

"We would miss him, of course, but I know he would be happier here than with us. He's got a life of luxury with you. No children to disturb him, lots of love and affection when he wants it, a nice warm house."

"Well, he certainly does get spoilt rotten. We'd feel so awful keeping him from you, though."

"Please don't. It's honestly the best thing for everyone. So, what do you think? Do you think Chris would be happy if he stayed here with you both?"

"I know it would mean the world to Chris. She was devastated when I told her you were all moving. I mean, obviously, she will miss you, but she was particularly sad about losing Basil. No offence."

"None taken," I laughed. "We know how important he is to you both. We feel so sad to be leaving Derby Road, and the thought of taking Basil away from you two is horrible."

"Well, if you're absolutely sure, then we would be delighted. Thanks, kiddo. I can't wait to go and tell Chris."

"Thank you for looking after him. It gives us another excuse to come and visit you whenever we are back."

We accepted an offer on our house and found a place to rent down in Devon. Moving day had arrived.

Rachel and the kids went on ahead of me, and I stayed behind to help the removal men.

It was staggering to think of everything that had happened since Rachel and I had bought our first house together 11 years ago. We moved in as an unmarried couple, working in badly-paid temping jobs. This house has seen us get engaged, get married, have three children (two of them born IN the house), have pets, go through several jobs, Rachel's teacher training, parties, arguments, laughs, tears, and creating 11 years of amazing memories.

It was just a house.

A pile of bricks and mortar.

But it has been the venue for so many of the key events in our lives. No other house that we live in will ever be able to match the significance of this one.

But, surprisingly, I didn't feel any real emotion towards the house as I took one last tour, pausing only briefly in each empty room, and taking it all in. I thought I would find it hard locking the front door for the very last time and knowing I wouldn't be back. But I was ready. The time felt right. All our belongings and possessions, and the four most important people in my life, would be waiting for me down in Devon.

"So long, Derby Road. Thanks for all the memories," I said to myself as I pulled the front door to, and heard the familiar click of the latch as it locked.

Saying goodbye to Doug and Chris was far more difficult.

"So, this is it," said Doug. "What can I say? I don't know what we'll do without you."

"You've been the best neighbours for the last 11 years," I said. "But we'll keep in touch, and you'll be seeing plenty more of us, you can be sure of that."

"Do you promise to come and visit?"

"I promise."

He squeezed me tightly.

"And I know you'll take great care of Basil," I said, picking up Father Dougal and giving him a big cuddle too. He started purring which was a rarity in recent years. It was almost as though he knew what was happening. Or more likely, he was hungry and hoping I would feed him.

"Take care, kiddo. And don't forget about us," said Doug, leaning through the car window.

I started the engine and set off down the road. I gave the horn a double-beep and waved my hand out of the window. I watched in my rear-view mirror as Doug stood on the pavement, cradling Basil in his arms, until I had reached the end of the street.

A few weeks after moving down to Devon, I had a call from Doug. I could hear Basil purring away in the background. Doug and Chris liked their new neighbours and had been getting on really well. Shortly after moving in, they had announced that they were expecting their first baby. Doug and Chris were both delighted with the news, and it was comforting to think we had almost gone full circle, with a new family beginning in the house where we began ours.

About the Author

George Mahood, UK
Website: www.georgemahood.com
Facebook: www.facebook.com/georgemahood
Twitter: @georgemahood
Instagram: georgemahood
George Mahood is the author of five non-fiction books. This story is an extract from his second book, *Every Day Is a Holiday*.

Taffy's Tale of Broken Hearts
By Jo-Anne Himmelmann

Hi, it's Taffy here. I could say I'm a standard cat, but I prefer to think I'm more than that. How about a loveable, long-haired, tortoiseshell ball of fur of a very sensitive nature? That's me and this is my story.

It started about two years ago when I was abandoned, by my humans, in a big, busy city. I don't know why I was abandoned, but I don't think it was my fault. At first, it wasn't such a bad thing because I could chase butterflies, birds, mice and all kinds of moving things, but as the days went by it wasn't such fun anymore. I got hungry and it became dark and cold. The basement I slept in was dirty and all kinds of other animals lived there. I had nowhere to go. Dogs and humans chased me and I was almost hit by cars. I had to beg for food, some humans fed me but others chased me away. It was a big, scary world.

One day, a very nice lady brought me food and placed it inside a crate with a bed. At first I wasn't sure if I should go in the crate, but hey, what the heck? What could I lose? It was room and board. So, I went inside, ate my lunch, and curled up in the soft, cosy bed.

The lady picked up the crate to take me home, but first we made a stop at the local veterinary practice for a check-up. We had to make sure I had no fleas, worms or parasites as we didn't want those little crawlies invading the house. The vet, a very nice gentleman whom I call Doc, told the lady I was emaciated.

"Hey, Doc, I'm skinny," I said. "That word you used sounds really bad. It takes away from the cuteness."

My fur was missing in places and my skin was dry and scaly. I had lots of dander, whatever that was, but I could still purr with the best of them and I was free from fleas. I was ready to go to my new forever home.

That's when I heard of the problem. My new home had a dog and I didn't have a good track record with the canine kind of animal. I needed to be introduced to it slowly and from a distance. This dog was known to dislike cats. The lady (let's call her Mom) put my crate, with me in it, in the living room with the dog. It was a big room with a cat in a closed crate at one end and a dog in a crate (with no door – can you believe that?!) at the other end. My crate had all the necessities of home – built-in water, food, bed, and litter box and so the dog and I co-existed for a few days.

During that time, I found out the dog's name was Mocha. She was very sad because she had just lost her brother Mick. Mocha and Mick were together for over ten years and there wasn't one thing they didn't share. When Mick was six years old he became sick with epilepsy. He had to take medicine for a long time but in the end it didn't work and Mick crossed the Rainbow Bridge. I heard Mom and Dad talking about how Mick was a leader and Mocha a follower. With Mick gone, Mocha didn't understand how to do things on her own. She didn't want to go for a walk, play or leave her bed because something was missing. Every time I looked over I could see her sad face lying between her paws.

After a while, Mom decided it was time to let me out, but she always stayed by my side just in case Mocha decided I wasn't welcome. The odd thing was that Mocha didn't care. She didn't care about anything but her food, and the first day I was out of my crate, on my own, I discovered what would happen when I tried to eat it.

I have a little secret. I love chicken. Baked, barbequed, pulled, boiled, in pasta – just as long as it's chicken. It is my absolute favourite and it was just lying there in that bowl calling me. How could that be? Unattended chicken! Well, it was time it was eaten. I quietly and slowly manoeuvred my way to the dish and came eyeball to eyeball with a tender, moist morsel. A growl broke my concentration. Feet and nails quick-tapped on the wooden floor and a brown and white, teeth-bared Mocha face dared me to munch.

"One little taste," I pleaded but she was having none of it. It didn't matter that I was a 'starvin Marvin'.

I saw the lips curl and terror struck – time to skedaddle. From that time on, I knew I was safe so long as I left her food bowl alone.

122

Mocha's sadness was wearing on me – I like it when there is no sadness in the world. I wanted to see her happy, playing and going for walks. I had to develop a happy plan. Mocha loved her crate which also served as a bed. Day after day, I lay on the chair next to her (you know, just so she knew she wasn't alone), I sat on top of her crate and leaned over to pet her nose (cute, huh), purred and ran my tail over and under her chin (no one can resist that) and finally slept beside her. She started to like me and I think she was glad of my company. I watched over her constantly and we became inseparable, she was my friend.

She liked to watch me look out the window for birds and squirrels and bounce off the glass when I tried to catch them. We went to the treat cupboard together because she knew we would do better in that department if we joined forces. We slept on the same bed even though I sometimes risked life and limb if she laid on me. I know she liked having me around; she wasn't on her own anymore. Mom said I was a pretty smart cat and I had given Mocha a second chance.

Mocha was a senior dog; she was 13 years old. Me, I don't know, the vet said I was between two and five years old, but both of us were ready and able to have adventures. For instance, humans have a holiday called Halloween when kids, and some adults, dress up in costumes. Mom thought it would be great if we could dress up too, what did I know about dressing up? I found out very soon. Mocha had already experienced 13 Halloweens so she knew dressing up was a yearly ritual. It was pumpkin hats first – I really did try to cooperate but I'm a cat, what does a human expect? It slipped, the elastic tangled in the hair under my chin, I jumped and turned circles to get it off. After many attempts, Mom got her photo.

Christmas was a special treat. It was my first Christmas so it was game on. Mocha watched me as I promptly scaled a tree taller than my Dad. There was much ado about that. Mom and Dad hung on to the tree and tried to extract me. I almost made it to the top. Christmas ornaments jingled, garlands dropped and bells chimed. I jumped, scrambled and ran over to sit beside Mocha. While I got a lecture from Mom and Dad, Mocha looked at me as if to say 'I told you so.' She had a habit of tattling when things went wrong.

We even got Christmas presents, Mocha had lots of homemade human peanut butter cookies in a fancy tin and I had salmon treats with lots of toys in a sock. For about two weeks we had that fantastic tree in the living room. I loved watching the ornaments swing when I hit them.

Mom let me play with them as long as I didn't knock any off. Mocha would lie on her bed and watch all the while, waiting for me to knock one of the expensive ornaments off. It was all great fun. Finally, the tree came down and it was back to normal antics for Mocha and me.

As I said, Mocha was a senior dog and as months passed I knew she wasn't feeling well. She lay on her bed all day and wouldn't eat unless Mom fed her. In fact, she even let me eat her chicken. She had a hard time walking and fell a lot. She slept most of the time. Mom cried and Dad hugged her. It was so sad. I stayed with Mocha because I knew soon something was going to happen. I didn't know what, I just knew I wouldn't like it.

One day, my vet came to our house. I was very glad to see him – you could tell by the purring and strutting I did. It turned out he wasn't there to see me. He petted me and reassured me my best friend would be in a better place and no longer suffer any pain. Mom took me out of the room and closed the door. I didn't know what was happening but I knew it was going to make me very sad and lonely. What I didn't know was how much pain Mom was in. I heard Mom crying – hard. I couldn't help, I was in another room. When I returned to the living room Mocha was gone. She had crossed the Rainbow Bridge, was no longer in pain, and was running and playing with her brother Mick and his friends. She would be waiting for me when I crossed that Bridge. That made me happy. I know you may not believe this but we cats know all about the Rainbow Bridge and the good time we will have when we cross it. We will still miss our humans but not as much as our humans will miss us. You see, we live moment to moment while humans live for the present and the future, sometimes even the past. They get sad when they don't see us as part of their future. Their life is missing our constant presence. We give them peace – most of the time.

Days passed and things settled into a pattern for me. We got ready for the big move from a house to a condo. Moving was such fun, I helped with packing – packing my toys into boxes, sleeping and spending time in small, medium and large boxes. I had to be careful because sitting in a packing box when humans are in a rush means no one sees you and you end up part of the package. I tore the packing paper into smaller pieces making them easier to handle, and learned sticky tape was something to be avoided. When I got it in my fur I couldn't get it out no matter how many times I turned circles. In the end, I had to stand still while my humans cut it out. I looked like a patchwork quilt, especially being a tortoiseshell.

The new condo was on the sixth of twelve floors. Mom warned everyone to keep the patio door shut as I may get out and jump off the balcony. Why would she think I would do something like that? I'm insulted! Maybe for a bird but only that. I spent many days on my ladder, supervising the construction workers next door. I was Queen of the Condo.

My fun was limited though because Mom didn't laugh, no matter what shenanigans I got up to. She screened her telephone calls and even dropped out of her Facebook social page. She wouldn't go out and most times sat in her chair reading or looking out the window. She didn't even want to get out of bed to see Dad off to work or to feed me (very important). She would go into her bedroom and cry by herself. There were many nights she never slept and would put on coffee and look into space, or go outside. She would ask Dad if she did the right thing – maybe there was something else she could have done? She said she wanted her Mocha back. I knew from cat sixth sense she felt alone – 13 years is a long time to be with someone and not feel lonely when they're gone. Her heart was broken. She even said our nice new condo wasn't a home because it didn't have a heart.

What to do, what to do? I wanted her to be happy and enjoy life with me. I went into action. I was the love machine. Mom was going to know how special she was. Where she went, I went. I slept in her bed (she moved too much and Dad snored a lot), I let her rub my belly and purred very loudly (sometimes she even fell asleep). I stopped lifting her eye lids in the middle of the night to get fed, I dug holes in her plants so she had a spot to store water, I helped her prepare meals (carrots roll off the counter very easily), I corrected her letters on the computer and laid on her notes just to look cute (that usually made her smile). I allowed her to feed me as many treats as she wanted and I never complained. I let her know how important it was to play with my toys (love that laser thingy) and I sat on her lap whenever she read, her favourite hobby.

I was with her constantly and it started to work. She cried less and smiled more. Truth be told, I liked being with her. I knew she was getting better because she started picking me up, hugging me and telling me what a good kitty I was (that's an aww moment folks!). At times, though, Mom still tears up but she tells me not to worry, it is just a puppy memory plucking at her heart.

And so, time passed. One day, the hallway door opened. There was a real racket, little paw sounds coming down the hall, panting, a bark…whaaaa…

A PUPPY!

I'm exhausted.

About the Author

Jo-Anne Himmelmann, Canada
This is my initiation into the world of memoir writing. This short story was narrated by Taffy, my precocious little rescue cat, and written by her adopted Mom (me). Taffy quickly became a loved member of this human and canine family, mending broken hearts along the way. She is a rescuer in the truest sense.

Sparky the Very Nervous Cat
by Frank Kusy

In 2009, my life was at something of a crossroads. I had just broken my leg, my export business from India was falling apart, and my second career as a travel writer had ground to a halt on the moot point of which hotel in Bombay had the better bathroom – the Taj Intercontinental or the Oberoi.

Worse still, my new rescue cat, Jack, aka Jack Kusy or 'Jacuzzi', was proving a disappointment. Every evening, as my wife, Madge, and I gathered for relaxation in front of our 42-inch flat-screen TV, Jack would sit bang in front of the screen looking miserable.

"Hmmm," said Madge, "I'm trying to watch an educational film about juggling Romanian dwarves, and all that patch-eyed monster wants to do is block my view and stare at me accusingly. What does he *want?*"

What Jack wanted, we soon found out, was to have his feet massaged. During his third night with us, he waited until we had settled down on the futon and adjusted a warm Turkish blanket over our legs, and then he trotted forward, dumped himself on my lap, and stuck one of his paws in the air.

"Good lord!" I exclaimed, as I found myself massaging the offered paw. "He's actually *purring!*"

"Rather you than me," sniffed Madge dismissively. "Try touching him anywhere else and he just walks away backwards again."

It was unfortunate for Madge that I liked cats. I had put 'must like cats' on the dating agency form that had got us together a few years earlier, and she hadn't taken this seriously.

She really should have. On our second date, I invited her over to my house, dressed both my previous cats in costume, and started singing to them on the staircase. Thomas wore a jaunty sailor's cap and looked both dashing and truculent. Henrietta was 'Madame Rhetty, Cat of Mystery', with an Indian prayer shawl draped round her whiskers and her eyes all droopy with sleep.

Madge looked on horrified.

She learnt to like, even love, both cats eventually, but she had real issues with Jack. "He eats his weight in food, he takes up half the futon, he even gets his ruddy toes massaged. And what does he give back? Nothing! He's so spiky and unresponsive, unlike our sweet little Rhetty who followed us everywhere. I wish he'd go – he's a real downer."

The very next week, she got her wish. Jack was run over by a car and laid to rest in the garden he had regularly – and defiantly – pooped on.

Madge felt bad about that, and so did my best friend, Phil, who had also spoken ill of Jack. Jack had sprung out at him and taken a chunk out of his ankle. Though this turned out to be a good thing, since Phil, by way of recompense, got me writing again. He turned up one day with a huge monitor, about two feet across, and he encouraged me to buy a computer for it.

I wasn't keen on this idea to start with. I had been scared off computers by a horrid writing course at the University of Westminster, but a week or so later I waltzed down to PC World and bought myself a brand new, state-of-the-art, Hewlett Packard to go with his massive screen. It changed my world.

So, what was I going to write about? About my cat, of course. I had lost poor Jack, but the cat Madge gave me to replace him, on my 55th birthday, became the love of my life. I had loved Jack in some weird way, but he was seriously damaged and never really felt my 'own' cat.

Sparky was my own cat from the very start. I reached into the pet shop cage, pulled out the tiny bundle of black and white fluff, and laid it on my shoulder like a baby. "This is it," I said firmly. "This is the one I want."

Madge was very pleased about the bond that formed immediately between me and Sparky. "Frank loves Sparky," she told her mother, "because Sparky is exactly like him: cautious, good-natured, highly-strung, and very nervous."

The reason I was very nervous was I had a long-standing sleep problem. I hadn't slept well since my mother died on my wedding day ten years before, and was consequently very jumpy and on edge during my waking hours. Fortunately, there was a hope on the horizon – the John Radcliffe hospital in Oxford. This was supposed to have the best sleep clinic in the country, and my GP had secured me a three-day stay there.

"Finally," I thought, "they're going to get inside my head and find out what's going on there."

Unfortunately, I didn't sleep at all the first two days. And when I finally did drop off, at 7am on day three, I fell into a short restless sleep full of *very* strange dreams.

In one of these dreams, my new cat Sparky, or what I *thought* was Sparky, lay cradled in my arms, his little furry head burrowing into my neck and purring fit to burst. But then, as the light slowly entered my room, I realised it wasn't Sparky at all, but a brownish female cat with two tails.

I only knew that it had two tails because a nurse knocked at the door asking what I wanted for breakfast. I stumbled up and, still with the cat attached to me, retorted, "Blow breakfast. What's this cat doing here?"

"Oh, that's the hospital cat," she casually replied. "Has it got two tails?" She checked for the second one and said, "Oh yes, that's definitely ours."

This wasn't quite the end of the story, since when I woke for real at 8.30am and groggily rang for breakfast, the call was answered by a chubby gay guy called Jason. And the first thing I said to him was "Where's the hospital cat?"

He took a nervous step back, and I followed up with, "You know! The one with *two tails!*"

Whereupon he legged it, never to return.

***

Wired and tired, I was left alone to do something I had rather neglected of late. My Buddhist chanting. And what came out of this chanting? Well, for some reason, the need to write.

I hadn't written a word in a year, not since the demise of my last tortured travel guide. It was like the muse, which had turned its face away from me when I'd got stuck on the subject of Bombay bathrooms, was suddenly all smiles again. I scribbled away on anything I could find – scraps of paper, loo rolls, even the back of the calendar on my wall – and by the time I'd finished I had the draft of my first fiction book, *Sparky the Very Nervous Cat*.

Back home again, I excitedly transcribed all these scribblings onto my computer and loaded the first few chapters onto a Harper Collins website for aspiring writers called *Authonomy*. I was keen to hear what people thought of it.

Well, people weren't keen at all. My first comment ran just thirteen words and said, '*No plot, no narrative arc, no target audience, no chance of being published.*'

I was crushed. My first attempt at fiction writing, with all my hopes and dreams tied up in it, had been totally trashed. But having drawn the curtains in my room and sat there sulking for three days, I realised the commentator had been right. My book didn't have a narrative arc, it was just a series of funny (to me) anecdotes about a cat. Okay, it wasn't just any cat, it was Sparky, the cutest cat in the universe, but he needed a plot, he needed to *do* something.

Then, of course, he did.

He went missing.

For the first six months of Sparky's life, as he grew from a tiny kitten with huge bat ears into a sturdy young cat with 'daddy issues', he followed me everywhere and even slept on me at night. We kept him indoors; the pet shop had strongly advised it.

But then came the day we had to let him out, his plaintive parps and squeaks became too much to bear. I picked him up, opened the back door, and took him outside.

It was a cold winter afternoon, the garden unnaturally silent and covered with a layer of frost. Sparky was entranced by all the snowflakes slowly floating down, and tried to catch them, hopping around like a little bunny, leaving his paw-prints everywhere. One particularly large flake landed on his pretty pink nose, and he took fright and dashed back inside again.

***

That was the last that we saw of him – for three whole days.

Had he got himself lost? Had he – worst case scenario – got into the street and been run over?

I was beside myself with worry. I didn't know what to do.

"Oh, he'll come back," Madge said for the first two days, but by the third even she was concerned. "Maybe you should chant to get him back," she suggested on the phone from work. "We've tried everything else."

Indeed, we had tried everything else. We'd searched the whole neighbourhood, we'd rung dozens of doorbells, we'd stuck posters on every tree and lamp-post for miles around. And every night, as we went out with a torch and shouted out for our little lost cat, it got colder and we thought he was frozen to death somewhere and couldn't get any food because the ground was now covered with snow.

"Chant right now, darling," Madge encouraged me. "What have you got to lose?"

The answer was plenty. This was it. This was when I had to put my Buddhist faith, my whole *raison d'etre* on the line. The Japanese word *jihi* is the same for doubt and faith. I had no time for doubt now. I had to place my faith in faith.

"*Nam-myoho-renge-kyo!*" ("I devote myself to the Mystic Law of the universe") I shouted at my Buddhist scroll at the wall. "I want my cat back in fifteen minutes, or I'm packing this whole thing in!"

To this day, I don't know why I said fifteen minutes. But the sun was hanging low in the sky and it was getting dark. If I waited any longer, I might not find my little Sparky at all.

I checked my watch. It was 4 pm.

Then I ran downstairs, hopped in my van and drove round to the block of flats to the rear of my house. I had a hunch. Ignoring the complaints of the old people residing there – I was stomping all over their frozen flower beds – I came to the fence overlooking the bottom of my garden.

"Sparky! Sparky!" I called in desperation. "Where are you, Sparky? It's Daddy!"

There were a few moments of silence, then a thin squeak, and a small black and white face appeared from under a bush.

"*There* you are, baby cat!" I cried with relief. "Did you jump over the end of our garden? Couldn't you get back? Have you been sitting here all this time? Golly, you must be hungry!"

And with that I whisked Sparky home in my van, put him back in his kitchen, and watched contentedly as my long-lost (and nervously constipated) cat leapt into his litter tray and did the biggest poo of his young life.

I looked at my watch again.

It was 4.15 pm.

***

The following day, with Sparky sitting by my side, I began imagining what would have happened if my precious little cat *hadn't* been found. Oh yes, he would have been catnapped by a fat, ginger Fagin of the feline world, wouldn't he, and put to work as a feline Oliver.

My tenuous *Sparky the Very Nervous Cat* book now transformed into an altogether more complex *Ginger the Gangster Cat* book, with the ever-greedy central character, Ginger, abducting Sparky and taking him to Barcelona to score a lorry-load of tapas treats 'fresh off the table.' Yes, it was a mad concept, but I finally had a plot in mind and when I told Madge I wanted to go to Barcelona to develop it further, she couldn't stop me.

Two weeks later, and off the plane in Barcelona, we hit an immediate roadblock. All the banks were closed by the time we arrived, and we had stupidly left our credit cards in our out-of-town hotel, for fear of theft.

So then, with no local money to spend, we trooped down to the main tourist drag, *Las Ramblas*, and tried to buy euros with pounds, which we should have done at home, from a *very* reluctant currency exchange booth.

The po-faced Spaniard behind the booth wanted identification. "Passport, driving licence, anything with *photo!*" he insisted.

We had left our passports in the hotel too, and Madge was all for giving up.

"I am *not* going back to the hotel," I told her. "There has got to be a way round this!"

First I rummaged furiously through my rucksack and came up with an old bank statement and an ancient photograph of myself. "There you go!" I said with a look of triumph. "I can glue these two bits together, and there's your photo ID!"

The official tiredly shook his head.

"Okay, then." I dived back into my bag. "How about a photo of my *cat?*"

132

And with that I flourished, as my last resort, a crumpled picture of Sparky.

"Is good, *vale?*" I asked hopefully. "Look, I can attach it to my flight documents!"

The girl in the adjoining booth tittered and said, "Sorry, no, but nice cat."

"Yes, he *is* a nice cat," I agreed, deflated. "And talking of cats, do you have any? I've been in Barcelona for hours and I haven't seen one. Where *are* they?"

"*Perdon?*"

"*Donde...esta...los...gatos?*" I repeated, delving deep into my rusty Spanish.

Madge's eyebrows began to arch in annoyance. Here she was, all set on some serious sightseeing, and her silly hubby was obsessing about cats again. Yes, she knew I was keen to find material for my new book, but this was going too far.

"Ah, *donde?*" said the girl happily. "Inside."

"Inside? Why...*porque*...inside?"

"Barcelona is big city," explained the girl. "Many people live in...how you say...flats. Keep *gatos* inside the flat. Outside the flat, they die soon. *Mucho traffico.*"

"That's crazy, *loco!*" I said. "There must be some street cats somewhere. Have you been to Istanbul? They're all over the place – even sleeping on cars and in mosques!"

"*Que?*"

"Mosques. Muslim mosques. We saw a *gato* sleeping in one. On the altar. On a cushion."

"You want to see mosques?"

"No, I don't. And I don't want to discuss them either. I came here to change money, which you won't allow me to do, so where are the bloomin' *gatos?*"

The girl thought a bit and then said brightly, "Oh yes, you can find them in hospital."

"Hospital? Is that a place for sick cats?"

"No," giggled the girl. "Hospital *Street*, very close to here." And with that she pointed me to a road directly opposite, just below the huge indoor food market that was *La Boqueria.*

"Many *gatos* there," she cheerfully informed me. "They live in park."

I wrinkled my nose in anticipation.

"Don't tell me," said Madge, rolling her eyes at me. "Our first day in Barcelona, and we're going cat-spotting. Why can't we see some Gaudi?"

"What, a whole load of unfinished houses and cathedrals?" I pouted. "We haven't even got the price of admission. Besides, this holiday is my birthday present, isn't it? So, bear with me on this – I can't *believe* all the stray cats in Barcelona live in one small park."

And with that I had a mission. It was called 'Spot the Stray Cat in Barcelona' and I went to it like a man possessed. Without even consulting Madge – she only followed on because it was my birthday – I walked briskly across the road.

What we found there surprised even me. Instead of an open park, with lots of carefree cats lounging around under trees and sniffing bushes, I came across what looked like a maximum-security prison. Inside, behind 15-feet-high double fencing, and overseen by brooding watchtowers and searchlights, sat four miserable cats. One was parked on a bench, another on a kindergarten slide, and two others were huddled up in a corner, gazing hopelessly at a football.

"What have they done to deserve this?" I marvelled. "Killed someone?"

"No," said a passing Spanish student. "This is charity home for cats. It is miraculous and wonderful."

Peering through the fencing, Madge spotted a little wooden sign. It was nailed to a tree and said *El Jardinet dels gats.org.*

"That is one weird website," she muttered curiously. "We must check it out when we get home."

"Why wait?" I said. "I saw an internet cafe back there. Let's do it now!"

Minutes later, staring at a screen, we were rewarded with the following information:

El Jardinet dels gats – the Garden of the Cats – is an excellent sanctuary in the heart of Barcelona, in a square just off the Carrer de l'Hospital. Run entirely by volunteers, it is well worth a visit and to make a donation. Strictly no kill, it does some amazing work. It is home to nearly 20 abandoned or feral cats who would otherwise find life on the streets hard and lonely. It was originally the playground of a nursery, which is the reason why there are some children's swings. They are still there, but adapted to felines, with scratching posts and special toys. Some benches are favourite sunbathing spots for our cats. The most brave of them even climb the trees!

"Climb the trees?" Madge snorted. "I don't think so. Every tree is wearing a little green plastic skirt to stop them climbing up!"

"And what's that about 20 cats?" I said suspiciously. "How come we only saw four?"

Back at the hotel, and happily reunited with our credit cards, we tried to imagine an answer to this question. Oh yes, the 16 missing cats, bored to distraction and led by a particularly disinterested cat called Miguel, had staged a daring getaway only the night before. Miguel, a big fan of *The Great Escape* movie, had dug a tunnel under his cell and let them all out. All, that is, but for four moggies too old or too blind to follow on. They were on the loose now – 16 furry fugitives – and they were in the mood for food.

Before you say it, we were both quite mad, we had lost the plot.

But I had just found one.

***

As the Ginger book progressed, Madge and I became more and more convinced that 'Ginger' was real. For one thing, Sparky brought in a dead mouse.

"That's strange," I told Madge. "He's never killed anything before. All he's ever brought in was a dead leaf, a dead worm, and an almost-dead ladybird. I was at the point of finding an elderly pigeon somewhere, tying it to a post, and wheeling it out to the garden for Sparky to lick to death."

"It's more than strange," said Madge suspiciously. "Look, he's ignoring the mouse completely and tucking into his cat food instead. I bet that mouse was dead already!"

"What are you saying?"

Madge shot me a knowing look. "I'm saying Sparky has a contract killer."

The contract killer turned up next morning. He was large and fat and orange, and he got stuck in the cat flap.

"Well, who's *this?*" I addressed Sparky. "Have you brought a friend? My, he's a big one, isn't he, and he doesn't look too comfortable!"

This real ginger cat looked spookily like the fictitious 'Ginger' I had been imagining for my book, and he was not happy. His head and the front half of his body had made it into the kitchen, but his swollen orange tummy had become solidly wedged in the open flap. It was only with the greatest of effort that I managed to push him back outside and then let him in through the back door.

"I think I've got an extra bowl," I said, ferreting around in the cluttered kitchen. "Now, I've got you rabbit, Sparky, I know you like that. But what about your friend? He looks like a fish man."

He was indeed a fish man. I was just reaching down to tempt 'Ginger' with a shiny pink prawn when a bright orange fireball leapt at my chest, grabbed the whole pack, shot out of the kitchen and up the stairs. He was eventually located under my Buddhist altar, gobbling down every single prawn and growling to himself with selfish pleasure.

"It's not his fault he's a mad, greedy piglet," I told myself. "He must be another feral cat like Jack and doesn't know whom he can trust. And if Sparky likes him, well, he can't be *all* bad – can he?"

But I was wrong. Ginger *was* all bad. He sat under the Buddhist altar all day, digesting his prawns, and then, simply because he felt like it, raced down the stairs, scratched around on the lawn round the back, and laid a large sausage right in the middle.

I was appalled. My nice, neat lawn was scratched and pooped on, and I only had minutes to sort it out before my wife returned from work. So, I dashed inside, returned with some rubber gloves and a trowel, and furiously removed all evidence of Ginger's deposit.

Madge's key turned in the lock the moment the offending sausage, now safely bagged up and odourless, dropped into the bin.

"What kind of a day have you had, darling?" she enquired casually.

"Well, Sparky's found a new friend!" I said.

"What *kind* of new friend?"

"A big, fat, orange one. Look, there he is out on the lawn, sniffing your rose bush."

"*Sniffing* it?" howled Madge. "He's *eating* it! That's *Dawn*, my favourite rose bush, and he's just chomped down all her blossoms!"

Ginger, hearing the commotion, stopped in his tracks and threw up the rose blossoms with a series of loud burps. He sat waiting to be forgiven.

"He's not staying with us," said Madge with finality. "He's got to go."

"But you're always saying Sparky needs a friend!" I protested. "He's bored, you said, of toy mice and jingly little balls and could do with a proper playmate."

"Yes, but not *this* guy. He's the spawn of Satan. See the way he's staring at me? If looks could kill, I'd be dead right now!"

Ginger, as if sensing he might have overdone it, rolled unhappily onto his back. He shot Madge a look of tired affection, and licked the naked rose bush in a gesture of belated apology.

"See, I told you!" I said, secretly relieved. "He's a good cat after all!"

Madge shrugged and went back in the house. "It's your call," she warned darkly. "But I'm telling you, you're making a big mistake."

The next day, after months of rain and dreary skies, the sun shone brightly and spring finally arrived. Madge flung open both garden doors and swarms of insect wildlife promptly invaded the breakfast room. "Oh look, there's an ants' nest right by your feet!" she told me happily, and a cool breeze ushered in a large, inquisitive bee, along with a couple of lost beetles and a cloud of newly-born flies.

Sparky's eyes flitted back and forth, nervously surveying both the bee and the vast expanse of sprawling lawn full of creepy-crawly things. He waited until Madge began poking a gigantic spider with a stick, and fled upstairs to hide.

Where was Ginger, I wondered? I had last seen him in the kitchen, scouring the floor for stray prawns. And why wasn't he out in the garden, when it was such an obvious field-day for crunchy little bugs and insects?

The truth of it was, Ginger wasn't sure he wanted to spend another night in our house, but once he had, he'd wandered out the front door behind me as I nipped out to check my van battery, and then, since nobody had seen this manoeuvre, he'd found himself back on the street again with no more prawns on offer.

"Ginger's gone," I said three hours later. "I can't find him anywhere."

"Good riddance too," mumbled Madge, nursing a big angry scratch on the back of her ankle. "That nutter came at me out of nowhere this morning, and tore a lump out of my leg!"

As night drew in, and Madge retired to bed, she had occasion to eat her words. There was a strange little tip-tapping sound above her head, suggestive of a small animal running back and forth, and she couldn't go to sleep.

"Where's Sparky?" she demanded crossly, getting out of bed and summoning me to her side. "Here, hold this ladder, I'm going to shove him up into the attic and let him kill whatever's up there."

Sparky was calmly snoozing in his basket when he was rudely plucked into the air and thrust into a cold, dark loft. Ten minutes passed, and another ten. Madge returned and shone a light up into the attic. What she saw there vexed her greatly – Sparky was sound asleep against a small baby squirrel. The two of them had been cuddling up to each other for warmth.

"Well, this won't do!" she raged at me. "I told you Sparky was a coward. He can't even kill a baby squirrel!"

"One day," I responded calmly, "Sparky will bring you a gerbil, or a robin, and you will be horrified as it gasps out its little life on your carpet. What do you want of him anyway? To be ultra-cute or a killer? You can't have both!"

"So, what do you suggest?"

I considered. On the one hand, I was glad to be shot of Ginger, but on the other, if we didn't get him back I wouldn't be going to bed at all.

"I suggest you go outside and find Ginger. I hate to say this, but he's the man for this job. Mister Squirrel won't have a chance."

"And then I can sleep again?"

"Well, I can't get up the attic with my bad leg, and you, with your fear of blood and torture, wouldn't kill a fly."

Grumbling under her breath, Madge snatched the torch, threw on some clothes, and went out into the street.

"Ginger! Ginger!" she called without much hope, and wandered down the road silently cursing to herself. But she needn't have worried. Ginger had positioned himself under a bush, just three doors down from the house, and as soon as he heard Madge's voice he dashed out to greet her.

"I don't like you," Madge informed him. "But I guess we both need each other. So, let's get out of this rain, and try to patch things up."

Sparky was delighted to see his lost friend back again. He watched as I dried Ginger off with a towel, and looked on, very gratefully, as Madge shoved Ginger up into the attic. There was a surprised squawk of terror as Mister Squirrel departed this world, and then Ginger returned to the mouth of the loft, licking his lips with cobwebs all around his mouth.

"Good boy!" we cried in unison, and carried Ginger down in triumph.

In my mind, the final piece of my Ginger cat book slotted into place. "Well, at least I'm good for *sumfink!*" I invented a Cockney geezer voice for him. "If I'd known they liked dead fings, I could have been 'good boy' a lot sooner!"

About the Author

Frank Kusy, UK
Website: http://frankkusybooks.weebly.com/ Twitter:
https://twitter.com/Wussyboy Facebook:
https://www.facebook.com/frank.kusy.5?ref=tn_tnmn
Email: sparky-frank@hotmail.co.uk

Born and raised in the fog-shrouded streets of 1960's London, and with more than 30 years of travel writing experience under his belt, aspiring Buddhist and incorrigible cat-lover Frank Kusy's story is excerpted from his latest memoir *The Reckless Years: A Marriage made in Chemical Heaven.* If you want to read more about Sparky the cat, and his fat slob of a sidekick, Ginger, these two furry friends feature in two other books of Frank's: *Ginger the Gangster Cat* and *Ginger the Buddha Cat*, both available on Amazon, Kobo, ibooks, and most other sales channels. Prrrrps!

Alfie
By Zoë Marr

I arrived home from work on a blisteringly hot day in Auckland, New Zealand. My husband's car was in the drive but he didn't answer my greeting as I walked through the front door. That wasn't a surprise; it was so warm he'd likely be outside. I walked through the house and into the garden, and there he was, to my surprise, holding a ginger kitten.

"I found him on the fence and it looked like he couldn't get down," Ray explained as he stroked the kitten. This was a happy surprise, they looked lovely together. The kitten wasn't struggling to get away and Ray appeared to have been holding it for a while. They were certainly content.

The kitten was about 11 weeks old. He had a big white bib, huge ears and ginger stripes like a tiger. He was very friendly, happy to be held and obviously enjoying the attention. As we stroked him, we noticed the tip of his tail appeared to have been broken. He was also crawling with fleas and other tiny bugs. It seemed the poor little chap hadn't had the best or easiest start in life.

Ray eyed me suspiciously. "We're not keeping him," he stated firmly. He knows me too well when it comes to cats. "We already have two and we've never wanted a kitten."

This I had to admit. We've always adopted older cats, ones that have been socialised and are less likely to shred the house, or our arms, to bits. But before you think I'm likely to kidnap anything with four legs that walks into our garden, I should explain we already knew about this little character.

A few weeks previously, late one night, I was watching TV in the living room and Ray was upstairs watching a delightful drama series about serial killers. There was a knock on the door. We don't live in the nicest area of town and I felt my pulse quicken as I checked to make sure the door was locked, thankful for the solid wood preventing the visitor from seeing what I was doing. I took the stairs two at a time and ran breathlessly into our bedroom. Ray was wearing headphones, he hadn't heard a thing. I motioned for him to take them off and he could see from my expression something was up.

"Someone's at the door and I'm worried about answering it by myself," I whispered, mindful all the windows were open to catch a little breeze.

Ray checked the bedside alarm clock – 10 pm. That was unusual. Who would be coming round this late at night? Our friends always send a text if they're going to visit unexpectedly. He got up and walked downstairs, turning off the hall lights and pulling the living room door to, so the inside of our house wasn't easily visible to anyone hoping to case the joint. My husband is 6'4" and solidly built. Hopefully being confronted by him would encourage a would-be criminal to move on. With scenes from the serial killer drama flashing through his mind, Ray prepared to defend his house and home.

He opened the door.

I lingered behind in the safety of the dark hall, trying to spy who was calling.

"I'm sorry to bother you this late," said a friendly female voice, "but have you lost a kitten?"

Immediately a feeling of relief washed over me as I realised we weren't in any danger. But the mention of a kitten piqued my interest. A confirmed cat lover my whole life, I felt terrible for the little thing wandering the streets at night. But in our case, we'd never had a kitten, let alone lost one. The lady explained to Ray that it was very small, bright ginger and extremely cute, but no one in the street knew where he might have come from.

"Poor thing," Ray said, "I wonder if his owners know he's missing. He doesn't sound old enough to be out."

After the lady left we thought little more of it. We hadn't seen any sign of him and assumed he'd found his way home.

It seemed that was the wrong assumption to make.

Now the poor ginger mite was standing in our garden, staring up at us pitifully, and squeaking for all he was worth. His squeak was an extremely high pitched sound, nothing like a meow, but not having had much to do with kittens before I thought this was normal. He was very chatty but obviously hungry so we took him inside and gave him some cat food, much to the disgust of our two cats, Socks and Izzy, who regarded him with open hatred.

He was a confident little chap, and tucked into some cat biscuits as the older two sized him up for their dinner. This was their territory, how *dare* such an imposter arrive and eat their food, from their bowls no less. They kept their distance but didn't let him out of their sight. There were no hisses but low-slung bodies and stares of horror told us they weren't impressed. He completely ignored them.

By the evening, he was still with us. It was a warm night so we'd left the garden patio doors open. Our little newcomer stayed close by as we watched rugby on TV, sometimes going for a wander outside before returning, probably in the hope of more biscuits. Although he didn't like to be cooped up, he certainly seemed to enjoy our attention and getting to know us. Then he was gone. We hadn't noticed him leave – but gone he was.

Saturday came and went with no sign of him so we assumed he'd found his way back from whence he'd came. We hoped he'd found his way home to his family and they were taking care of him, although he'd obviously been sleeping rough for a while judging by his hunger and fleas.

On Sunday morning I was in the middle of video calling my parents back in the UK, and had just mentioned the disappearing kitten, when I spotted him walking along the fence again. I shot off to scoop him up. I brought him inside and held him up to the computer screen.

"Here's the kitten I was telling you about," I said as he wriggled around in my arms. He knew this was where he'd been fed before and seemed more interested in having breakfast than being paraded in front of my parents. "We've no idea where he's come from but want to help him find his way home."

"He's certainly gorgeous but definitely too young to be out on his own," Mum replied. "Why don't you keep him in until his owners are found? Far better than him getting run over or attacked by a dog."

She was right. We couldn't leave it to chance that he'd go home anymore. If he even had a home.

Ray went to see the neighbour who had knocked on our door.

143

"Did you have any luck finding the owners of that kitten you found a few weeks ago?" he asked. "Only he's been hanging around our garden lately and we'd like to make sure he gets home."

"No luck at all," she replied. "I think he's a bit of a free spirit, he just seems to wander around the neighbourhood."

Free spirit my left foot. As Ray relayed his conversation with the lady, I looked down at the little kit who was now curled up fast asleep on our armchair, fleas and all, showing not the slightest inclination of moving. Socks and Izzy continued their vigil of disgust but he wasn't bothered in the slightest. I got the distinct impression he'd moved in. We fed him some more, fussed over him, and decided on a plan of attack. We'd keep him in that night so he'd be safe and advertise him as found on TradeMe (New Zealand's version of EBay) on Monday.

When we went to bed, we took him upstairs with us so we could keep an eye on him. But it wasn't a peaceful night. He got up several times to poo and vomit in the bath. How such a little thing worked out that the bath was a good place to do these things I don't know, but it made the clean-up job far easier than had it been on the carpet. I felt terrible though, I didn't know what was wrong. I may have overfed him and he couldn't handle so much food. I was learning kittens are very different to adult cats. After a few trips to the bath, I was concerned he'd become dehydrated, so I offered him a drink from the glass next to my bed. He lapped at the water with vigour and was soon off for yet another trip to the bath, fortunately only to wee this time, not more vomiting.

Monday morning arrived and we were fast becoming attached to him. The deed, however, had to be done. I fired up my computer and scrolled through the list of lost cats. Most were adult cats who had wandered off after moving house, and each advert made me terribly sad as I read pleas for the return of a much-loved pet. No sign of any lost ginger kittens though. With great reluctance, a slight shake in my hand and my heart pounding in my chest, I wrote a description of him and posted it online under 'Found Cats'. I thought about putting a photo up but, as he was so young and super cute, I was nervous someone would claim him as a way of getting a free kitten. I wanted to keep some of his distinguishing features to myself. The anxious wait began.

That was food, shelter and advertising for his owner sorted, now onto the next major issue – his health. Being riddled with fleas and other tiny critters, in our house and around our cats, a trip to the vets was a major priority regardless of whether he would be claimed. I made an appointment and explained he was a stray about whom we knew nothing. He trotted happily into the cat box, being too young to understand the link between cat boxes and the V-E-T, and took everything in during the 15-minute car journey to the surgery. He was very well behaved and kept the box clean during the journey – so unlike our other cats. We have been going to the same veterinary practice since we arrived in New Zealand and feel very fortunate to have found them. They are incredibly up to date with the latest advancements in technology and treatments, and their care of Socks and Izzy has been second to none.

When we arrived, I gave my name to the receptionist. That felt strange as normally we make appointments using the cats' names, but we didn't know what this little one's was.

"Oh, is this the stray?" the receptionist asked.

I held the box up so she could see him over the counter. She cooed over the tiny little thing sitting proudly in his box, squeaking. He didn't seem fazed by the experience at all.

Before long, we were called into the consulting room and the vet checked him over. The vet pronounced him a fine chap, confirmed his tail was broken but he wasn't in pain and the tip was still alive. He was given, what we assumed to be, his first injections and wormer, and we bought some kitten and adult flea treatment – our cats would need another dose now. The vet also advised us on where else to advertise him, but he didn't seem to think there was much chance of us finding an owner. If he was still in our care in another month we would book him in to be neutered.

As well as checking more lost pet sites online, we visited all the local vet practices and read their lost pet notices. Nothing.

The longer the advertisements remained up with no sniff of interest in him, the more attached to him we grew. Granted we'd never wanted a kitten, but his antics were enchanting to watch. He chased his toys around the house, attacked anything that moved, and sometimes things that didn't move, especially pouncing on our toes first thing in the morning. OK, that bit we could live without.

He liked to sleep in an old shoebox, and every day he grew just a little bit more, slowly outgrowing the box. Before long he didn't fit in it at all, but he was so determined to still sleep in it. The contortions he got into were hilarious, our phones soon filled up with pictures of him sleeping in seemingly impossible positions. He really appeared happy to be with us and grateful for the food, shelter and care he was now getting.

As the days passed, we decided the little chap needed a name. We were becoming ever surer he'd be staying with us and we couldn't keep referring to him as 'The Kitten' or 'Little Boy'. We searched online for suitable male cat names. Toby – no. Milo – no. Leo – no. Cassidy – what? Blade – seriously? Garfield – um, no. On and on it went. He was such a little character, into everything. He loved being around us, he could hold his own against Socks and Izzy, he needed a name worthy of him. The names were getting weirder. Ace – no. Duncan – definitely not. Zeus – don't go there. Alfie – no. Hang on. Alfie? Actually, that's pretty good. We looked at him, our heads cocked to one side. Alfie stared back at us.

He settled into our lives and we began to assume he'd be staying with us. It was hard to imagine life without Alfie entertaining us with his toys, squeaks and complete fearlessness. He loved to play and would chase balls all over the floor with no regard for anything that got in his way. We spent plenty of time poking around under the sofa with sticks trying to retrieve whichever ball had been batted under there last.

A few weeks later an email thudded into my inbox.

"I think you've found our cat."

My heart raced, I could feel it thumping in my chest as I read the rest of the message. Please no please no please no please no please no please no please no please no.

I rang Ray. He was just as upset as I was but was hopeful the enquirer was not Alfie's original owner.

"Well look, it might not be his cat. He hasn't seen a photo, there must be lots of ginger cats around," he reasoned. "Ask him for some more info."

I exchanged several emails with the potential owner that afternoon. There were some details that didn't quite add up about his age and location but he was insistent that I show him a photo.

"OK," I said reluctantly, "but first I need to you to tell me what's unusual about him."

"A torn ear," came the reply.

His ears were both in one piece and his broken tail was hard to miss. After our email exchange I was much more confident this was a genuine enquiry. We exchanged photos of his missing kitten and the one we'd found and, no, they were very different indeed. His was a little older and didn't have the distinctive stripe markings that Alfie had. That was it, Alfie was staying with us. The adverts had been online for weeks with no results, so that evening I took them down, and Ray and I opened a bottle of wine in celebration of the new addition to our clan.

By now it really was as if he'd always been with us. He slept on our bed at night, on the sofa during the day and gradually Socks and Izzy tolerated him eating at the same time as them. Occasionally we'd see him snuggled up next to one of them, but his playful nature soon turned a catly snooze into a fight. But still, we'd never wanted a kitten and, although we loved him dearly, we were soon reminded why.

We were just dropping off to sleep one night when we heard banging, crashing and squeaking coming from the family bathroom. I got up, dashed across the landing, turned the light on, and little Alfie stared up at me, a picture of pure innocence.

"What are you doing?" I asked.

I got a blink in reply.

Back to bed for five minutes before the noises started again. Oh so quietly, I crept out of bed and tiptoed down the hall. FLASH! I hit the lights. Alfie stared up at me, no evidence of misbehaviour to be seen. I gave up and went to bed, stuck my iPod on to drown out the squeaking and drifted off to sleep.

At 4 am we were woken by a tapping noise. Every time we made to get up it stopped. We knew he was up to something but what? I was soon aware the noise had moved and was now coming from my side of the bed. I reached down in the dark and my hand found the small bundle of fur. I felt him drop something. Lights back on.

"Oh, heck," I cried. "I can't believe what he's just done! You're not going to like this. He's chewed through my phone charger."

We checked the other power cables in the bedroom. Some were shredded, others had bite marks. Alf was certainly staking his claim. We bundled up all the cables we could, stuffed them in drawers and went back to bed.

"There's a reason we were never having a kitten," Ray reminded me as we lay awake in bed.

"I know, but what could we have done? He needed a home," I replied.

"If we find another one, we're taking it to the SPCA," he said.

Reluctantly, I agreed we'd approach the SPCA (Society for the Prevention of Cruelty to Animals) if we found any more kittens.

Five minutes later the squeaking started again. I ignored it. It got worse.

I climbed out of bed to investigate. Turning the bathroom light on, I was met by a sea of white. He couldn't hide the evidence this time – he'd shredded an entire roll of toilet paper overnight and was clearly besotted with his new skills. There was shredded paper everywhere, including in the bath and sink. The worst part was he'd destroyed all the paper he'd pulled to the floor, cleaning up the tattered fragments was going to be a huge job.

Exasperated, I shut him out of the bathroom.

The next day I woke to see Alfie in a slightly strange position at the end of the bed. The duvet felt unusually heavy – and damp. I reached towards him. The duvet was sodden with cat wee. I'd shut him out of what he considered his night time toilet and, although capable of using the litter tray during the day, he was too young to realise he could go downstairs at night to use it. I felt like a complete fool as I stripped the bed sheets and soaked the duvet. I'd been outsmarted by the little guy's intuition. He could easily have been weeing all over the house at night but no, what he'd chosen had been easy for me to clean. A quick swish of bleach and hot water every morning was all it took to clean up after him until he got the hang of using the tray at night, and purely out of frustration I'd taken that option away. What an idiot, another littler tray would have been the answer!

The day soon came when it was time for Alfie to be neutered and chipped. As responsible pet owners, we've always been strong supporters of neutering, particularly as we have no idea where our cats go during the day. The last thing we'd want was for one of them to contribute to the thriving feral population, or produce unwanted litters amongst our neighbours' cats. We dropped him off at the vet and duly collected him later, minus a couple of parts. We had to go out that evening and I was worried about leaving him alone after his first surgery. He hadn't seemed any the worse for wear when he came home but I thought he'd probably get dozy later on. We went out and I fretted about him throughout the evening. Returning home, we opened the front door and I caught a glimpse of him – halfway up the living room curtains. Any concerns I'd had about him being groggy were swiftly quashed and he spent the rest of the night running full pelt around the house.

Alfie was now protected by his vaccinations and prevented from increasing the local feline population. It was time to let him out.

We've had cats for several years but I always get nervous when a new one goes outside for the first time. Will they remember where home is? Will they even want to come home? Will they get run over the first time they encounter traffic? Alfie was the youngest cat we'd owned so I was even more nervous than usual. As it was, he was a little trooper. I shouldn't have been surprised given how we'd found him, he was always confident going about his day amongst the distractions and dangers of the outside world. We hung around watching nervously as he stepped back into the world he'd known as a tiny youngster. True to form, he sauntered out into the garden, sniffed around, and lay down in a patch of sunlight. He didn't want to run away after all.

Not long after he'd first started going out, I was in the kitchen cooking dinner when I spotted a flash of red out of the corner of my eye. Turning around I could see Alfie was playing with a red foam ball, made to look like a basketball. That was strange, we didn't own anything like that. Where on earth had it come from? He chased it around the living room and seemed far more interested in it than any of the toys we'd bought him. Had he stolen it from someone's garden? I felt a bit guilty knowing he probably had, but it was quite sweet to watch him playing with his find and I forgot about it after a while.

The next day another pop of colour caught my eye. This time it was purple and covered in sparkles. It was obviously a cat toy, but again I wondered if he'd been into a neighbour's house and stolen it. Many of our neighbours have cats, so which house was he going to? I felt awful and had no idea what to do or how to stop him. Over the course of the next few weeks, a string of not-so-new cat toys entered our home.

Our Alfie was a thief!

But it didn't stop with cat toys. A blue pair of baby's socks arrived and was batted around under the dining table. At least we knew which neighbour had recently had a baby so they were easy to return. Then there was the well-used make up sponge, caked in orange foundation, which he left in the middle of our kitchen floor – I wasn't going to go door knocking with that! By now my concern was that he was rummaging around in people's homes, not just taking a cat toy that caught his attention. My fears were confirmed when a yellow silicone egg poacher arrived, followed swiftly by a half-eaten breakfast sausage.

This clearly had to stop, but how?

In the end, we settled for a mail box drop, with 'Wanted' posters depicting Alfie. We always notice when another cat is in our garden or sniffing at the door so we decided alerting the neighbours to his sticky-pawed ways was the best idea. We left his ill-gotten gains in our mail box for the rightful owners to collect. Since then his thieving has stopped. I don't know if he's just grown out of it or the neighbours followed our advice and didn't let him in, but I suspect the latter.

Alfie has been a part of our lives for several years now. He's grown into a huge ginger cat and is the dominant animal in the house. I sometimes watch him sleeping and, as I stroke his thick, ginger fur, wonder about his start to life. Was he dumped or did he escape from somewhere unpleasant? Why did no one claim him? How long had he been on the streets? All these are questions we'll never know the answers to but one thing's certain. His home is with us.

About the Author

Zoë Marr, New Zealand
Ant Press Website: http://www.antpress.org/
Completely Cats Website: http://completelycats.weebly.com/
Facebook: https://www.facebook.com/CompletelyCats/

Zoë moved to New Zealand from the UK in 2011. She retrained as an editor and proofreader, before joining the team at Ant Press in 2016. Confirmed cat-lovers, she and Beth Haslam decided to use their combined skills to help cats in need, and so Completely Cats was born.

Moet the Blind Cat
By Emily Shotter

I was brought into a country called Oman from my birthplace, but I'm not sure where that was, and taken to a place called the pet shop. All the other fluffy kittens at the pet shop said it was a horrible place but I'd soon be out of there. One by one, my companions left the shop, but one of them had given me cat flu, which made me very ill so nobody wanted me. The mean people at the pet shop didn't care about me and I was often left without food and water, in a dirty cage with no bed to lie on and no toys. Nothing.

I was so miserable and I got more and more sick. Eventually, the things I could see started to go fuzzy, until one day I woke up and I could only see shadows and light. It wasn't too long after that I could see only darkness. My world was miserable and I lay down to find eternal sleep.

My cage was opened and a lady's hand reached in for me. There were loud, insistent voices, as well as a lot of scuffling, and I was put into a carry-box. I was so tired and low by this time I didn't move a muscle. I just lay there thinking perhaps I was going to the Rainbow Bridge the other cats had spoken of.

I felt the cold of a metal table, kind voices, the sting of an injection and a soft bed. I ate the food I was offered and slept…waiting and waiting for the kindness to take me to the Bridge. It didn't come, and after a while I drifted off, waking every now and then for more food, some water and a stroke from the hands belonging to the kind voice.

After a day or two, I was taken again to the cold metal table and given another sting that made me drift off quickly.

When I woke up I knew something was different about my eyes. They felt sore on the outside but inside they didn't hurt so much and, oddly, they felt better. The nice voices said I had stitches and so I had to wear a horrible plastic collar. I didn't mind because I felt more energetic and stronger, and generally felt a lot better. The kind voices came and went, I was given the most delicious food I had ever eaten and I always had a soft bed to lie on. Maybe I had crossed over the Rainbow Bridge? No, this was real!

I didn't much like the daily stings, but the nice voices said they would make me feel better and one day I might have a home of my own. A home? Really? But I also heard some whispers about it being difficult to find a 'good' home for a blind cat. I wasn't too sure what that meant, but I was happy and purred loudly at the kind voices and strokes that came my way. In fact, they said I was one of the happiest kitties they'd ever met. I didn't know why, but that made me even happier.

Six days after my surgery a new lady appeared. She also spoke to me in a very kind voice and stroked my cheek. I rolled over for the next stage – the belly rub. She cooed and ahhh-ed and said, "Yes, I'll take her."

Two days later, after my stitches were removed and I was finally free of the annoying collar, I was again put into a carrier and taken to a new place. I knew there was another cat there because I could smell her, but the lady didn't let her get to me and we had our own separate areas for about five days. I loved my new place. I had strokes and cuddles every day, great food, lots of different beds and so many toys I kept forgetting which one was my favourite. I also learned that if I lost a toy, my human would go and retrieve it if I let out the merest squeak (which is all I do by the way, I'm not into shouting loudly).

I've been in my forever home since September 2014. My mum is just the best and loves me lots. I think maybe I'm her favourite, which annoys sisfurs and brofur – two of whom arrived after me.

Mum rescued Lily after me, from a tiny birdcage in a horrible local market, where she was being left to die. She could not move in her small cage, had no food and only a dish of slimy water. Her poor eyes were crusted shut and her paws were sore from the wire floor. Worst of all, she had birds above her and she was covered in their droppings. It took a lot of work to get her out of there without paying the ridiculous sum of money the sellers were asking for her. But Mum managed it

154

and took Lily home. She didn't intend to keep Lily, just take her to a vet to get better and rehomed, but Mum fell in love.

During Lily's first night in the house, Mum gently cleaned her eyes and cut the worst of the mats out of her fur. Lily purred and purred throughout. Mum had set up a litter tray, food station and bed in her bedroom and shut the door to keep Lily separate from us as she was to go to the vet the next morning. Little Lily sat on her cat bed with a wistful expression towards Mum as she climbed into bed. Mum tapped the bed for her to come up and Lily bounded over, rubbed her nose against Mum's hand and lay on the bed next to her. She purred all night. That was it, Mum was sold. How could she give her up?

Cosmo arrived about a year after me. Mum said three was enough, but cats are like potato chips, you can't just have one and, in fact, you want the whole packet! Well, she saw a boy for adoption in Abu Dhabi, and his face struck Mum's heart instantly, but she knew that four cats were too many. Weren't they? He was a Maine Coon with a black and grey coat and a mostly black face, which was why he wasn't being adopted. However, Mum adores black cats. His beautiful eyes standing out from his luxurious fur, along with his sad and needy look and cute poses, kept Mum looking at him for almost six months. Eventually she gave in and the man of the house arrived. He's certainly different from us; more vocal, more 'boyish' and very possessive of Mum, but we all get on fine, despite the odd scuffle.

We are a happy family, but Mum says I'm full of beans and constantly want attention and playtime. I'm not a lap cat at all, but I love my chin strokes, brushes and tummy rubs. My favourite sibling is Luna and I just love it when I creep onto the bed at night sometimes, and she washes behind my ears for me and lets me snuggle up to her. I love to play with her too because she doesn't play as rough as Cosmo. Although sometimes I have to tease her to play with me because she can be a bit of a princess.

Mum says I never sit still. I do though, and I like sleeping too because there are so many nice places to curl up – Mum's bed, five cat trees (one of which is like a real tree) and two comfy sofas. Mum also has a nice balcony, which she made safe by enclosing, and we're allowed to go onto it whenever we like. However, the balcony wasn't always plain sailing.

I'd been in my forever home for about four months and I was so happy. I know how much Mum loved both of us – it was just me and

Luna then. I had every luxury, and Luna and I had bonded well. We used to play chase and pounce around the apartment. Although she was a bit rough at times, I loved her company and the madness.

We weren't allowed on the balcony for ages. I didn't know about the outside, but Luna used to look longingly through the patio doors. It got to winter, when it's cool enough in Oman to go out, and Mum decided to put up a six-foot wire fence on the balcony to make it safe for us to go out. We live on the fifth floor and there is a drop down to the first-floor quad, so she needed to make sure we wouldn't go over the edge.

Once I tasted the outside, I loved it. I'd spend ages (under the watchful eye of Mum) sunning myself, listening to all the noises, the birds, people walking around other corridors, and I even had a stool and a custom-made shelf to sit on so I could feel the breeze. It was magic.

After we'd had the balcony available to us for about a month, and Mum was comfortable it was safe, she'd leave the patio doors open overnight for us to go out and get some fresh, cool night air. Some nights I even slept out there for a while. I also learned if I sat on the balcony when it was time for Mum to come home from work, I'd hear her walking down the corridor and could rush to the front door to meet her. Ahhh…bliss.

One night Mum went to bed as usual. We normally came onto the bed during the night and Mum says she remembers Luna appearing immediately for her bedtime cuddle before she jumped off. We started the usual tearing round the apartment running here and there, jumping up onto things and generally keeping Mum awake for a while.

At around 2 am Mum woke up and thought it was odd that neither of us were on the bed, but she eventually went back to sleep. Perhaps we were snuggled up in one of our cosy cat trees. Our usual wake up time was 6 am, so when the time came Luna appeared for her breakfast and woke Mum up with her usual paw on face and nose-licks. But I wasn't anywhere to be seen. Mum was baffled at first. Perhaps I was hiding or had got into a cupboard or another place that I couldn't get out of. Once she had looked everywhere, she started to get worried.

A voice told her to look out of the window, she wasn't sure why, and she was convinced she was just being paranoid. Surely a six-foot fence would be too high for me to climb? She was wrong.

What she didn't know was I had scaled that fence – Luna and I were chasing each other and I rushed up it and over to the other side. It was a bit odd and I couldn't cling on for long, but hey, the ground wasn't so far, so I just let go. The ground didn't appear. I was falling. I was frightened. Then came the hard ground. I don't remember much of the rest of that night, but I knew I wanted Mum so badly. I didn't know where I was, I felt dazed and pain was tearing through my body. I crawled a little way into a corner and just lay still. It hurt too much to move and I knew Mum would come eventually.

After several hours, I remember Mum calling my name and I tentatively looked up a long way to where her voice was coming from. MUM! I heard her retreat and she fled out of the door in her pyjamas, rushed down and came to me. I responded with a head movement, but I couldn't move. Mum didn't want to leave me now she'd found me, she gingerly put her hands underneath my body and started to lift. It was uncomfortable, but not too bad, so I didn't flinch or meow. I just wanted Mum to make everything better. We slowly went up to the apartment and Mum put me down on the mat inside the door and I moved gingerly, but pain ravaged my body so I lay down again.

I heard Mum dialling the emergency vet. She told them she'd be there in 15 minutes and explained briefly the seriousness of what had happened to me. I'm not sure how she thought she would manage to get there so quickly, since our home is about 12 minutes' drive from the vets with no traffic, but she did. In fact, when we got there the vet hadn't yet arrived. As it was a weekend morning nobody was on duty.

Once the vet arrived, Mum carefully lifted me out of the carrier and placed me on the table. I knew the smell, since this was the vets that rescued me, but instead of saying hello, I lay there scared, listless and without any energy. The vet checked me over and it was uncomfortable, but I remained quiet. He told Mum that although there seemed to be no broken bones – a miracle – they would keep me in for observation and to do an X-ray. I desperately wished I could go home with Mum, but they put me in a cage and Mum left. I felt forlorn and still in some pain.

I was taken a short while later for an X-ray and I was so listless they didn't even need to restrain me, I just lay there. The X-ray showed that nothing was broken, but still I felt awful and didn't understand why. I had no appetite and could only take a few sips of water. They told me I had to eat, but I just couldn't, so they got this horrible syringe filled with something called recovery paste and made me eat it. Oddly, I felt no better afterwards, but I did seem to gain a little more energy.

After what seemed like days, not hours, Mum appeared. Oh, I was so happy but still so uncomfortable, my body hurt and felt weak. Shouldn't it be better if I was going home? I was tired, I just wanted to sleep. Still, they told Mum that I might do better at home, so off we went. She had clearly been told to make me eat with that awful syringe again that evening, but I resisted so hard that eventually she gave up. I took a few laps of water and Mum settled me on the bed next to her for the night.

During the night I knew things weren't right. I decided perhaps now was my time to go to the angels and so, as is typical for us cats, I gingerly crept off the bed and hid myself underneath it, on the side where Mum wasn't. Now I could sleep.

The next morning, I heard Mum get up and call me, searching and searching as she had done the morning of the fall. She spotted me under the bed. My head was fuzzy and I couldn't get up. I vaguely remember Luna washing me, which was comforting, but I couldn't move despite Mum's coaxing and gentle strokes. Mum sounded so worried and immediately rushed about making calls to the vet again and getting her clothes on. I heard her tell the vet, her voice full of sadness and fear, that she thought I was dying.

Mum again put me into the carrier and rushed me to the vets. After an unpleasant blood test they found I was severely anaemic and guessed I must have internal bleeding. They began a pin cushion exercise of pushing needles into various parts of my body to find out where. It didn't hurt as by then my whole body had begun to shut down, and finally, they found it – a haemothorax. I was bleeding badly into my chest cavity and my anaemia reading was practically off the charts it was so low.

You see, being blind, I didn't manage to anticipate the landing, even though I did what came naturally, I righted myself. On the plus side, it meant that I didn't have the broken limbs one might expect after that kind of fall. On the down-side, I'd landed on my chest.

They immediately admitted me and gave me two injections for blood clotting and haemoglobin, and there began a long and agonising two-week journey for both me and Mum. The two weeks really did feel like years, but Mum came in to see me after work almost every day to give me some strokes and tell me how brave I was. I perked up every time she called my name. It was the most wonderful sound and each day I thought, "I wonder if I'm going home now?" It was during that time that Mum developed her pet name for me, Mo-Mo, which has stuck and I respond to just as well as Moet. Each day Mum told me how much she loved me and how fond she'd grown of me over the four short months we'd been together. She wanted me to live so desperately.

After the wonderful care, lots of TLC and more nasty injections at the vets, I pulled through. Finally the day came when I could go home. It felt wonderful to climb on my cat trees, play with Luna and have chin strokes and brushes from Mum again.

However, it wasn't plain sailing in those early weeks. After about three weeks at home, I started to feel weak again and went off my food. Mum again took me to the vet for more tests, only to discover I'd had a small relapse and had developed something called immune-mediated anaemia, which is when the immune system destroys its own red blood cells. It was only down to the expertise and experience of the lead vet that they discovered this, and it meant, much to my distress, that I had to have two injections every two days for a fortnight. Oh my.

The wonderful practice conducted at least two of the treatments at my home to reduce my stress, but I hated having to get in my carrier and go back there so often. Eventually it was over and my body recovered. Since then, I've been back to my old bouncy self. Mum says I'm such a survivor.

For those of you wondering, that balcony is now totally fenced-in, all 12 feet right up to the ceiling, and it is finally a fun and totally safe area for us all to play. In fact, Mum has even put a cat tree and some cat-friendly plants out there for us to experience – it's my favourite place to hang out.

It was a few months after that incident that Mum started taking lots of photos of me. She wanted to share me and my amazing stories with the world and so she signed me up to several social media platforms. I started out on Twitter, but soon after I joined Facebook, Instagram, YouTube and finally, Snapchat (although we're a bit slack on the last one – something to work on). I first joined in 2015 and since then, I've made some furrtastic friends, and some are so amazing that they even send me gifts. I've received gifts from furriends both on Twitter and Instagram and from lots of places all over the world, and every single one has delighted and entertained me.

It would be rude not to model my new gifts, especially when they are wearable. Although I must admit, I'm also partial to trying on treats, toys and cards for size as well. Soon, Mum frequently had a camera in her hand and I got used to a constant clicking sound.

However, my times as a cat model were not, and still aren't, plain sailing. Firstly, you must realise I'm a rather restless girl, who never sits still and thinks that everything presented to me is a toy – that is, until I can smell it's something to eat. With that in mind, Mum's first challenge is to adorn me with the item. Never easy. However, once it's on, I try my hardest to scrape or roll it off. Mum tells me how beautiful I look in that silly cat-voice of hers. That does help. I may have a very small vain streak, and eventually I'll stop trying to remove it and start strutting around. It's at this point that Mum grabs the camera or her phone, or if one isn't to hand there's a frantic search before I get too frisky and run off.

Finally, she has her camera, but now the lighting isn't correct because I'm posing under the table or in the least photogenic spot in the flat. Every now and then, I might play ball and sit looking demure on one of my scratchers or cat trees. Or I may flirt with the sound of the camera clicker to 'look at me'. But I guess I'm not really a natural, yet. Mum says she'll train me by getting me more used to it, however, I'd much rather keep it as a game of chase and shoot!

Once I was on social media with my lovely gifts and photos, Mum realised I could be an ambassador for special needs cats, animal welfare and Trap Neuter Release programmes. She found a group in Oman called Omani Paws, who are a group of volunteers who rescue strays and ferals. Mum knew she had to be involved and so did I.

As we have no animal welfare legislation in Oman, the pet shops (like the one I came from) are appalling. There's no other word for it. Cats, dogs and other furries are cramped into small wire-floored cages with sparse food and water, no toys, no bedding, filthy surroundings and dirty litter trays. I remember my early life, a whole year in fact, in one of those awful places. I was rescued, but most are not and many will suffer a worse fate if they get sick – they'll be put out onto the streets in the fierce heat to either starve, be run over or attacked by humans or other animals.

Pet shops aren't the only dreadful thing here. The stray cats and dogs are left to breed unchecked and to control the population, one official body goes out to shoot dogs (cruelly and often unsuccessfully) and poison the cats. Mum has also witnessed, through social media or directly, shocking cases of cats being physically abused.

There are also the abandoned pets. Oman is a country with a churn of expats, and a rather high churn at that. Many people adopt or buy pets from those awful stores and when they leave, they either dump them at a local vet in a box or simply abandon them to their fate outside. Many of these abandoned cats can't survive outside, it's too hot, we're not hunters and fighters and we invariably end up in a desperate state, if we survive at all.

There are no shelters, no charities (they're not permitted) and no programmes. So, Mum channelled much of her passion for rescue into the group, focussing on using her skills in marketing, writing and social media, as well as a few cat rescues. The group relies solely on donations from local communities and operates extensively to provide TNR for cats and dogs, medical care for sick and injured stray animals and help for abandoned or abused animals. They also foster and rehome where possible, always advocating 'adopt, don't shop'.

I also help to promote the group and raise funds through social media. I've even donated some items from my online store of Moet goodies to raise money too and I donate all profits from my online store to Omani Paws. I so enjoy being a part of the group. However, individual funding from me, Mum, group members and donations from friendly humans can only go so far. So, I set up (with Mum's help) a Go Fund Me campaign to raise much-needed funds. Crowdfunding has helped many in the past and so I figured this would be the way to continue supporting my fur-relations in Muscat.

One day I hope the situation here will be different, but for now, me and Mum will keep raising awareness and funds to make a difference for those without a voice, who are so desperate for our helping paws and hands. And who knows, if I make enough from my own ventures, my dream may well come true: to open Oman's first ever cat shelter.

About the Author

Dr Emily Shotter, Oman
Website: www.moetblindcat.com
Twitter/Facebook/Snapchat/Instagram: @MoetBlindCat
YouTube: www.youtube.com/c/MoetTheBlindCat

Moet is a truly amazing, spirited, happy girl and I'm honoured to be her 'mum'. We hope, through this story and her online presence, to be able to raise awareness about the amazingness of blind cats or any with special needs, in the hope that more will be adopted into loving forever homes. Since Moet's fall, we have learned she has three spinal injuries, including a crushed disc, which will cause her a few chronic problems. However, it has not dampened her sense of adventure and my aim is to make her life as happy and full as possible.

Genus Marmaladus
By Margaret Eleanor Leigh

I cannot comment on the finer qualities of the feline nobility, because I've never had a Japanese bobtail, a Cornish Rex, or a blue-point Persian. I can only speak from my considerable acquaintance with your average moggies, and out of these, I have found one that stands tail and whiskers above the rest. That's *Genus Marmaladus*, more commonly known as the regular ginger tom.

For as long as I can remember there's been a cat about the place, usually more than one, and they've come in all shades of the cat-spectrum: black, white, black-and-white, striped, striped-and-white, black-and-striped, grey, tortoiseshell, tortoiseshell-and-white, and so on. Crowning them all has been the wonderful *Genus Marmaladus* (and yes, I did make that up).

As often as not they've found me, this clowder of cats. Sometimes they've just turned up at the door, although it must be said Miss Fluffy Cat made a far more dramatic entrance – a drama queen from day one. She appeared at the top of a tree in the garden one day, wailing piteously till I sent a sturdy tree-climbing boy up to rescue her. No previous owner was forthcoming and so of course we adopted her.

Another time I found an abandoned kitten stuck deep in the stairwell of an apartment building in Johannesburg. And then there were the cats where there was no choice but to whisk from unhappy or insalubrious surroundings.

That's how it was with Vincent. When I first saw Vincent, he was a marmalade scrap of matted fur, hunched miserably in a faeces-brimming cage in the window of a seedy Johannesburg pet shop.

No! said Common Sense. *Don't you dare! You do not have a suitable life for a cat.* I was 19 years old, working as a cadet-reporter for a newspaper, and living in an inner-city apartment. It was not a suitable life for a cat, as Common Sense rightly pointed out. But of course, Common Sense didn't stand a chance against the haunting image of that sad little face.

My feet retraced their steps, almost of their own accord, and in less time than it takes to tell, I found myself with a box of panicking, filthy, wild-as-can-be, blood-red marmalade kitten. I got him home and opened the box, whereupon he flew out in a freak, claws at the ready, paws flailing in all directions. He disappeared behind a bookcase and there he stayed a full week. I coaxed and pleaded, and put down saucers of food, but he only ate when I wasn't there.

One day it was as if he had had a revelation. He emerged from his hiding place and sat on the plain wooden floor, some five metres away, and stared at me measuringly. Without warning, and taking us both by surprise, he launched across the room and flung himself into my arms, where he lay purring and nuzzling as if his little heart would burst.

From then on, he stuck like glue. When I stood up, Vincent stood up. When I walked away, he wrapped himself around my ankles. When I sat down, he jumped onto my knee. When I lay down, he curled himself into my neck and stared lovingly into my face. No cat had ever looked at me like that.

Six months later, I had to go away for a couple of days, leaving Vincent in the care of flatmates. The night before my return I woke in tears. I'd been dreaming about Vincent; it was an unspecific dream, but I knew at once what it meant.

I drove back to Johannesburg with a leaden heart, and so it was. Even though I searched high and low for weeks, put up notices, and walked the streets calling him, he did not come home. I howled over the little cat that broke my heart more thoroughly than any other cat before or since. And in the process, I discovered it is not the length of time one knows a cat that determines the depth of the love. I also learned it is easier to bear the death of a cat than the disappearance of a cat. (I can still feel the pain of Vincent's vanishing, even after all these years.)

Flash forward a year to my second encounter with *Genus Marmaladus*, only this time an encounter more comic than tragic. Karen, an old school friend and I were hitchhiking around Britain. We were 20 years old and very stupid. It was our big Overseas Adventure. Once done with Britain, we were going to head south to Greece and

164

work as waitresses for a while. Then we'd move on somewhere else – Italy perhaps, or the south of France.

You will notice the absence of a cat on this agenda, and looking back, I still can't quite believe what we did next. Somewhere near Inverness, in the Highlands of Scotland, we chanced upon a ginger kitten wandering alone down a country lane. I forget exactly how events unfolded immediately thereafter, but I do remember the outcome. We travelled by overnight train to London, and arrived in the capital with a ginger kitten in our jacket pockets.

Our kitten was a girl, which was something of a surprise, since I'd grown up thinking all ginger cats were toms. Apparently, this isn't so, although 75 percent are. I'm told it has something to do with the ginger gene and the male chromosome. Whatever the science of the matter, we had found one of the exceptions to the ginger rule, and with considerable imagination we called our exception 'Pussycat'.

There was now a very pressing problem which you have also no doubt noticed. It isn't possible to hitchhike to Greece with a kitten. A kitten needs a settled home, even if that home turns out to be a tiny, squalid London bedsit, which ours did. And so there we were, stuck in London with our dreams of Greece growing dusty on the shelf. But we had our ginger kitten and London on our doorstep, and in our chaotic, ill-considered way, we were more-or-less content.

Karen moved out a year later and I made plans to return to South Africa. I flew Pussycat on ahead. It seemed like an excellent idea at the time. I was to realise later that it wasn't an excellent idea at all, at least not for Pussycat. While some cats may recover from the trauma of inter-continental travel, Pussycat never did. The sound of an engine, any engine, even a car engine, would send her in a panic beneath the bed. Next time, I decided, if ever there was a next time, I would rehome her.

But there was a next time. Three years down that road of chaos that was my life, and at the age of 24, I found myself pregnant. Well I didn't exactly *find* myself pregnant, it wasn't the immaculate conception, after all. I *got* myself pregnant. Pregnant, unwed, and living in South Africa in the turbulent days prior to the transition to majority rule did not add up to a suitable baby-raising environment. I would relocate to the United Kingdom, I decided, and with this decision came the painful necessity to rehome Pussycat. She went to old family friends. It wasn't easy, leaving her. No, it was unspeakably hard leaving her. *Never again, no more cats. No more partings. All just too hard.*

Fast forward the tape another three years and you will find me no longer in the United Kingdom, but living in the beautiful city of Auckland, New Zealand, with my son, Michael, then two years old. It was at this point that *Genus Marmaladus* came into my life for the third time, where he was to rule for the next 14 years. The gene in question belonged to a fluffy marmalade bag of fleas I called Fleabag.

"You can't possibly call him Fleabag," protested a friend. "It's so demeaning!"

Thus Fleabag became Beabag, which in retrospect was probably only slightly less demeaning, but he bore his name, along with everything else, with the greatest possible dignity.

Possession of the fluffy gene along with the ginger gene, meant Beabag was even more good looking than your average ginger tom, but he had far more going for him than mere good looks. Beabag had Personality with a capital P, and Gravitas with a capital G.

It wasn't long before he and I had that connection going, that telepathic connection I'd only ever had with Vincent. Like Vincent, Beabag was my shadow. Soren Kierkegaard once said, "Purity of heart is to will one thing," and that was Beabag in a nutshell. Pure of heart, and willing just one thing, and that one thing was to devote himself to me with what I have come to recognise as customary single-minded ginger-gened passion.

When Michael was nine, we moved from Auckland to Wellington, along with Beabag, Miss Fluffy Cat, Sammy, and my mother, Polly. There I wrote an appalling doctorate and managed to fail spectacularly as a bookseller. Polly took care of everyone when I was away on doomed book-purchasing expeditions. Beabag, she'd tell me, would fall immediately into an extended mope and refuse all food. More strangely, and without fail, an hour to the minute before I was due home, he would plod gravely down to the garden gate to wait for me. We never could fathom how he knew to the very minute when I was due home, but know he certainly did.

Beabag was the patriarch of our family of cats. No-one messed with Beabag. No-one. If a neighbouring dog was foolish enough to enter the property, Beabag would fly out the French doors no matter what the size or breed, he took on a German Shepherd once, and the dog would turn tail and flee. Neighbouring cats weren't allowed either, with one

166

notable exception: hungry strays. Beabag treated hungry strays with kindness and respect, and issued an open invitation to dine at the cat-family table. He was a true gentleman, was Beabag, or perhaps should I say, a true gentlecat.

He lived 14 years. When it got to the point that he could barely walk, or climb through the cat flap, I called time, and so awful was it, I swore I would never give my heart to another cat. After Beabag, life became cold and bleak. Michael left home, too, and one by one the ties that bound me to New Zealand were severed. So it was, at the age of 40-something, I indulged in a spectacular mid-life crisis, bought a one-way ticket to Europe, a bicycle and a tent, and cycled solo from Holland to Greece, living the life of a gypsy, the life that had been pre-empted by the advent of Pussycat, all those years ago.

Then God, or fate, or whatever you will, moved me permanently back to the United Kingdom, at least I thought it was permanent. First to Scotland and then to the former coal mining district of South Wales. I lived in the UK some eight years in total, and the vow of no-more-cats got broken once again. This time I shared my life with Charlie and Nelson, boy brothers, black and white, and not a ginger gene between them.

I loved Charlie and Nelson, there's not been a cat in my life I haven't loved. I just didn't love them the way I loved my two ginger boys and my ginger girl. It was starting to look as if only the *Genus Marmaladus* could find its way into the depths of my heart.

The move to South Wales was a disaster and heralded the bleakest and darkest of years. So, I hatched a plan and the plan was simple. I'd buy an old campervan and become a gypsy in France, much as I'd been before, only this time in a little more comfort. You can't take two cats abroad on a bicycle, after all, and of course Charlie and Nelson were to come with me. There was no question of parting from them.

They'd need to become gypsy cats, mind, no small ask, but other cats had managed it. I'd read stories on the internet about successful gypsy cats. Cats are adaptable, cats are smart. They wouldn't like it at first, but they would get used to it. There would be consolations. The cuisine would be excellent – this was France we were talking about, after all. They would have me, and they would have each other. I would keep us all in the finest rabbit and duck, since my work allowed me to live anywhere, even in the middle of a field if I so wished, so long as there was wireless internet.

But so much for plans. Something nasty intervened. Endometrial cancer to be precise.

"You'll be in hospital five days, maximum," the surgeon assured me. "Nothing to worry about."

A fortnight later I was in the Intensive Trauma Unit at Cardiff University Hospital fighting for my life. The first operation had gone horribly wrong and I'd developed septicaemia, or peritonitis or some other such nasty complication. I'd had two operations now, not one, and in the second they'd removed just about everything they could lay their hands on.

I did not die, you will have gathered. Yet while I did not die, the dream of France had to. With apologies to Marianne Faithfull, I knew Charlie and Nelson and I would never ride through Paris in a campervan, with the warm wind in our hair (fur).

Instead I would go back to New Zealand, where there were people who cared what became of me – my son, for instance. I could not take Charlie and Nelson for reasons I won't bore you with. But apart from those reasons, I'd never forgotten the trauma international travel caused Pussycat.

Charlie and Nelson were rehomed the day before I came home from hospital. The depressing little flat in the depressing little Welsh village I hated and had always hated, was, on my return from hospital, cold, dark, dank and *empty*, e*mpty, empty*. It was devoid of the furry warm living comfort of Charlie and Nelson.

Stretching ahead were six months in which to recover from my near-death experience and prepare for the long-haul journey home to New Zealand. Every time I looked out the kitchen window I half expected to see Charlie sitting there, waiting for me to let him in, the way he always used to do. Once or twice I even thought I did see him.

It was an unspeakably awful time. I had a great gaping wound in my abdomen that took months to heal. I could barely walk. I was weak as a kitten. I was incapable of even the simplest physical activity – vacuuming, for example – and so to add to the misery, I was soon living in squalor.

Worst of all I had lost my companions of eight years. The only way I got through it was by a decision of the will. *I will not allow myself to grieve. I will trust that God answered my prayers, and that Charlie and Nelson's new home is a happy one. If I grieve over them, I will die. I am not in any condition to grieve.*

So, I put the pain on ice. I ring-fenced it, and marked it *Do Not Enter Here*. It is possible to do this and sometimes it is even necessary to do so. Eventually the grief must come out, though, otherwise it stays locked up in there forever, festering away. I guess that's what I am doing now, as I write this tale of cats loved and lost. I am grieving at last for Charlie and Nelson, and for the way they had to start all over again with new people.

At last my solitary Welsh ordeal was over. My wound closed over, I thought it never would, and I made the difficult journey back to New Zealand, the only place in the world I had ever felt truly at home.

Postscript

"Let's get a cat," says Michael. "I hate living without an animal."

He is saying something I've been thinking every day since we moved into our overpriced rental in Auckland. ("Overpriced rental in Auckland." Ha! Now there's a tautology if ever there was one.) I am working all day and every day to cover expenses. But I am working from home, and I am home for good, so is there any real reason *not* to get a cat?

There are several. I am scarred and burned by the loss of Charlie and Nelson, the loss of all of them, over many years. Reason no. 1.

"You will move on," I say to Michael. "You will probably go overseas when you've finished your studies." He is young. He has his life ahead of him. I will be left carrying the cat, so to speak. Reason no. 2.

Who knows how long I have? With two further operations scheduled and no guarantees, it's too risky. Reason no. 3.

So of course, we get another cat.

It is Michael who finds him. He finds him on Facebook. Yes, I know you aren't supposed to adopt cats from random strangers through Facebook. You are supposed to go through the proper channels. But the minute I see Norman's photograph – he's stuck in a tiny cage in someone's back garden, staring at the camera with a look of mingled despair and terror – I simply have to rescue him. He's a little *Genus Marmaladus*, perhaps three months old. It is Vincent all over. It is love at first sight.

Michael isn't so sure, especially when we meet Norman in the fur, so to speak. Norman nearly tears the cage apart in his terrified bid to escape. But I have had feral kittens before. I know they need only love, time and patience. I know that love, time and patience will be rewarded a million-fold once trust is won.

While I did not allow myself to love Charlie and Nelson in quite the same way I'd loved Vincent and Beabag, with Norman it is different. I have nothing left to lose. I give him my heart and he gives me his. When it dawns on him that he's safe and loved, the transformation is dramatic.

He now leaves me only to dart into the bushes to perform his ablutions. He spends his days on my knee, his nights on my bed. He purrs constantly. He retracts his claws when we play because he has realised claws can hurt. He wraps his little paws round my neck and stares lovingly into my face. He follows me everywhere. He is the reincarnation of Vincent and Beabag. I love him exceedingly.

I have a Roman Catholic friend with whom I argue regularly about whether animals have souls, and whether there are animals in heaven. He says no, and trots out some complicated Thomist argument about the soul being rational, and animals lacking rationality, *ergo* animals lack a soul. To which I say, minus the sophisticated argumentation, "Bollocks! It simply wouldn't be heaven without animals."

I know I shall see all my cats again, in that place where there are no more partings, no more tears. I'll be with them forever, all of them, my *Genus Marmaladus* lovelies, and the others too – Charlie and Nelson, Sammy, and Miss Fluffy Cat. The latter are with Polly now, who waits for me also.

And, if you'll pardon the pun, there's at least a part of me that's just dying to be with them all again.

About the Author

Margaret Eleanor Leigh, South Africa, UK and New Zealand
Website: www.books.wordwinnower.com
Facebook: www.facebook.com/margaret.e.whibley
Twitter: Twitter.com/MargaretLeigh8

Margaret Eleanor Leigh is a New Zealand-based writer of memoirs and crime fiction, a freelance proofreader specialising in theology, and perhaps most important of all, the devoted slave of Norman, her beautiful, gentle, marmalade cat.

Lucy
By EJ Bauer

I was aware of Lucy before we met. Our local vet had rescued two litters of kittens and they were playing in a large enclosure when I went to collect food for Toby, our black and white tuxedo cat. There was a beautiful champagne tabby cavorting with her siblings, a silver tiger, several ginger boys, two black and white mites, some tiny tabbies and a timid little tortoiseshell. When I returned two weeks later, the champagne girl was no longer in the wire cage and several other kittens had been claimed. The remaining furry balls rolled, played on and stalked each other.

It was several weeks before I returned. A juvenile humpback whale had been found in a waterway in the north of Sydney and it was not expected to survive. The media outlets had followed the youngster's progress and we received daily updates. As I parked the car, the newscaster announced the decision had been made to euthanise Colin the whale. Volunteers and veterinarians had fought hard to save the little fellow. It must have been so difficult to finally decide he couldn't be repatriated. I imagined most of the city would be feeling upset at the outcome and I pushed the surgery door open, feeling sad and even a little teary. Without even thinking, I checked the enclosure and made eye contact with the last kitten. A loud chirrup came from this tiny, tortie creature. I was being summoned.

The vet was managing the front desk as it was quite early. I looked at him and said how sorry I was that the baby humpback hadn't made it.

"The marine vets' decision was for the best." I knew he was stating a measured, professional view but even he looked downcast.

I sighed and looked back at the bossy little lady who was demanding my attention, talking and trilling.

I turned to the vet again. "Well, this is hardly fair. Here I am feeling sad about the whale, then I come in here and you have this young lady all alone. I actually think she's calling for me."

We had quite a conversation through the mesh of her cage and I felt wretched that she was the last of the two litters.

"That's Lucy," I was informed. "Staff members always name the kittens when they're caring for them. Her sister was Annabel and the ginger boys were George and Henry."

I looked back at her. At this point I knew little, if anything, about tortoiseshell cats. Indeed, I had been known to misname their sister calicos, calling them torties as well. She was a classic example, with split patterning down her midline. She had half an orange blaze down her nose which extended to beneath her chin. Across her little chest, a creamy yellow band finished at the middle of her sternum. She had black whiskers, a black nose and the rest of her coat was in the characteristic brindled pattern. Later I would discover she had white and gold fur on her tummy. She trilled again and this time when we made eye contact, I felt a strong pull from this little morsel. But it was time to go. I hastily paid for Toby's food and reluctantly headed to the door.

I was late for work but the germ of an idea was slowly taking shape. I mentioned Lucy to my husband and for once he said, "Let's talk about it when we get home."

He had always countered any request for a kitten from me with a kind but firm negative. We'd had cats ever since we were married, and we'd always had more than one. Since our bossy grey, Meg, died, Toby had been all alone. Maybe a new addition would be good for him? Hmm. Discuss this tonight? I honestly couldn't wait that long. Strangely, I felt dreadful that I had walked away from Lucy that morning after our amazing conversation. As soon as I finished work, I drove straight back to the vets. Lucy was not in her cage. I was beside myself. Surely she hadn't been adopted since we met this morning? I should have asked the vet to hold her until I could get away from work. I was feeling stressed and guilty.

I approached the desk and shakily asked if they still had the little tortie kitten.

"Let me see, I think someone took her for a quick check-up."

The receptionist made a call to the staff in the clinical area at the back of the practice and I heard her ask about Lucy.

"Evelyn has her. She'll be with you in a minute."

She was behind the scenes with one of the nurses. I was so pleased and slowly exhaled. I asked if I could meet her as I was interested in adoption.

I was ushered into one of the examination rooms and the nurse arrived with Lucy. She handed her to me so we could get better acquainted. The little girl made all the right moves for an adoption interview. She snuggled and purred and rubbed her head on my wrist. She even tried chewing on my watch band. To the practice's credit, the nurse was conducting her own survey. I wasn't the only one being screened. I had seen the staff refuse a young couple adoption about a month ago. They had no proof of a fixed address and had expected the puppy they were interested in would be free, so I knew that they were very careful about the placement of their precious charges.

The nurse looked at me and then at Lucy. "You do realise Lucy is not really a tiny kitten anymore." She was waiting for my reaction.

I glanced down at the little lady who was pushing her head into the crook of my arm. She was a lanky five-month-old and growing fast.

I looked back at Evelyn. By this time, Lucy was pulling at the buttons on my shirt cuffs with her sharp little teeth and I gently removed the temptation. "I don't really want a kitten – I want a cat." I was pretty convinced this was the right answer.

"Besides," I added, remembering our exchange earlier in the day, "she's an amazing talker."

The nurse looked askance at me. "Lucy never talks. We've had her since she was very tiny. We had to hand rear the entire litter as their eyes weren't even open. No. Lucy doesn't talk."

Now that really was incredible. I had spent at least ten minutes that morning, talking and answering her trills and chirps, when I should have been heading to work. I simply couldn't believe the staff had never heard her communicating. Unless… The whimsical (some would say crazy) part of me was whispering that maybe she had been waiting for the right person to engage in conversation.

I quickly enquired about all the necessary adoption details, asked if they would please hold her until the next morning, and hurried home to convince my husband.

"I went back to the vet practice to see that kitten."

He was reading and didn't look up. "Oh yes. And how was it?" He was still reading but listening.

"She's gorgeous. She's the only one left from the two litters I've been telling you about. She called to me when I went to buy Toby's food and she talked to me. The staff said she never talks. She's perfect and, besides, I think Toby needs a friend." I paused to catch my breath.

He looked up. "Well, perhaps you need to adopt her."

I was caught unawares. I still had quite a few very persuasive points sitting unused in my arsenal, but he was being curiously amenable. On reflection, I think he missed having a two-cat household and he was perhaps hoping she would be a companion for Toby.

The next afternoon after work, Lucy and I became an official item. There were forms to complete and quite a sizeable adoption fee. She needed kitten food and I was handed flea treatment and a noisy bell toy. The staff pointed out that Lucy was likely to come into her first season soon.

"Annabel, her sister, was de-sexed late last week. So, she may well follow suit. Watch for the signs. She will call relentlessly, possibly roll on the floor and rub herself on you or on furniture. Bring her in then. She'll need to be spayed."

I added this delightful snippet of information to all the other instructions I had received and eventually gathered Lucy, the food, registration papers, the tinkly toy, flea treatment and a booklet on rearing a kitten and stowed everything safely in the car.

Lucy had been rescued from the side of the road. The litter had been dumped in a hessian sack, but fortunately someone had retrieved them in time and taken them to the local animal welfare office. They passed them to our vet's surgery for treatment, care and finally adoption. She had spent all her time in a cat enclosure, so I decided to start her off gently with her own little room with all the basics: a bed, food, litter, water and toys. I would head in every half hour or so and sit on the floor with her while she sniffed, played and explored. She loved hiding under the bed and would crouch and pounce when I jiggled a toy for her. I don't think she could believe her luck. No more cage or yucky vet smells.

That night my husband and I could hear what can only be described as cat Olympics as she bounced and jumped and skittered in her new, very own space. She settled into using the litter tray with very little trouble and scoffed her kitten food.

Our next task was to introduce her to Toby. He was interested in her, but she put on her best firebrand impression and made brave noises, with much hissing and spitting. Within minutes they were firm friends. Given that Toby seemed quite impressed with his kitten (I know he thought Lucy was his), I felt comfortable leaving her with access to the rest of the house after about three days. I made sure she knew where her tray, food and water were and left for work.

I needed several items at the supermarket and was heading down the tea and coffee aisle when my phone rang. I stepped past a wide platform ladder where two female staffers were stacking high shelves and answered it.

"I can't find Lucy." My husband sounded quite frazzled and I knew he wouldn't call me unless he had exhausted every possibility.

"What do you mean you can't find her?" I had checked before I left and she was happily playing with Toby.

"I've looked everywhere. I just wanted to make sure she was OK before I left the house."

"She's a kitten, she can't have gone far. Did you check the bedroom?" I tried to think where she might have gone.

"She's nowhere. I think she might have slipped out when you left." Well this wasn't going to end well. We'd lost our kitten and she'd only been with us for three days.

"I don't think she escaped. I'm pretty sure she was with Toby when I shut the front door." Now I began to doubt myself, but I was sure they had been playing together. "Did you check the lounge room thoroughly?"

"Yes. Oh, wait a minute. She's under the leather chair." He sounded very relieved and I was almost in tears.

"What was she doing under the chair?" As soon as the words were out of my mouth I heard two voices above me.

"Oh, thank goodness."

"I was so worried."

The two staff members arranging merchandise had been listening to every word. I looked up at their smiling faces.

"That's wonderful news."

They shared my elation and as I paid at the checkout I realised Lucy was already making her presence felt.

Naturally, Lucy began calling, trilling and shimmying on our first weekend together. This went on constantly all night. I called the surgery and she was booked in to be spayed the following week.

I took her in for her surgery and felt horrible. This dear little girl had spent but a few short days with us, and I was carting her through the vet's door and back to all the familiar sights smells and voices she knew so well. I fretted. Would she think she was being abandoned? Did she imagine she had not been the best cat she could have been and we had decided we didn't want her anymore? It was dreadful standing in the waiting room with all these thoughts chasing around in my head.

I spent an awful day at work worrying about my baby, waiting for the surgery staff to call and let me know how she was. They'd had a busy day and didn't call me until quite late. In the meantime, I had worked myself into a mild panic imagining all sorts of dire outcomes. The nurse told me Lucy was fine and I could collect her anytime. When she was carried out to me in her little wicker basket, she trilled and chirruped the minute she caught sight of me. I had already been forgiven.

She arrived home with a shaved tummy, stitches and instructions about keeping her quiet and rested while she recuperated. The nightly Olympics resumed immediately. She did not miss a beat; she really seemed to revel in her new world. No longer confined to a small wire cage, she had an entire house at her disposal and a beautiful black and white boy to keep her company. After listening to all the leaping and bouncing over the next few nights, I was very glad that she hadn't managed to rupture her sutures.

Lucy slipped seamlessly into our lives. She adored Toby, loved my husband but was obviously my kitten. They were both indoor cats, Toby because he had a little pink nose and Lucy because Toby lived inside. Wherever he went, Lucy was usually trotting in his wake, his little shadow. They played together, slept together and watched the world through the large front window. Occasionally I would find Toby snuggled under my comforter all by himself. He loved *his* kitten but appreciated a little down time as well.

Each morning she would jump onto the bed accompanied by her lovely trilling calls. We would snuggle and I was first gently, and then more insistently, encouraged to start her day with food and litter duties.

One morning, her cuddles varied a little. She leaned across me and pushed my left breast with her head. I moved her away, as I was about to get up and attend to her breakfast. We collected Toby from the end of the bed and headed to the kitchen. She repeated this behaviour the next morning but this time she was much more assertive – annoying even. I reached across to stop her and as I moved her head my hand brushed a lump. A lump I should have found myself had I not been so haphazard in my own breast examinations. A lump that was not going away. I was reluctant to acknowledge what I had just felt and cautiously palpated my breast several more times before admitting that I should see my general practitioner.

Everything changed in seconds. My doctor saw me without an appointment and I spent a harrowing day at the Sydney Breast Clinic. I arrived with about 20 other women and had my mammogram. My results were read by a doctor and I was called in to be told I would need further tests. I returned to the waiting room, where the number of other women was now down to eight, and I headed in for my ultrasound. As I waited for my report, there were three other women still seated with me, but when I returned from my second consultation with the specialist I was the last patient. The waiting room was empty and the sharp reality of my situation was slowly sinking in. I had cancer. I underwent a biopsy and my pathology tests were performed while I waited, confirming the diagnosis. By the end of the week I was in theatre.

There are numerous accounts of surgeries, chemo and radiotherapies. Breast cancer is all too common and many women choose to share their journeys. I won't go into any great detail. I spent months dutifully following every instruction I was given, attending every appointment and downing every medication. My dislike of injections and cannulas quickly faded as there were too many to keep track of. They were all too commonplace by the time I was finished with chemotherapy. Eight months later I was pronounced fit for work. Five years later the powers that be were tentatively pleased with my progress.

So – was it sheer happenstance? Dogs are known to sniff out cancer – but cats? I honestly don't know, but Lucy found my cancer. I don't care how she did it, Lucy essentially saved my life. At the very least she hastened my diagnosis and treatment.

She has tortitude by the bucket load. She loves my husband and me unconditionally, and occasionally my daughter, but Toby always. I have friends who do not believe Lucy lives in my house. All strangers

179

are to be hidden from, but supervision of the tradesman working on our renovations is deemed necessary, albeit from a safe distance.

I knew very little about torties before I met Lucy. I know a lot more now and have become one of an elite group of enchanted tortie lovers. It's an exclusive club, by invitation only, and I am so glad I was asked to join.

About the Author

EJ Bauer, Australia
Website: http://www.ejbauer.com/
Facebook: https://www.facebook.com/ejbauerauthor

Elizabeth has lived in Australia all her life. Her working career began as a speech pathologist and subsequently morphed into the unrelated field of retail management in a university. Travel has always been a passion and after a diagnosis of breast cancer, her illness nudged this interest to the fore. She began chronicling her trips with extensive photography, promising herself she would also write about her exploits. She is happily married, a mother of two, grandmother of five and devoted assistant to a bossy tortoiseshell cat, Lucy, the subject of this story.

Kitty Up the Curtain
By Leanne Roger

Saying goodbye to a pet is never easy. Although I use the word pet, what I actually mean is 'animal family'. Animals are SO much more than being 'just pets'. They are furry members of family that share our homes, and permanently burrow into our hearts. A year ago, my heart was broken when I had to say goodbye to my much-loved ginger cat, Apricot. He was in his 19th year, but due to ill health I had to make the heart-breaking decision to have him put to sleep. Even though I know it was the best thing for him, I was devastated. My house felt empty without him, and my heart was torn.

Initially I didn't intend to get another cat, but as time went on, I gave into my heartbreak. No pet is replaceable, but I could learn to love another kitty. Each one has different qualities and characteristics. I felt I needed to learn to love again, and start to mend the cat shaped hole in my heart.

One day, I was contacted by a lady who was having to rehome her five-month-old (large) tabby kitten quickly for personal reasons, and so on the 13th Feb, exactly a month after losing Apricot, Gizmo came into my house and my life hasn't been the same since – in more ways than one. He started to mend my broken heart, found ways to make me laugh every day, and he reminded me how easily a kitten can climb curtains, amongst other items.

The first things to strike me about Gizmo were his enchanting green eyes. He can look directly at me, and I'm instantly under his spell. Thanks to his eyes, he can do pretty much anything, and I forgive him when I look at him. He frequently uses this to his advantage. Another thing that stands out about Giz, is his stunningly sleek and soft tabby coat. I've never seen a cat's fur reflect sunlight quite like his. When the sun lands on his back, it looks like glitter as it shimmers in the light.

When Gizmo first arrived in my house, *any* noise terrified him, and he spent days hiding underneath the dining room table, only venturing out a few steps before legging it back under the table if anyone looked in his direction, breathed too heavily or dared to make a noise. To cut an 11-month story short, Gizmo is now a totally different kitty. He is full of fun, and *always* up to naughtiness of some sort. Thanks to his constant mischief and personality, I started writing a blog about his behaviour a month after getting him. All his stories are true. My imagination is awful, and I wouldn't stand a chance of making things up, but quite honestly, some of the things he's got up to in the last 11 months are hard to believe.

One of Gizmos skills is climbing. To Giz, our bungalow is an elaborate assault course, specifically laid out for him to challenge his athletic abilities in every room. As a kitten, he could climb the indoor clotheshorse better than an Olympic gymnast performing a gold medal routine on the uneven bars. He could launch himself up the clothes horse, with impeccable balance and speed, jumping from bar to bar, without so much as a wobble. This is also applied to other items of furniture such as the sofa, display cabinets, various wardrobes and his current favourite obstacle, the living room curtains.

For anyone who hasn't witnessed a large kitten climbing up full-length vintage curtains, it's an impressive sight. The speed and fearlessness Gizmo shows when climbing curtains is extraordinary, at least the first time you see it. After the first few times, human emotions quickly go from amazement and joy, to frustration and annoyance, and ultimately fear for the molecular rigidity of said vintage curtains. This leads to the human muttering expletives, especially if the curtains are starting to appear frayed and battered from the constant kitty traffic, and will continue to endure until kitty either gets too heavy, or the curtains give way. So, 11 months after Gizmo arrived, the curtains have seen better days, and now have almost as many holes as the kitchen sieve. Thankfully, Gizmo doesn't climb the curtains with as much exuberance as he used to now he is much heavier, and ever-so-slightly lazier. Phew!

And that leads me onto another talent. Gizmo frequently expresses his creative talents on my kitchen wallpaper. My kitchen walls now display an abstract 3D 'work of art' thanks to Gizmo's claws. And if one wall wasn't enough for Gizmo to express his creativity on, he now has three canvases on the go at the same time. I can't say that I'm a big fan of abstract art. If I have to squint, and still can't see what the artwork is supposed to resemble, it doesn't appeal to me. This is where the problem lies for me with Gizmo's creations; they're all straight lines that don't look like anything.

In fairness to Giz, redecoration was needed long before he moved into my house so he's trying to do me a favour by making interior decoration improvements. I'm considering getting Gizmo his own wallpaper canvas he can scratch to his heart's content, without being at risk of going on Santa's naughty list. This 'Gizmo Art' could be sold off to the highest bidder, and the money raised might help to cover the cost of redecoration. His artwork seems to appeal to quite a niche market though, however I'm yet to find anyone who is begging to buy an original piece.

He is also my personal alarm clock. I have to get up at 5 am, six days a week. Until I got Giz, when my alarm went off I would groan, begrudgingly drag myself out of bed, put my uniform on and get ready for work. Since he arrived, things have changed very slightly. The alarm still goes off at 5 am and I still groan, but before I have time to drag myself out of bed, Giz has usually appeared at my head, purring loudly, eagerly rubbing my hands as I struggle to find the button to turn the alarm off before it gets so loud it wakes the entire neighbourhood. Giz throws himself on me several times, the volume of his purring increasing to maximum, and I struggle in the dark to find an escape route from the bed without knocking him off or sitting on him. I realise he's keen to get me out of bed so he gets his breakfast as soon as possible; I'm under no illusion he is pleased to see me at all. As Gizmo's human slave, I know my job is *only* to serve his needs.

When he first came to me, Giz was an indoor kitty, having never been allowed outside in his short kitty life. However, I decided after he had been fully vaccinated, and had his 'crown jewels' removed, he could go outside and see if he liked it.

During his first experience of the wider world, I sat outside as he worked his way around the edge of the patio, sniffing everything and getting worried by some unfamiliar noises and running back inside the house at lightning speed. He was terrified by birds flying overhead, and regularly crouched on the ground before running back indoors. After about an hour, he began to explore the garden a bit more. He was unsure what to make of the grass, as he lifted each of his paws to shake them after placing each of them on it. He discovered the wheelbarrows with old leaves in them and made his way down the grass towards the garden shed. He also (to my horror) got much closer to my pet ducks than I would advise.

Trevor and Tulip, the ducks, are ferocious. Honestly, they are terrifying! They chase anything that appears in their garden. This includes pesky squirrels, neighbourhood cats, various birds, wild deer and of course, humans. I once witnessed one of the ducks grab an unsuspecting pigeon flying too low over the garden, pull some of its feathers out, before releasing it and quacking loudly (shouting ducky insults I imagine!). If you see a partially bald pigeon in central Cornwall, it's probably the one my ducks attacked. Said pigeon hasn't been back to our garden since. It took Gizmo a few months to understand the boundaries of the duck/Gizmo relationship, but after getting his bum bitten on more than one occasion, and being chased up the garden at speed, Giz learnt quite quickly that the ducks are to be avoided at all costs if he wants his dignity (and his tail) to remain intact.

He soon learnt to love being outdoors, especially when he discovered the apple trees in my back garden. I was optimistic that if Giz could climb to his heart's content in the garden, he might not attack the living room curtains, but unfortunately for my vintage curtains, Giz still enjoys climbing them, especially when the weather is a bit wet outside. He doesn't like getting his paws wet under any circumstances.

During the warmer months, Giz regularly spent all afternoon playing hide and seek in his favourite tree with me, whilst climbing at speed. He scared the life out of me as he had 'wheel-spin' on several occasions when he went up the tree trunk too fast and bits of bark flew off where he lost traction.

He can climb trees even faster than he can climb my curtains – shocking, but quite impressive, to watch. He is definitely skilled, and as yet, he hasn't needed any assistance to get down from trees either, but I'm sure that day will come. I just hope that if or when it does, there are some good-looking firemen on duty!

However, Gizmo was devastated a few months ago when his beloved apple tree had to be cut down. You see, this was Gizmo's favourite tree. He used to climb it frequently, and stare over the wooden fencing into our lovely next door neighbour's garden, spying on her and her group of dogs. Without his favourite tree, he would need to find another way to spy on Mrs E. The six-foot-tall tree had started to look unsteady in the wind, and before the winter weather set in, we decided to cut it down before it fell in the winter weather. During the ordeal, Giz stared out of the conservatory window, watching as his favourite tree was reduced to a heap of branches in less than an hour. He was not happy. He looked so miserable that our friend, who was cutting down the tree, was concerned Gizmo was going to go out and slash his tyres, or scrape his claws down the side of the truck and trailer. If looks could kill, our tree-cutting friend would have been missing at least one limb of his own.

In addition to climbing, Giz has proved himself to be a successful hunter. He started off bringing home the discarded elastic bands our postman regularly drops outside the house. Although I thought this was a little unusual, I was pleased Giz was doing his bit to keep our neighbourhood litter free. I did consider selling the huge stash of bands back to Royal Mail, but after Giz has left his teeth marks in them, I'm not sure they're much use now. I keep them in a drawer, and I will probably never need to purchase new elastic bands – ever.

Of course, being a good hunter, Gizmo also brings various types of 'livestock' into the house at frequent intervals. These have included mice, shrews, plus the odd bird. Oddly, Giz doesn't kill his gifts, and never attempts to eat them. However, he usually releases the very-much-alive gifts into the house and leaves them for *me* to catch. He seems to want to demonstrate how difficult it is to catch these offerings and encourages me to join in. He makes it look so effortless. On more occasions than I dare to think about, I have been found, kneeling on the floor in my pyjamas at a dark hour of the night, trying to catch Gizmo's latest gift and release it back outside. It is not as easy as Gizmo makes it look.

This game of 'human mousetrap' seems to be an activity that Gizmo enjoys watching, but he does get annoyed when I confiscate the gifts and release them into the garden. Thankfully, I have been successful in catching several different species of live present, including a robin. Yes, a robin. A very much alive, flying around the house at 6 am, perching on top of the cabinet, red-breasted robin. Somehow, with more luck than judgement, I managed to catch it and release it back outside, much to Gizmo's annoyance.

The most unusual gift I have received is hay. As in animal bedding, dried grass, that sort of hay. One day, I found Gizmo lying on the living room, next to a pile of hay, looking quite pleased with himself. I praised him, before wondering where it came from. A few days later, it happened again, proving this might be part of a series of gifts I didn't understand. I'm still trying to work out if the hay was supposed to be the gift wrapping for another gift, like a pet hamster, for example. Or is the hay the gift? I'm just concerned there was a distraught child in a nearby street who has had their pet hamster(s) stolen, along with some of its bedding, twice in one week. I never did get to the bottom of this puzzle.

One gift I'm hoping I don't receive is one of the four pesky squirrels that regularly taunt him from my garden. On his first encounter with a squirrel, they seemed to be having a staring competition, and Giz somehow got within six inches of it before breaking eye contact. The squirrel took the opportunity to run down the garden, leaving Gizmo sitting on the grass, wondering where his new friend had gone. This encounter seemed to annoy him, and every time he's seen a squirrel since, he has attempted to chase it – with varying degrees of success. I have twice witnessed him get within a whisker of catching one, but, thankfully, the squirrel has outsmarted him on both occasions.

Within the first three months of Gizmo moving in, I successfully managed to train him to come home when I whistled. This came in very useful when he was outside and I wanted him to come home for dinner, before shutting him inside for the night. Those were the rules when he was younger, he could go outside during daylight hours, but must be home before dark. However, he tested the boundaries of his curfew on one memorable occasion.

Just before dark, I went outside to call Giz. I whistled a few times at the back door as usual, but when he didn't appear I was a little shocked. Hmmm. Maybe I didn't whistle loud enough? Not to worry, I thought, I have a second plan. I called his name, quietly the first time, but louder, and probably with some annoyance in my voice the second time. Still there was no sign of him. Hmmm. That was concerning. So, short of me wandering the streets and neighbours' gardens in my unflattering pyjamas (yes, they do have cats on them) to find him, potentially being reported to the police for snooping in bushes, looking up trees and generally acting quite oddly, I had a cunning plan to entice him home.

Gizmo is not able to be bribed with food or treats. Unlike previous cats I've had, Giz is notoriously fussy, so rattling his food bowl, or a packet of treats was not an option.

My plan involved standing in my doorway, whistling once and immediately rattling one of his loudest toys. Thankfully, this was immediately successful. Gizmo came speeding up the garden and straight in through the back door within 20 seconds. As soon as he ran through the door, looking for his toy reward, I quickly slammed the door and launched his toy mouse across the room. Big sigh of relief.

However, this sense of achievement didn't last long. Enticing the little monster home using a toy meant he wanted to play with the toy mouse for the next two hours, and I most definitely did not want to join in. Unfortunately, Giz wasn't deterred by playing alone. I think he was secretly hoping to convince me to join in but he didn't succeed. So instead, I lay in bed for the next two hours, listening to him launching himself off various items of furniture, literally throwing his toys out of his toy box and having a wonderful time without me, being as loud as he possibly could. In fact, Gizmo frequently wakes the humans up by demonstrating each of his favourite toys at a dark hour of the night. It's not everyone's idea of fun, but I've got used to it.

Getting a reputation for being quite mischievous, Gizmo developed quite the fan club, and even landed himself a job as 'Chief Product Tester' for a luxury online cat website. After this, he was regularly sent products to test from a variety of companies including toy, food and gift companies. It got to the point where all the parcels that arrived at my house were addressed to Gizmo. The delivery lady knew him on first name terms, he received that many parcels. Gizmo was getting regular job offers, and being his human, I started to feel pretty unsuccessful about my employment. Why couldn't I get job offers like Gizmo?

Touch wood, until very recently, Gizmo was in good health. He'd been to the vets on a few occasions since I'd got him, as I've had him fully vaccinated, and he's regularly treated for fleas and worms. During previous visits, he was surprisingly well behaved, despite not enjoying the car journey. But recently, his behaviour has not been as tolerant at the vets.

It was a stressful festive period in my house. Not because of the pressure of Christmas, but because Gizmo was quite poorly. And how did I know he was ill? He was being too well behaved. He hadn't stripped my wallpaper or climbed my curtains for a few days and he didn't want to play with his favourite toys. Those were the first things I noticed, but this rapidly got worse over the following days.

To cut a long and stressful story short, between 24th Dec and 29th Dec, I took Giz to the vet on four separate occasions. His was getting more lethargic, he stopped eating and he was starting to lose weight. For the first three visits, the vets were unable to find anything abnormal: his temperature, gum colour and vital signs showed very little to suggest ill health. The vet told me it was probably a tummy bug that might take a few days to recover from.

In true Gizmo style, even though he was feeling very poorly and hadn't eaten for a few days, he still managed to lighten the situation slightly on his third visit. I can only assume he was fed up with having a thermometer inserted up his bum during each visit, and was trying to get out of having it done again, at any cost.

Firstly, I struggled to get Giz into the wire cat carrier, despite him being quite weak and lethargic. Once I succeeded getting him in, I placed the carrier in the truck, on the passenger seat. I got into the driver's seat and gently drove out of my street and started the five-minute journey to the vet. In the time it took to drive out of my road, Giz somehow managed to slide out the long pin that fastens the carrier lid. The first thing I knew about it was when his head popped out of the corner of the carrier as he looked for the best direction to disappear in. I wasn't quite sure what to do.

Before I had time to think the situation through, he was out of the carrier and loose in the truck. I considered turning around and heading home, but I didn't want to be late for Gizmo's appointment so I reluctantly decided to continue our journey, driving even more carefully than before. I made it to the vet, having watched Giz avidly explore the inside of the truck, from the leather front seats to the boot, before ending up on the back seat behind me. When I parked at the vet, I knew I had to somehow get Giz in the carrier before opening a door. As luck would have it, I was able to catch him quite easily, and put him back in the carrier within a few minutes. His truck adventure must have exhausted him temporarily. Note to self: find another way to secure Giz on journeys to and from the vet, and not rely solely on the pin.

Once we got into the consultation room, blood tests were needed to investigate his illness further, as his condition wasn't improving. The vet went to get the assistance of an experienced veterinary nurse, and let's just say that Gizmo was not happy about having blood taken. We tried for several minutes, restraining him in several different positions, but still Giz was not going to allow anyone to take his blood. He even had a hood put over his head to stop him from seeing the needle coming, but that made things worse. The vet suggested giving Giz five minutes in his cat carrier to relax and we would try again, but I had a better idea. I suggested keeping Giz at the vets and trying again once he had time to calm down.

I remember the vet clearly saying that they would contact me in about an hour, to come and collect my cat, but five hours had passed by the time I got that call, and they still hadn't managed to get any blood. The vet suggested another appointment in two days' time, and Gizmo would be sedated for blood to be taken, and possibly have other tests at the same time if his condition hadn't improved. But the very next day, Gizmo deteriorated again and was sick, so I immediately rushed him back to the vet, making sure that the lid was secured with additional string reinforcements this time.

On this fourth visit, the vet immediately admitted him, sedated him, ultrasound scanned and X-rayed him, and diagnosed pancreatitis within a short time. Gizmo was hospitalised straight away, put on a drip, given medication and monitored closely. Despite being poorly, Gizmo was still living up to his reputation of being naughty, as the nursing team quickly realised. He successfully managed to chew through his leg bandage and drip tube in a short space of time. Because of his continued chewing, he was made to wear the cone of shame, a symbol of naughtiness and defiance in his case. I was also told he seemed to like the sound of his own voice, as he was repeatedly singing a strange rendition of a song that none of the nurses could identify.

After being on fluids and medication, he was starting to feel better, and he used every opportunity to try and escape, at one point, launching himself at a veterinary nurse's head when she went to check on him. Thankfully, the nurse was not psychologically scarred by this experience, but Gizmo's naughtiness ensured he wouldn't be forgotten by the nursing staff anytime soon.

After 48 hours on fluids, and being monitored closely by the wonderful veterinary team at Penmellyn Vets, Gizmo was eventually deemed well enough to come home on New Year's Eve and he continues to recover at home. Personally, I think his repeated naughty and challenging behaviour got him booted out of the practice, but the nursing team were far too polite to say this. Since 31st December, Gizmo has been recovering at home, using me as a source of heat due to his current bald situation thanks to the extensive shave he had prior to the ultrasound scan.

A few days later, I took Giz back to the vet for a check-up. He was not happy about going back, and he was very relieved to come home again. Thankfully, the vet is pleased with his progress, and Giz is currently showing no discomfort from his pancreas, so fingers crossed we have found a way to manage the situation. Gizmo is now on a very strict, and expensive, diet for the foreseeable future. He always did have expensive taste in food, but at this rate, I will be considering selling one of my limbs each month to fund his food bill. He is on a veterinary diet, and not allowed any treats at all. Luckily for Giz, he's not a treat fan, so he won't notice the difference.

When Gizmo and I got home from the check up, he found the postman had delivered a parcel for him. It was a lovely blanket from his friends at Tillypops Toys. This blanket has been keeping Gizmo comfy and warm all afternoon, he is such a lucky kitty. Not only is he feeling better, but he's also getting gifts from his friends, helping him on his road to recovery.

Always trying to find a positive outcome, I want to raise the issue of having pet insurance. Until I got Giz, none of my cats were insured, but with Giz I was encouraged to get insurance, and I'm so glad I did. If I hadn't taken out the policy, I would now be facing a bill of almost £1350, which I couldn't have paid, from consultations, investigation, treatment and specialist care over the space of six days. I assumed Giz was a young, healthy kitty, but this experience has shown me that any cat can get ill for no apparent reason, and unless you have adequate funds to pay for any treatment your beloved kitty needs, insurance cover will be vital should they need medical attention. The speed of Gizmo's deterioration was so fast. But luckily for Giz, because I know what his 'normal' behaviour is like, I knew he wasn't feeling well.

Between the time Gizmo first went to the vet and today, I have been overwhelmed and touched by literally hundreds of messages from people on social media, wanting to know how he's doing. These messages are from people across the world who have never met Gizmo or me, but have gone out of their way to send messages of support and encouragement to us both. The cat community have helped me stay positive through the past few weeks, and I thank every single person for taking the time to contact me. Cats have always been special to me, and as I've found out recently, cat-loving people are pretty special too.

I'm so grateful to still have Gizmo in my life. The last 11 months have been full of laughter, disbelief and fun, and I hope he will continue to bring happiness into my house and continue to help me find reasons to smile every single day. Gizmo has a very special place in my heart, and put several holes in my curtains...long may it continue!

About the Author

Leanne Roger, Gizmo's Human Slave, UK
Website: https://kittyupthecurtain.wordpress.com Facebook: @kittyupthecurt1
Twitter: @kittyupthecurt1 Instagram: @kittyupthecurt1
Gizmo is a naughty, but adorable tabby kitty, living in Cornwall with his human slave. He is always getting up to something he shouldn't. You can keep up with his adventures on his blog and social media feeds.

192

Lobezno
By Charlotte Moore

It was the end of July and the heat was rising above 40 degrees Celsius (104 degrees Fahrenheit), before the August holiday month in Spain. Early mornings were the only time anything could get done, before the heat rendered working an impossibility. It wasn't cool even then, around 27 degrees Celsius (80 degrees Fahrenheit), but it was manageable. The locals dealt with the heat by assuming a natural, measured pace with not a bead of sweat forming on their brows. The men were up for work at 4 or 5 am, some breakfasting at the coffee bar, before heading into the fields or down to the coast. No one in this small village worked in the nearby city of Granada, manual rural labour or hotel work within the town was what they knew.

By 7 am the locals were out on the street. Two middle-aged Spanish ladies chatted as they swept their front step and their section of the street in velour slippers, tights and long aprons covering their simple skirts and tops, despite the summer heat. They wandered to the fountain to fill their bottles, then ambled back to water the plants by their door. Large rubber plants with glistening leaves and brightly-coloured pots of geraniums, a riot of colour owing to the care and attention from the ladies, hung from wall brackets and on railings.

The peace was shattered as Juan Peseta rattled past on his 50cc scooter at full throttle, his squat form topped with a helmet, its straps dangling down, and a roll-up cigarette clamped firmly between his lips. He bellowed a greeting in his guttural Andaluz, the women smiled and he was gone, off for breakfast and to arrange his day's work.

At the side of the street, a dog raised a lazy eyelid and went back to sleep. There were so many stray dogs and cats in these small towns and villages that people had to drive around them. This was no stray dog though, this was Bailey, and he was happily lying in the full sun as his master, David, worked inside the garage repairing a very decrepit scooter. All things mechanical took a battering in these small towns. Once off the main roads, there were tracks of clay soil which twisted left and right, and clouds of dust rose in a vehicle's wake during the summer months. A car that was clean and sparkling at the start of the track quickly turned a red oxide colour within a few yards. The rainy months hammered the ground hard and left great gouges in the track where it thundered down the mountainside. It was often a hazardous drive at any time but it could be interesting trying to dodge the extra channels too.

Everything became choked with dust and so it was inevitable that David had a queue of customers, desperate for him to wave his magic wand over their little work horses. He opened his workshop front to let the light in as he worked on the scooter, allowing Bailey to slumber in the sun in as David worked away.

The small town was quiet in this part of the *barrio* (neighbourhood). A distant hum of voices from up the street and the burbling of the fountain on the corner blended with the sound of the Spanish radio station in the workshop. David was absorbed with the scooter repair, sweat already forming in the centre of his back, as Bailey basked in the sunshine – both absorbed in their own lives.

A mangy cat eased its way around the corner of the building. She stopped, eyes right as she spotted Bailey basking in the sun. Her back started to arch as she studied him, her fur raising into spikes. She relaxed as she realised he was no harm to her – he was sound asleep. She strode purposefully across the street to the water fountain, her pregnant belly swaying as she walked. She was due to give birth any day now. Totally ignorant of the blue inscription on white tiles at the back of the fountain, penned by Garcia Lorca, *As I have not worried to be born, I do not worry to die,* she paused before she hopped up onto the edge and dropped her head into the flowing water to drink her fill. Sated, she sat a while to rest in the shade that the fountain gave, and her eyes scanned the street for anything that could do her and her unborn harm.

Meanwhile, Bailey slept peacefully in the sun, his paws twitching as he dreamed. David worked away, totally unaware another stray cat was about to have kittens that she would probably be unable to feed and care for. Her only hope was that someone would find them and look after them. If they were born deep in the countryside the chances of survival were low. The mother cat knew no different, she was born in the wild and fed from whatever scraps she found or small rodents she killed. Her life and that of her kittens would probably be short unless she kept her wits about her.

It was 2 pm and the temperature had risen to over 35 degrees Celsius (95 degrees Fahrenheit). Even Bailey had admitted defeat and retreated inside the garage to a shady corner. David closed the garage and went to the gym. The pregnant cat had gone, un-noticed by anyone. She was just another cat. The rest of the week at the garage went by in much the same way. The days were hot and the nights not much cooler. The shutters were down on the windows during the day to keep the sun out and flung open wide at night to catch any gasp of air that might blow by. Sleep was hard to come by in such high temperatures however used to it you were.

As David opened the garage up one morning there was a horrid smell in the air; a smell of decay and death, rotting flesh. The garage was large and had many nooks and crannies that were either empty or stored bits and pieces that might be useful one day. David sniffed the air and grimaced, something had died and he needed to find out what it was. Finding a torch, he went around the garage, shining the light into the dark corners but he couldn't find anything. He went up to the storage level and the stench got stronger. He dreaded what he was going to find. Shining his torch around he saw a dark mass in the corner, he walked over and sighed. Kittens curled up together but sadly no longer living. The mother must have given birth in here and left. It was a sad sight and he had to deal with them. Where was the mother and were there more kittens he hadn't found yet?

With a heavy heart, he searched for more of the family before he went to work on a customer's bike. He turned up the radio to distract himself from the sad find as he worked, Bailey, as ever, taking up a guard position at the open door. Every so often David glanced up, hoping for a glimpse of a stray mother cat without her kittens. He was worried she may be too weak to fend for herself – if she was still alive. Bailey's ears pricked up and he began a low growl, then a whine. But he wasn't looking down the street, he was looking fixedly into the corner of the workshop. He rose and stood transfixed. David stopped working and looked over at him wondering what was wrong. He turned off the radio and listened. A plaintive mew was coming from near the office door. More kittens? David's shoulders dropped, what was he going to find?

He peered across to the corner but couldn't see anything. He moved a bike and saw a tiny ball of fur on the floor. A pained mew and a little pink tongue revealed itself. Bailey whined but stayed back, his head to one side and his tail gently thumping on the floor. David bent down and gently scooped up the bundle of fur and it mewed again. It was no more than a few weeks old and was fluff and bone. It locked a milky eye on David and mewed again. As he cradled it, David looked into the corner for any of its siblings but there was nothing there. He leant on the seat of a bike and felt something wet underneath his hand. Blood. He looked at the kitten again, it was jet black so it was hard to see anything. David moved towards the light and could see the kitten's right eye was shut and swollen and there was a little blood on its cheek. David was puzzled, what had happened to it? He looked around, there were no more kittens but the kitten had been directly below the ledge where David had found the dead kittens earlier. The poor little thing had fallen off, and by the look of it, his landing had been cushioned by the bike seat before it fell to the floor.

David shut the door on the unit and headed upstairs with his furry bundle, Bailey at his heels eager to see what this tiny new thing was. In the light of the kitchen, David could see the damage to the little fella, but first, a little milk. He poured some into a cup, dipped his finger in and offered it to the kitten. It sniffed a little at first, then sucked on his finger and mewed for more. David stood dipping and feeding, the kitten slowly bringing its paws out and grasping onto his finger suckling happily. With what seemed like a sigh, it stopped suckling and fell asleep, time for David to wipe the eye with some warm water. He gently raised the eyelid, the eye was a little red but looked OK. Would the little fella last the night? All David could do was get some kitten milk from the vet and ask about the possible eye damage.

All this time Bailey had sat patiently at David's side, waiting to find out what the fuss what about. "We need a box for this fella," David said to him. "It looks like we have a new member of the family."

Bailey gave a gentle yelp and thrashed his tail on the floor in happiness. David headed back to the workshop to find a box, lined it with an old jumper, and popped the kitten in to rest. Bailey sat guarding the box, waiting to see what this little bundle would turn into. He had a new pal.

Over the coming days, David diligently fed the little kitten and Bailey continued to watch and protect the little wriggling black fur ball. The kitten was becoming more active now it was getting regular food. Its eye had healed and it was wobbling around the apartment exploring corners, before collapsing into a heap and falling asleep wherever it felt like, usually in a patch of sunlight. David would pop up and check on it during the day and Bailey still wondered what this little bundle of fur was, it was unlike any other dog he had met and it smelled different too. He was beginning to wonder if it was one of those cats he saw in the street, but surely Dad wouldn't have one of those, would he?

Of an evening, Bailey would lie at David's feet, the kitten happily curled up on David's chest enjoying the warmth. Its paws would stretch out, claws searching for something to grab. Often those needle-like claws would grab a bit too hard at David's skin. As the days went on, the kitten got stronger and demonstrated its lion-like personality, jumping on dust balls and stalking beams of light as they shone through the windows.

It was time the kitten got a name, it seemed he would be staying. As David played with him one night, the kitten was in his comfy place on David's chest as he lay on the couch. David was teasing him with a feathery toy and he biffed the little plume. He rose up on his back paws and tried to snatch the toy before David pulled it away, his tiny white claws grasping at thin air until he caught not the feather but David's cheek. *Time we gave you a name to go with your personality,* thought David as he wiped his cheek. *You've fought hard to survive and you're feisty with claws like needles. I know. You're Wolverine. Lobezno.*

Lobezno continued to grow and began going into the workshop with David and Bailey. Bailey was like a protective parent, if Lobezno explored too far outside the workshop, he would gently pick him up and put him back inside. Lobezno would try to sneak out again but Bailey just hauled him back in. Instead of staring out into the street, Bailey sat at the open doorway and watched over Lobezno as he played. Lobezno stalked his own shadows, jumped on fluff balls as the breeze caught them and wound himself around David's ankles as he worked. There wasn't much that could distract David but Lobezno was proving to be a dab hand at it.

Meal times were a noisy affair. Whilst Bailey was trained to sit and wait patiently, Lobezno would mew and mew as if he hadn't been fed for days, not just hours ago. He watched as David opened the kitten food, plaintive cries issuing forth. He hindered David as he walked across to the feeding area, his head held high and his little pink mouth open and continuing to mew. Before David had even put the bowl on the floor, Lobezno was weaving a figure of eight around his ankles again. Once the bowl was down, he devoured the food as if he might never see another meal. Meanwhile, Bailey sat patiently waiting for permission to eat, a slight drool appearing at the corner of his mouth until David nodded at him and he began to gently eat his food.

David went to his gym, turned on the music and began to warm up. He was lying back on the bench press when Lobezno jumped onto the end of the bench, his paws delicately tested each step, stalking as he moved forward. David lay still to see where he would go next. Lobezno looked up and then leapt onto David's tummy before starting to pad. He lay down, dropped his head onto his paws and went to sleep. David tried not to laugh, but he couldn't help it, Lobezno gently bouncing up and down on his abs. He didn't stay asleep long! He stretched and began to stalk up to David's chest, one tiny, white edged paw at a time, with each step his tiny claws needling through David's tee shirt. One step, two steps, he flopped down again. He started patting at David's chest, wondering why it was moving and enjoying the movement of his chest hair.

His ears pricked up, it was something to play with, it was moving, it must be prey! His head came up and back as he cupped his right paw and wafted at the chest hair. He lay back down, head up again and cupped his left paw. Bum up in the air next, his head lowered and his eyes narrowed into diamond shapes. Before David could move him, Lobezno was in for the kill. POUNCE! His claws went in as he caught his hairy prey. David winced as Lobezno's face registered it was 'Dad' who was connected to this hairy bit of prey. He sat up and looked guilty, waiting to see what David would do. Lobezno was scooped up and popped onto the floor next to Bailey, and not for the first time, David smiled as he wondered why he had kept this kitten. Having something to care for was doing him as much good as he was doing for Lobezno.

Days rolled into weeks and Lobezno was growing into a healthy cat. He still hankered after David's attention but seemed to enjoy spending more time with Bailey. His mannerisms were noticeably dog like: the way he sat, the way he pawed at his bed. David chuckled as he looked at them sitting side by side in the sunshine, watching the world go by. Bailey, David was sure, thought Lobezno was a dog and he felt sure Lobezno thought he was a dog too. He had certainly become a firm part of the family.

About the Author

Charlotte Moore, Spain
Website: www.charlotte-moore.com
Artist, writer and designer with a love of Spain and its traditions. I've published short stories and a memoir about yes, you've guessed it, Spain. *Calamity Spain*, available on Amazon, is my journey of buying a rural house in Spain and the events that unfold.

Oliver Poons
By Lauryn Wendus

From my cage, I dreamed of what my home would be. It couldn't possibly be these wire walls. Then, one day, she arrived with ringlets in her hair and bright green eyes just like mine. I had no idea she had picked me out online. I didn't even know my profile was out there. Our first meet and greet went well. Luckily, I was well groomed, fluffy and used all my charm. I concealed my darker traits, the scratchy and slightly whiny side, until I was sure of my adoption.

I had all my shots and walking papers, and the day had arrived for her to come back to pick me up and take me to my new home. I loved everything about my new life. My soft bed; teddy bear friend, Emma; soccer ball; string toys; and lots of attention made me one happy cat.

Little did I know that one day I would become the protagonist in *The Adventures of Oliver Poons* children's series. These books were written when Lauryn (my lovely human), got very sick with Lyme disease, which lasted for years. I stayed right by her side watching over her. When Lauryn's mother came to take care of her every day, I'd let her know how Lauryn was doing. I gave her the full report. However, my vocabulary is a tad limited, so from here, I'll let Lauryn fill you in on the details.

Being a cat, Oliver's version of my Lyme disease meant watching over me and lots of cuddle time. But there was much more to this story. Lying in the hospital bed that fateful night in 2012, I knew I had crossed some type of pivotal life threshold.

Amidst all the sickness, the doctors, and the frantic friends and family members by my side, I vividly remember thinking to myself that this was surely the beginning of a life-altering chapter. At the very core of my being, there was part of me acutely aware that my life was about to take a drastic turn into the unknown. I had been sick for months prior to finding myself in that hospital bed. My symptoms started so subtly I couldn't quite pinpoint a problem at first. I vaguely remember starting to feel more tired than usual, but it wasn't enough to stop me from carrying on my life. I was 23, at a relatively new job that was fast-paced and demanding, and I was determined to prove myself worthy of the seemingly limitless financial and career opportunities dangled before me. I was putting in some serious hours learning a new industry, studying for licensing exams, traveling, and taking on as many projects as I could handle. There was no time for sickness, until there had to be.

I first tried to address my fatigue with simple things. I stayed in on weekends, cut out some social engagements, went to bed earlier – all to no avail. This was a different kind of tired than I had felt before, it was all-encompassing and imprisoning. No matter what I did to rest, there was no way to escape the exhaustion.

As time went on, new symptoms slowly crept up on me. I had a few swollen lymph nodes, my knees began to ache as I walked up flights of stairs, and it felt as if I was losing control of my body. My appetite was up and down, I was losing weight, and I felt so weak that some days I seriously questioned if I'd be able to hold myself up in the face of a blustery wind.

I had begun to visit the doctor's office as my sickness worsened, but my ambiguous symptoms kept the diagnosis wide open. While I awaited the results of countless blood tests, it seemed endless possibilities hung in the balance: an obscure virus, an autoimmune disease, fibromyalgia, something cancerous – or maybe something psychological?

As I attempted to juggle doctor's appointments with my fledgling career in the investment industry, it quickly became apparent to my boss and co-workers that something wasn't quite right. I admitted I was having a few health concerns, and it wasn't long before the symptoms permeated my life to a point where I could no longer hide the fact that I was sick.

One day while driving during my morning commute, my near vision suddenly blurred to a point where I was unable to read the controls on my dashboard. This was my first of many moments of mental and emotional upheaval. My boss and I were supposed to meet a potential investor for a 9 am meeting, and not being able to see clearly wasn't on my checklist of things to deal with that morning. A little before 8 am, I called my boss to tell him I may not be at the meeting. When I told him why, he immediately rushed from his house to the office, shirt untucked with his suit jacket and tie in hand. He handled the situation with grace and kindness, drew upon his fatherly side to comfort me while I got hold of the doctor's office, and insisted his executive assistant drive me to the appointment the second she arrived to work for the morning.

By the time I was seen at the eye doctor it was a few hours later, and my vision had returned to normal. I went through some testing, but everything checked out fine, and I was told it was likely just an ocular migraine. Short-lived, unpredictable symptoms were becoming an ongoing pattern for me. While physical issues were more common, they came in waves, varied in severity, and seemed to change at the drop of a hat. I began to question if this sickness was all in my head. Could it be possible that these symptoms were not physical at all, but only a manifestation of my mind? This thought started to rock my foundation. I considered myself a mentally strong person and if anything, thought I was directing my mental power to push through the physical symptoms and keep my life in order. But what if it was the other way around – was I simply imagining it all?

Surrender. It's a word that packs a punch and, at the time, I associated solely with defeat. As my blood tests began to return, results generally showed more signs of health than illness. My initial Lyme test came back negative, and so did the results for a variety of autoimmune disorders. Further bloodwork for certain cancers seemed to take ages to return and I was referred to make an appointment with an oncological surgeon for evaluation of my swollen lymph nodes. For what seemed like the longest few weeks of my life, my diagnosis swung between the possibility of cancer or nothing physical at all.

In the meantime, I was becoming sicker by the day. My body would almost shut down from exhaustion and I was experiencing episodes of mental incoherence. I couldn't remember basic facts or spell simple words, and struggled to communicate functionally for significant periods of time. My head felt like a heavy storm cloud, full of fog and ready to collapse at any moment. I had severe headaches at the base of my skull, low-grade fevers, episodes of vomiting, and my weight had dropped from 112 pounds down to only 92.

Soon, it was fourth of July weekend and I knew I was going to be sick. My head was pounding, I was mentally foggy, nauseous, and incredibly weak. I went to a walk-in clinic, but was told my case was too complicated and to consider taking myself to the Emergency Room. In an attempt to avoid the hospital on a holiday weekend, I opted to stay with my mother, who wanted to keep an eye on me. Within a few hours, I was in the midst of a violent vomiting episode. A family friend who was an EMT came to visit and immediately called for an ambulance.

While I was too sick to recall many of the details from the beginning of that evening, once the vomiting ceased and I had returned to some level of mental clarity, I immediately felt defeated. I had ended up in the hospital – a place I dreaded to be. It was the ultimate reality check that there was something seriously wrong, and I could no longer win the fight to keep my life going amidst illness. I had to surrender.

My potential diagnosis changed with the shifts of attending Emergency Room physicians. I remember the comments vividly and their phrases swirled around in my head. "There's a possibility of leukaemia or lymphoma." "She presents with symptoms similar to malaria." "If she can stop vomiting and keep something down, we could send her home tonight." It was quite the gamut of medical opinions.

I was officially admitted as a hospital patient somewhere around 4 am, and the next day wasn't any better in terms of a diagnosis. While I still felt incredibly weak, I could keep down a few sips of ginger ale and had returned to mental coherence. I even sent my boss an email from the hospital bed saying I was a little held up and likely wouldn't make it in to work on Monday, but perhaps by Tuesday, things would be better.

Clearly, my feelings of defeat were short-lived. While I by no means felt healthy, I remember thinking for a fleeting moment that perhaps these past few months had really all been a fluke. Could all my unexplained symptoms have culminated into this crucial moment and forced themselves out of my body? I thought to myself how lovely it would be to forget any of this had ever happened.

While in the hospital, I was sent for a chest X-ray and had a few teams of specialists perform evaluations, but wasn't receiving treatment beyond IV fluids. I met with the infectious disease team who first complimented me on my excellent cholesterol levels, and told me

I was a very mysterious case. I quickly began losing faith that anyone would find out what was wrong with me.

The final straw was when the new attending physician told me she remembered a case from a few months back where a young man presented with similar unexplained symptoms and remained undiagnosed after weeks of hospital stay. When I asked what had eventually happened, she replied she wasn't sure —he likely checked himself out, and as far as she knew, hadn't been readmitted.

I took the story as some type of foreboding sign from the universe to sign myself out from the hospital against medical guidance and return home to the comfort of my bed, even if just for the night to await remaining bloodwork results. I also could not wait to return home to my fluffy best friend for some reprieve. He always made everything better.

I did what I could. I greeted Lauryn at the door upon her arrival and then scooted quickly up the stairs to the bedroom ahead of her. This way, by the time she got into bed, her spot would be nice and toasty. I didn't entirely know what was wrong with Lauryn at this point, but eventually I kept hearing the words 'Lyme disease' again and again. From what I heard, the new bloodwork said it wasn't just Lyme disease either. There were a lot of other infections involved and it could be a complicated case to treat because it wasn't found right away.

Then I heard rumors some of the doctors tried to blame me! I was an indoor cat, though. No ticks on me. The nerve…

I did my best to make Lauryn smile during our long days in bed. Sometimes I'd carry my teddy bear, Emma, up the stairs to her in bed. She always seemed to think this was funny. Other times, I would sit on the neighboring pillow above her head to greet her when she woke up. Who wouldn't want my cute face to be the first thing they see upon waking? Lauryn and I would have our own celebration parties when she woke up feeling even just the slightest bit better. I would prance around and purr and meow. She would pet me. It was a win-win.

The only thing I wasn't entirely prepared for was the vomit. I didn't know I was a cat with a queasy stomach until this chapter in my life. Sometimes she would vomit and then I would vomit. Maybe it was sympathy pains.

If you told me before I became ill that a disease brought on by a tick bite would cause me to be so sick I would be unable to work for years, I wouldn't have believed you. Prior to becoming ill, I rushed through a good chunk of my life and tackled any obstacle in front of me with headstrong force. I was always trying to get to the next phase of my life as quickly and efficiently as possible, because it always seemed the land of golden opportunity lay ahead somewhere in the distance, never at my feet. I was not the person who savored the journey of the present; my eye was always looking off in the horizon toward the next destination.

Lyme disease very abruptly made me realize the type of force I used to overcome obstacles in my past wasn't going to work this time. The more I tried to push my body into functioning, the more it pushed back at me and the worse my symptoms would flare. Longer episodes of incoherence, more vomiting, hand and leg tremors, headaches, vision problems, and on and on. The headstrong 23-year-old in me who wanted to push her way back into her old life was going to have to adjust to a new mind set to accommodate her new body. I would be forced to learn the delicate balance between perseverance and daily accepting my physical limitations.

The headstrong 23-year-old in me did not back down easily. I was getting impatient. It was almost a year into my illness and I craved my old life. As much as I loved my extra cuddle time with Oliver, I was desperate to work, to socialize, to get out of the house. While I was still facing numerous symptoms and restrictions, certain aspects of my condition had improved slightly, and I thought maybe, just maybe, this chapter would finally be over and I could return to "normal" life.

It didn't quite work out that way. My condition regressed every time I tried to force myself back into a box my new body refused to fit. After multiple failed attempts to return to work due to my unpredictable flare ups, I struggled with where to turn.

The word again echoed in my head: *Surrender.*

Again?

Yes, again.

Just as the headstrong me had to surrender to the fact I was sick, I had to accept I would no longer be able to work in the traditional manner I once had. It was then I was given a huge blessing.

My case of Lyme disease had brought with it the onset of several neurological symptoms, most of which (like everything else) would come and go. It felt like my entire brain and nervous system would go haywire some days. Then, one day, I found myself suddenly writing with my left hand, even though I was previously only right handed. Of all the symptoms I had, this one certainly wasn't bad – just odd. I decided to embrace it and write left-handed during my time stuck back in bed.

Of all the things I could've written, I'm surprised it turned out to be children's rhyming stories. However, I'm not so surprised that the main character was inspired by my lovable Oliver!

I'm not surprised either. Who wouldn't want me as their main character? I'm cute, I'm fluffy, I'm funny, and I'm loyal. I also had an outside cat friend named Orange Kitty who I spied one day through the sliding glass door in the kitchen. We had the perfect tale and Lauryn was the perfect one to tell it. In the books, my co-characters, Orange Kitty and Myrtle, offer me much guidance on my adventures. With a little help from friends, anything is possible. That's always been my motto.

Since the books came out, Lauryn and I often brainstorm ways to help our fellow cat and human friends. I hear there are a lot of other humans who face health issues like Lauryn and can't work in traditional jobs. And I know first-hand there are a lot of cats still waiting for their forever homes amidst wire walls. Two of our brainchildren, localstrong.org and #YellowHatsforCats, help both causes. I always knew I was a smart cat.

What I've learned most throughout my illness and starting a business during my recovery is that I can't do it alone. Oliver brought fun and whimsy into my darkest days and it's his joy that shines through in *The Adventures of Oliver Poons*. I also could not have accomplished what I have without the help of my mother.

While the story thus far has focused mostly on me and Oliver, there's another layer to the story with my mother. At the time I was writing left-handed in a notebook from bed, my mother was still coming over every day to take care of me. Of course, she eventually asked what I was up to. It also just so happened that she mentioned a desire to get back into painting. Well, you probably know where this is going – she's now a mother, a retired teacher, AND a children's book illustrator.

However, it's not quite that simple. About another year from the time I initially started writing *The Adventures of Oliver Poons*, my mother and I were finally about 80% of the way through the illustrations for our first book, *Oliver Poons and the Bright Yellow Hat*. At this point, my health was better, but nowhere near normal. I was still severely underweight, barely weighing in at 90lbs some days, having flare-ups multiple times per week, and still needing hours of help from my mother on a weekly basis. Then, early one morning, the phone rang. It was an all-too calm call from my mother. "Lauryn, I think I broke my ankle."

My mental image of a broken ankle prior to this moment was of a cute, pink cast for six weeks or so and some crutches. Boy, was I off base.

As it turned out, my mother had fallen down half a flight of basement stairs onto cement. She did not have the cute pink cast kind of broken ankle. She had the three-surgeries-two-plates-17-screws-and-two-years-to-heal kind of break.

Our life quickly became an episode of the sick leading the injured or the injured leading the sick. Neither of us was functioning at anywhere near full capacity, but we still wanted to bring our children's book to life.

My mother and I learned through our own experiences how many other people are in similar unexpected life situations. There is an entire segment of the population who cannot participate in the traditional job market due to one circumstance or another and find themselves struggling. However, they have unique skill sets that, when combined with others, have the potential to turn into new work possibilities. This premise kick-started our efforts to create an online platform that would help harness the power of community. What started in our personal lives as illness, injury, and a series of children's books has led us on an even greater mission to unite and help others in new ways.

Now let's get back to the cats. None of this would've happened if I wasn't in the picture. There would be no book with a cute cat in a yellow hat to speak of and no alternative work options on the horizon. That's why it was important we find a way to give back to help cats too. Since launching our first book, all the Oliver Poons children's books and character-inspired accessories have incorporated into the

Oliver Poons Children's Company. It was through this company our #YellowHatsforCats campaign was born.

#YellowHatsforCats is the Oliver Poons Children's Company's partnership with animal welfare organizations, to which we donate a portion of our proceeds. It's great that we can do something a little extra special to help the organizations that help humans find their future best fur-friends. And, even better, everyone can show their support for this campaign by posting a picture of their cat in a yellow hat and tagging #yellowhatsforcats on social media.

I do love attention so I suppose it's natural I would want to start a new online trend, but it's for a good cause, after all. It's wonderful to see so many cats and cat lovers looking just like me these days and posing for a picture in a yellow hat!

As difficult as this period in my life has been in countless ways, when I look back on this chapter, I think I will ultimately remember more of its beauty than its struggle. Throughout all the darkness and the challenge, Oliver has been the guiding light for me to remain positive and he certainly never fails to brighten my day. The children's books he's inspired are meant to bring happiness and whimsy into everyone's life, and giving back beyond the children's books I hope will create meaningful change for others. As Oliver reminds me daily in all his infinite kitty wisdom: Bring a smile to others and your life will surely smile back at you.

About the Author

Lauryn Alyssa Wendus, USA
Website: oliverpoons.com / localstrong.org
Instagram & Twitter: @oliverpoons @local_strong

After a life-altering illness yielded me unable to work a traditional job, I ventured down a road of entrepreneurship to make a new life for myself. With a little inspiration from my cat, Oliver, I started the Oliver Poons Children's Company with the launch of my first children's book, *Oliver Poons and the Bright Yellow Hat*. My personal and business experiences have encouraged me to think of new ways to help others and have inspired my new online platform to harness the power of community, LocalStrong.org. My mission is to build businesses that inspire creativity, promote generosity, and strengthen community.

The Surprise Visitors
By Jules Clark

It all began on an ordinary weekday in March. My husband left the house early in the morning for his commute to work and our teenage son cycled off to college. I stood at the sink and filled the washing up bowl with warm, soapy suds in readiness to wash the breakfast dishes. As I looked out of the window, the bright, early morning sunshine warmed my face, and I noticed the first of the spring bulbs we planted last autumn were beginning to bloom. It had been a chilly winter with icy cold frosts, and it was lovely, at last, to feel the warm sunshine.

My phone rang just as I put my hands into the bowl of suds. I grabbed a towel and before I had even said hello I heard the panicked voice of my mum. She sounded a bit muffled as she was outside and her phone reception was breaking up. All I could make out was she wanted me to pop round as soon as possible. Sensing the worry in her voice, I left the dishes in the sink, grabbed my car keys, and headed straight out of the door.

My mum and dad live in a beautiful little village amid picturesque rural countryside. There are around two dozen or so houses, thatched cottages and bungalows, a village pub, which runs popular weekly quiz nights, and a grocery store that includes a Post Office. The grocery store is the hub of the small community and houses a small tearoom serving tasty lunches and sumptuous afternoon teas. In the summer months, they sell delicious ice cream sundaes of all flavours in tall glasses. It's a beautiful and quiet place to live, where not much usually happens.

I don't live very far away from my parents and grew up in the house they still own. As I rounded the corner, drove past the village duck pond and arrived in their driveway, Mum darted out from the side gate that leads into their back garden. I saw Dad reaching behind a large shrub, hammering some wood into the shed at the bottom of the garden and I waved to him. Their garden is large, landscaped on one side with leafy shrubs and perennial flowers, and the other half given over to tall apple trees. The two halves are broken up by a path that leads down to the shed.

Mum, looking flushed, explained that as it was such a warm day, my dad had decided to give the lawn its first cut of the year. He went into the shed to get the lawnmower while Mum took advantage of the warm weather and hung out some washing on the clothesline.

"There's something living in the shed!" Dad had shouted.

Fearing mice, Mum jumped up on the nearest wooden garden chair, visualising rodents running all over the garden. She has always been frightened of mice ever since her older brother hid one in her doll's pram when she was a little girl.

Mum standing on the chair made Dad laugh, which she took great offence to as he knew she didn't like mice.

"Just look inside the shed," Dad had said gently.

Mum knew Dad wouldn't lead her into something she wouldn't like, so she got down from the chair and cautiously made her way over to the shed. When they opened the door, they heard little scurrying noises and Mum quickly backed away. Dad encouraged her to take another look and they heard another small sound, then another, and saw something small and fluffy. Mum told me at that point she seriously thought it was mice and was about to make a run for it.

"It's kittens, there are five kittens in there!" Dad had said.

Like me, Mum absolutely loves cats, especially kittens. She explained the kittens were huddled together, cuddled up for warmth. All except for a little tabby with a white face, peering quizzically at them and meowing little baby meows quite noisily. There were two other tabbies, along with one almost pure black, and one black and white kitten.

Mum and Dad couldn't fathom out how on earth the kittens had got inside the shed as at first, they couldn't find any holes in the walls and there was no sign of an adult cat with them. Mum found a cardboard box for the kittens and took them into their conservatory to keep them warmer as she felt it was chilly outside for them. Dad fetched a warm, knitted blanket for the kittens' box and investigated how they could have got inside. He found a hole behind a large hydrangea planted underneath the shed's frosted window.

Having recounted what had happened so far, Mum took me into the conservatory and I instantly fell head over heels in love with each kitten. I've always loved cats ever since I was tiny. Mum once found me fast asleep in my tent in the garden surrounded by our neighbour's four cats, all curled up and also fast asleep. I now own my own cat, Purrley, a beautiful lavender point Birman, so named because he has the loudest purr I've ever heard.

I cuddled each kitten in turn. The tabby with the white face was the most alert and was very nosey. We decided to call her Noisy as she was constantly meowing. Next up was the almost pure black kitten, he had a little curled white moustache so called him Tache. One of the other tabbies had much longer, softer fur than the others so we named her Fluffy. The last tabby was smaller than the others so we called her Tiny. Finally, the black and white kitten had black legs with white markings on all his paws so we named him Socks. Dad was amused we'd named the kittens, he said he guessed we would.

Dad hastily repaired the shed and we stood in the conservatory trying to decide what to do. Mum had phoned my brother and he was on his way over. He has always loved cats and owns a mischievous black cat named Maggie. Sadly, Mum and Dad were unable to keep the kittens as they were going on holiday in two days. My brother and I both already had cats and we couldn't think of anyone we could rehome them with. I would have happily claimed them all but didn't feel it was fair to Purrley to suddenly arrive home with five kittens.

We called the local vet for advice and he gave us the phone number of an organisation that may be able to help find homes for the kittens.

"Keep an eye out for their mother, she'll still be feeding them herself," said the vet. "Have any cats come into your garden regularly?"

"I've seen a grey cat a couple of times, sitting on top of the shed," said Dad. "I didn't think much of it at the time, I thought it was a neighbour's cat hunting birds in our garden."

At that point, my bother arrived, Noisy greeted him straight away and nuzzled into his neck when he held her. I was cuddling Socks, Mum had Tiny who'd climbed out of the box and ventured underneath a table and Dad was making the phone calls with Fluffy and Tache curled up together on his lap.

Dad called the organisation, who took his details and a description of the kittens. They would send someone out later on, or even the following day. They also told us it may be best to put the kittens back in the shed to see if their mother would come back, so Dad went to undo his repair job on the broken wood.

We took the them back to the shed. The early morning sunshine had now all but disappeared and it felt chilly outside. We put them in the box and a few climbed straight out and ran all over the floor.

"I hate to leave them out here, they'll be so cold," said Mum.

"They must have survived here for some time," said Dad, taking charge. "I'm sure they'll be fine."

We reluctantly left the kittens to their own devices for the time being, hoping their mother would return as they must need a feed again soon. That was probably why Noisy was meowing so frequently.

When we returned to the house, Mum refused to leave the conservatory. She didn't want to be out of sight of the shed and she wanted to leave the door open so she could hear if the mother returned. By now the weather had turned very cold and, although Dad had turned on the radiator in the conservatory, it was still very chilly.

"Would you run upstairs and fetch for me another layer of clothing?" Mum asked me. "Oh, and my warmest winter coat too please."

I grabbed a thick jumper, leggings she could wear underneath her trousers and spotted some leg warmers she wore for her Zumba class. I also found her gloves, a scarf, some thick bed socks and her warm, padded winter coat that had a thick fluffy collar. By the time Mum had put on the extra layers, she looked ready for an expedition to the Antarctic.

Dad sat in the toasty warm lounge, reasoning he was staying near the phone, notepad and pen at hand in case the organisation called back. My brother and I decided to take a walk around the village to see if we could see the kittens' mother, and to ask the neighbours if they'd seen anything that could help us find her. Before we set off, I made Mum a flask of warming coffee and packed her up some lunch. She'd remembered there were some binoculars in the study, and Dad had just found them for her.

Mum settled herself down into one of the soft, padded rattan conservatory chairs, with the binoculars on a cord hanging around her neck and wrapped a warm blanket around her. Just before we left we heard a noise in the garden. Mum was straight up to the window, peering through the binoculars, but it was just a collared dove visiting the bird table near one of the apple trees. Mum settled herself down again and pulled the blanket back over her. We poured her a cup of coffee and set off for our walk around the village. She promised to call if there was any news of the mother or any updates from the organisation.

My brother and I walked down our parents' driveway and stopped at the village pond, the ducks enjoying a swim on the pond quacked noisily in greeting to us. From there, lanes ran in different directions so we decided to split up and search separately. I headed in the direction of the grocery store and the homes surrounding it, and my brother went towards the pub and the houses and cottages at that end of the village.

As I was walking towards the grocery store, I met one of my parents' elderly neighbours. She was the head of the village's Neighbourhood Watch so she was good person to ask if anyone had reported news about a cat. She hadn't heard anyone mention anything but knew some neighbours who owned cats and pointed out their houses and bungalows. She was making her way around the village delivering leaflets about an upcoming local baking competition, and she kindly said she would mention our search to anyone she met along the way.

Just then, my phone rang and I saw Mum's name flashing on the screen. I felt hopeful of good news, that the kittens' mother had turned up or someone from the organisation had arrived. Unfortunately not, she asked if we had any news and if we could pick her up some soup from the grocery store for her flask. It was getting colder and I was glad I was wearing my warm, padded coat. I thought about the poor little kittens having to huddle together for warmth, so I sped up my search and headed towards the store.

I had always loved visiting the grocery store; there was a little bell on the door that jingled when you entered. The tearoom was attached and there was always the wonderful smell of freshly made coffee and the tantalising aroma of delicious homemade cakes, meat-filled pasties and sausage rolls. Sometimes there was a smell of warm ginger cake or rich chocolate and cherry cake. Their Victoria sponge was light and fluffy and filled with homemade strawberry jam, which was produced by the owner – the fruit was even grown in their allotment.

My favourite purchases from the store were one of their Bakewell tarts and a frothy cappuccino. I'd walk to one of the benches on the village green, carved by a local carpenter, and enjoy the coffee and cake in wonderful relaxation. During the summer months, the villagers took part in a 'Best Blooming Village' competition, and went all out to decorate the village spectacularly, with pots of beautiful flowers and hanging baskets prettying up the lamp posts. The village green was usually the centre focus and was a wonderful place to relax with a picnic of tasty items bought from the tearoom.

I'd known the owners of the grocery store since I was a little girl and was always warmly greeted by them. Behind the main counter were jars of all kinds of colourful sweets, and I used to love spending my pocket money on a bag of mixed sweets and a comic. They stocked a wide range of magazines and newspapers, along with all the basic store cupboard ingredients, locally-sourced meats, freshly-laid local eggs, a good selection of cheeses, and locally-grown seasonal fruit and vegetables. You could also purchase knitting patterns, wool and household knickknacks.

I explained to the owner how we'd discovered the kittens, and he said none of his customers had mentioned a missing cat, or that their cat was expecting kittens. He suggested I put a notice in the shop's window so anyone could contact us with helpful information. After writing out the notice, I popped into the tearoom and bought Mum some of their homemade vegetable soup and bought us a Bakewell tart each.

I decided to knock on the doors of the homes at this end of the village and began with the ones I had been told earlier owned cats. Each home I visited was sympathetic to our plight but not one of them had a cat that had been expecting kittens or had gone missing. I had one more bungalow to visit and noticed a grey cat sitting on the dustbin in the back garden; it was a beautiful cat with bright gold eyes. Unfortunately, there was nobody home at the bungalow, and assuming it must be their own cat, I decided to call back later in the hope they might have noticed another wandering around.

My phone rang again and this time it was Dad. He said the organisation had called back and wouldn't be able to send anyone out that day. Mum was beside herself with worry for the kittens' health, especially as they were outside in the cold, waiting for their mother to return. By now it had been a long time since we'd found them and we didn't know how long their mother had been away.

I met up with my brother and he didn't have much news either, except that one of the villagers had seen a cat eating the remainder of a piece of a little girl's Victoria sponge. Apparently, some seagulls made her jump by swooping overhead fancying a piece of her cake, and she'd dropped it on the ground. My brother didn't take that much notice of that and presumed the cat probably belonged to one of the villagers.

When we got back to our parents' house, Mum was huddled up against the conservatory window with the binoculars at her eyes scanning the bushes and trees. Dad, on the other hand, was doing a crossword and listening to the local radio. The news reported it was going to be a frosty night and that only worried Mum further. I heated the soup up for her, handed out the Bakewell tarts and made some coffee. Meanwhile, my brother, still wrapped in his warm winter coat, went to have a quick check on the kittens. Mum watched closely through her binoculars and he reported they were all cuddled up sound asleep together.

My brother had to go to work, so I popped upstairs to borrow some of Mum's clothes to put on another layer and joined her in the conservatory. We took it in turns to keep watch through the binoculars and we shared the soup between us. There was still no sign of the kittens' mother, although we counted lots of different birds visiting the garden. It was now starting to get dark and Mum encouraged Dad to check on the kittens and to put a torch inside the shed so they had some light. She also suggested he turn on the outside light so it lit up permanently instead of when somebody stepped outside.

We decided that if the kittens' mother hadn't come back by 9 pm we were going to bring them indoors to spend the night inside in the warm. There was no way we would be able to tuck ourselves up in our cosy beds knowing they were in the chilly shed.

"Perhaps we should buy an oil-filled radiator for them?" suggested Mum. "We could heat it up in the house and, when it's warm, move it into the shed. I'm sure I've read they keep warm long after they're unplugged."

"I don't think we should disturb them too much," reasoned Dad. "It might stop their mother from returning."

We finished the soup, and by now it was too dark to see much with the binoculars, even with the outside light on. Just then, my mobile phone rang showing a number I didn't recognise. When I answered, the caller asked for me by name and explained they owned the bungalow I'd visited earlier in the day, the one where I'd seen the grey cat sitting on the dustbin. The caller introduced herself and said she had been out all day visiting a friend and had called into the grocery store to pick up some milk on the way home. She'd seen my notice and realised I might be looking for the grey cat.

It had arrived at her back door one frosty morning as she was about to put some seed out for the wild birds in her garden. She hadn't seen it before and didn't recognise it as a local cat, so she took pity on it being out in the cold and gave it some cat food. She went on to explain she had recently been looking after a friend's cat and had some tins of food left over. She said the cat had returned every morning since and some afternoons but never in the evening or at night, so I arranged to visit her to see if the cat was around.

It was getting close to 8 pm and we were all anxious about the poor kittens and worried about their mother. As I was about to leave to visit the owner of the bungalow, there was a knock on the door. Dad answered it to find a lady wearing a tag from the organisation he had contacted earlier. She apologised for calling so late but explained she had been busy trying to help another set of kittens. As Mum and Dad's house was on her way home, she'd decided to stop and help that evening.

We were so relieved to see her and Mum led her down the path to see the kittens. She obviously loved cats as much as Mum and me because she also fell in love with them all. She said we did the best thing for them, putting them back inside the shed to see if their mother would return to feed them. We reckoned by this stage they must be ravenous with hunger. Little Noisy was meowing and Socks was trying to hide behind my old bicycle.

She checked them over and we were relieved to hear they were all healthy. She explained that as their eyes were open they may have been there a little while, but she didn't think they had been born in the shed.

She looked at the hole Dad had tried to repair earlier and said she believed their mother had probably carried them in one by one, and had been returning to feed them and possibly sleep there overnight.

She went to her car and returned with a large pet carrier. It had a fleecy blanket on the base and two bowls for water attached to the side. Just as she was putting little Tache inside the carrier we heard a movement behind us. As we all turned around, there stood the beautiful grey cat with shining golden eyes I had seen at the bungalow earlier. She walked over to Tache and nudged him gently with her head in greeting.

The lady from the organisation gently approached the grey cat and after gently examining her declared she was the kittens' mother as she had recently given birth and was full of milk. We were so relieved that mother and kittens were reunited and explained we had searched the whole village for her and her owner. She didn't belong to anyone in the village and she wasn't wearing a collar either. The rest of the kittens were put into the carrier and their mother climbed in as well, laid down, and all five kittens snuggled around her. I remarked with amusement that the mother's purr was almost as loud as Purrley's.

It had been a long day and we were so relieved when we knew the mother would accompany the kittens to the organisation as it was best for them to continue to feed on her milk. As the lady prepared to drive away, she assured us they would be well looked after and all go to good homes. We leaned into the car to say our farewells and saw all five kittens feeding happily from their beautiful mother.

Following their departure, loud hammering noises could be heard from the bottom of the garden. Dad was making sure that the hole was well and truly blocked up and nothing else could get inside the shed. In daylight the following morning, he went around the rest of the shed to make sure it was all secure. Mum was relieved as, although she loved the kittens and their mother, she was glad there was no chance of any mice following suit and moving in.

About the Author

Jules Clark, UK
Website: https://crazycatladyukblog.wordpress.com
Instagram: crazycatladyuk2017
I live in the UK with my husband, son, and our fluffy, mischievous cat. I've been writing stories for as long as I can remember and I absolutely love writing. I hope you enjoyed reading my story and, if so, please have a look at my blog about my cat and his friends.

Finally Finding the Good Life: Our Story as Told by Ginger
By Anna Georghallides

It all started about 11 years ago, when I was abandoned at three weeks old, beside Anna's car, in her parking space under the block of flats in Pernera Gardens. She was away working as an international cultural photographer, so I was only discovered after I started meowing pitifully as she alighted from the taxi upon her return. I don't know how long I had been there but none of her neighbours bothered to see what was wrong.

What she found was a skinny, sorrowful, ginger mess. My head was out of proportion with my undernourished body, I had huge ears and was wet from my pee. She dashed upstairs to leave her luggage and brought down a carrier box into which I was unceremoniously placed. She was muttering something about the shops being closed, this is Cyprus after all and everything closes early, and where was she going to get formula and pads? I was taken up to the flat where her two rescue pups were very interested in me and I was left in her bedroom, door closed, with the heating on.

After what seemed like an age, I heard her park her car and speak to her good friend and neighbour, Sylvia, who had also been away and has now become a cat rescuer too. The front door closed and I heard her moving about the kitchen, talking to the pups and explaining they had to be nice to me because I am only a baby. I started meowing loudly, reminding her of my existence, for which I was rewarded with some lovely, warm formula that I guzzled before demanding more. Instead, she placed me in a new box, all warm and cosy, complete with pee pad, cuddly toy and pet hot-water bottle, and I snuggled down for my first comfortable night ever.

Over the next few weeks, I settled in, put on much-needed weight, became very good friends with my pup siblings and started to enjoy life. Because I had lost my feline mum so early I developed a habit of suckling on everything and everyone. Each time mum or her guests sat down they'd end up with a damp behind because I had suckled on the throws. I've grown out of it now but occasionally I still indulge on a pup tail or ear, much to their annoyance. Another habit I developed, which I refused to give up, was opening doors. I jumped up, hung on to the handle for dear life and let myself into whichever room I chose. So, Mum locked most of the doors, grrrrrr!

About four months later, after taking the pups for their second daily walk, Mum popped out again and returned with a black and white, two-month-old fur ball who was struggling ferociously despite a very swollen eye. Mum found him crying in the middle of a main road and took pity on him. A trip to the vet diagnosed a severe infection that was curable with a month's worth of eye drops and antibiotics. Thus, we welcomed Cheeky into our home. We took to each other immediately and I helped his recovery by licking his eye whenever I thought Mum wasn't looking, and showed him the ropes on how to play with two young dogs. Cheeky took after me by suckling, but only on Mum when she pats and cuddles him. He's very chatty and one of the sweetest kitty personalities I know.

Five years came and went and Mum's then-boyfriend left her – I didn't like him much. A new man came into her life and is now our Dad, whom we love, and we started to hear things like 'moving', 'selling the flat', 'moving above my parents into my Grandmother's house' and 'renovation'. Packing boxes moved into the spare bedroom, a huge truck came to get them and we were bundled into Mum's car to move into our new, much bigger, home. Noisy renovations lasted three months until finally the workmen went home and we were left to enjoy our new space. *Great*, I thought, *no more upheavals*. Little did I know it was just the beginning.

New faces appeared, of both the feline and canine variety. Lucky was next, a handsome, young, skinny boy who was abandoned by his mother in our back garden and who cried to be let in. By then, Mum had begun to help various rescue organisations on Facebook with fostering, and one day she came back from the vet having been to meet a gorgeous four-month-old kitten named Cindy. Cindy had been found three months earlier with her front paws half dangling, presumably having been run over, and had spent most of her young life in a vet cage. One paw was amputated and the other very deformed so she hops around putting on weight as she goes. We call her our bunny and Dad says she's a little barrel! She is a maternal type and 'mothers' all our siblings, both temporary and permanent, who come through our doors. I was always top kitty but for her I gladly relinquished the role. She may not have front paws but she knows how to pin us all down and viciously lick us spotless, it can get quite annoying at times when one is trying to snore!

We had so many disability cases arrive that Mum decided to turn our home into a mini-sanctuary for 30 lost souls. It was originally for 20 but when we're this cute, what is a human to do? Mum says if I cover each case I'll write a whole book so I'll concentrate on our more interesting feline residents. I'll also mention that we have nine doggy siblings too, the rest of us are the meowing species. And we also feed a family of hedgehogs when they appear.

To understand us better you should know we live on the small island of Cyprus in the Mediterranean Sea. An island that, although beautiful and with Aphrodite, the Goddess of Love, as her legend, has one of the worst animal rights reputations in Europe. Most of us kitties are too young to fend for ourselves and are cared for by volunteers, after been found abandoned in the various parks. Because of our humble beginnings we tend to develop, and in many cases, succumb to, various viruses. Our little bodies struggle with other medical problems, such as paralysis from abuse, or being run over, so it's rare that we win. Those of us that do are often left blind or with weak immune systems, and I have four siblings with these issues.

Our most unique brother is a kitty with a story Hollywood could get to grips with. He's had quite a rough ride but now is safe in our wonderful home with loads of love showered upon him, helping him forget the horrors of his past. He was born on a gentleman's veranda and had three sisters. The gentleman took really good care of Tommy and his mum, but Tommy was a bit of a wanderer and ended up with severely injured hind legs that became infested with maggots. He managed to crawl back to the house and was taken to the vet, who suggested he be put to sleep. His owner refused and saved his life by having his legs amputated.

All was going well and he was adjusting to his new situation, when his mum had another litter of kittens and decided Tommy was a threat. She chased him from the house and a nasty human threw him into an empty swimming pool with no shade, food or water. The summer temperatures in Cyrus are very high and Tommy was terrified. By chance, some animal rescuers found him and threw food to him over the high fence daily, as they couldn't get to him straight away. A route in needed to be discovered. Two weeks later they succeeded in getting to him but he was so scared he wouldn't let them catch him. Finally, out of desperation and exhaustion, he let them.

Tommy was rushed to the vet and a foster home was found. Posts on Facebook found his owner who wanted him back but, although he loved Tommy, his owner realised he wouldn't be safe and agreed to give him up. Once again, through Facebook, Anna heard his story and offered him a forever home with us. It turned out that, quite by chance, Anna knew the gentleman's brother, a well-known artist, and the two men have been supportive and follow Tommy's progress with interest. Tommy is an amazing soul who walks on his front paws with his back end wiggling in the air. I don't think I could do that!

He's very affectionate but not all that innocent. Although neutered, he's taken quite a fancy to our little Tinkerbell, who was born with cerebellar hypoplasia, CH, or Wobbly Cat Syndrome, so as a result had delayed growth and hasn't been 'done' yet. She came into her first heat the other day and, oh boy, you should have seen the commotion! She wagged her tail in Tommy's face and he pinned her down, at the same time trying to swat at Sammy, who has just arrived, and is very senior with no teeth. That's not easy to do when you only have two paws. Mum kept running in to separate them as Tinkerbell objected to her neck being bitten and finally she was put in a big doggy crate for her own protection. Now this has passed, Tommy and Tinker, as I affectionately call her, sleep together with his paws cuddling her close. She will be spayed as soon as we can safely do so.

Tommy: "Hey Ginger, I'm telling Mum on you! Who said you could discuss my private life?!"

Me: "Chill, if you don't want it mentioned, don't do it!"

Tommy: "In that case I'll tell everyone that Mum has to give you a bath every time you roll in the poop tray!"

I slink away embarrassed, tail between my legs. It's just something I like to do, OK?

Tinkerbell isn't the only CH kitty with us. A white girl with orange spots, Sally, was dumped at a cat colony and due to her condition, which was worse than Tinker's, she wasn't allowed to eat with the other cats. A volunteer, who had never come across this condition before, immediately called Mum to ask if she might know what was wrong with this poor creature. The best decision for Sally was for her to live in a home, so of course Mum opened our doors. I must admit, I wish she'd ask me first! Wobbly Cat Syndrome causes jerky movements, tremors and generally uncoordinated motion. The animal often falls and has trouble walking. To make sure Sally gets to eat, she feasts in the kitchen while Mum washes our dishes. After her meal, she stretches out full length on her belly and Mum massages her while she purrs away at top volume. Mum says it's one of her favourite times of the day, time with Sally.

I'll bore you all with one last very special case that arrived recently, something Mum hadn't come across before and is still learning the ropes, with my help of course. At least I try, by sleeping in her box and biting the sling she uses for therapy!

A video appeared on mum's Facebook profile of a tiny kitten who appeared to be swimming. At first, we assumed it was CH again, but looking closely, the kitten moved very much like a frog. The young girl who found her had no idea how to help her and no money for a vet, so Mum agreed to speak to our vet and have the girl visit him. The two-month-old kitten was diagnosed with Swimmers Syndrome or Splay Syndrome. Swimmer kittens have a muscular or tendon and ligament deficiency that causes their back legs to splay out and they cannot bring their legs under their body to lift themselves into position. They are called 'swimmer' because the kittens get around by using a swimming motion with their legs to scuff around instead of standing up properly. It's rare for the syndrome to affect the front legs too but unfortunately little Swimmer had this to contend with also. An urgent appointment was made with our physiotherapist and some exercises were recommended. We worked with Swimmer twice a day but she was so weak it seemed to be getting worse rather than better, again this is very rare.

To make matters worse, the girl who found Swimmer announced there were two Swimmer kittens but the sibling, also a girl, was in better condition. Mum brought her in too, hoping she would encourage Swimmer to fight. Unfortunately, we said goodbye to Swimmer as Mum and our amazing vet helped her to the Rainbow Bridge. I gather it is lovely there and she can now run free and be healthy. Abby, her sister, is still with us and doing well. She's certainly a determined little thing and she has figured out how to climb in and out of her bed unaided. Mum uses as sling to strengthen her hind legs and it seems to be working.

Living the Good Life

Living at Even More Special is exactly that, special. Mum and Dad have made sure all our comforts are catered for. We sleep indoors all snuggled up together. We did have our own beds but we had a kitty conference and decided we'd prefer fewer, larger beds we can share. It makes laundry easier for Mum also. Dad built us a wooden frame of various floors, complete with scratching posts and we have a kitty tree and loads of toys to chase. During the renovations, Mum and Dad had a large balcony enclosed with wire mesh so there is no danger of us falling. That means we have an outdoor space complete with plants, a large dead branch, which we love to climb and scratch, fake grass, a custom-built kitty house and wooden pallets for those who can't climb.

Breakfast is our favourite time of day. All that good, nutritious food boosted with vitamins to keep us extra strong. I'm not sure our humans are all that keen on our meowing and jumping antics while we wait for them to serve us, it can get quite chaotic and we enjoy getting under their feet as they put our dishes down. Paws and tails get trodden on, Mum gets annoyed and we jostle each other to make sure we get whatever special treat goes on top of our meal each day. My canine sister, Ruby, is a dab hand in the kitchen and she and Mum have set up Ruby's Kitchen, so we get to try all the delicious goodies they've been cooking up, all canine and feline healthy of course.

Mum loves to garden and of course it's up to me, and the rest of the gang, to make sure she does it properly. She spends time at the computer reading up on plants that aren't poisonous for us before making a trip to our favourite garden centre. They very generously donated some plants for the kitty balcony when they heard it was being done up.

The gloves go on, the pots come out and it's time to start digging. Mum pours fresh soil into the pots and I immediately jump in to make sure she's added just the right amount. "Silly Ginger," she scolds, lifting me out and brushing me off.

I wander off to sniff the other plants, pretending I just walked out to the balcony but keeping one eye on the activities so I can seize the chance to be helpful again. The plants go in and are watered, Mum goes inside to wash her hands, the perfect opportunity! I wander nonchalantly over to the pot and peer inside, it looks good but there may be a little too much soil. Mum's tired so I'll do my bit, I climb in and start removing some of the soil, all is going well until I hear "GINGER GET OUT NOW! D*** CAT!" Oh well, I guess I misread that one. My punishment? I get picked up and put in the bath before I can leave muddy paw marks all over the house.

As Mum and I type this, we are heading into the Christmas season. Another year has just flown by. Christmas is a favourite time for the Even More Special animals as Mum and Dad make it as exciting for us as possible. Each year we have new siblings who experience the magic of the holidays for the first time and even I, who has celebrated 12 of them, still feel like a little kitten on Christmas morning. Mum doesn't believe in decorating the house before December 1st but she starts putting away the usual ornaments about a week earlier to make space for the festive ones.

On the evening of December 1st, the Christmas music plays softly on the CD player, a glass of red stuff called mulled wine is poured, with the rest bubbling away on the stove and the Christmas trunk is opened. The tree is put together with all of us doing our bit, although it does look a little moth-eaten, and Mum gives us long-lasting treats to keep us busy as she displays her precious ornaments. Some she's had from childhood and we're under strict instructions that we are not to touch! She also has some lovely baubles of those animals waiting for us at the Rainbow Bridge and she tenderly places them on the tree once the fairy lights go on. Once the ornaments are up, she settles down with another glass of mulled wine and a plateful of her warming chilli con carne. Dessert is a mince pie and she has baked some feline and canine Christmas muffins, which we devour. We get to open the first window of our special advent calendar and share the goodies she's placed inside.

We spend December evenings replying to holiday e-mails, writing cards which we can paw stamp to animal-friendly friends, wrapping gifts – we get seriously involved with the paper and string – and baking all sorts of Christmas goodies. Before we know it, the 24th arrives and preparations for the following day start coming together. Mum cooks our special Christmas breakfast consisting of fish cakes for us felines, and chicken, liver, mashed potato, Brussels sprouts with a dollop of cranberry sauce for the canines. She sets her Christmas table with us sitting on it of course and late in the evening she puts us to bed before playing Santa. We each have a tiny stocking on the fireplace and filled with a treat and new toy. We go to sleep listening to carols and breathing in the aromas from the kitchen.

It's 7 am and that means it's time to wake the humans. The pups howl and we meow and scratch at the bedroom door. They roll groggily out of bed and give us each a good morning pat before letting us out to do our business while they serve our special meal. We're all too excited and rush back in making as much noise as possible until Dad tells us to be quiet or we won't get anything. We gobble breakfast as fast as we can and sit under the tree, mouths drooling in expectation. Mum and Dad join us with a mug of coffee and give us our stockings. We dig out our gifts with great enthusiasm, wasting no time on our treats before pouncing on and chasing our new toys and figuring out our new games. The humans open their gifts and have lunch with our grandparents. There are too many of us to join them, so we settle down to snooze, bellies full, until they return and the celebrations continue.

A few hours later, they are back and the canines go for their long walk. It's rather chilly out so we stay snug in our beds until we hear them stomping up the stairs. The Christmas music goes on, the mulled wine is poured and it's mince pie time. Mum has baked some pet safe ones for us and we munch away happily hissing at anyone who finishes theirs quickly and tries to steal someone else's. We have this silly tradition where we wear Santa and reindeer hats and Dad snaps photos of us. We even dance with Mum around the sitting room until one of us decides to sink the claws in. I gather this year Mum has ordered a special pet-friendly beverage for us over the internet, I can't wait to see what that is all about. A Christmas movie is played and we slowly head to our beds. Before long, you hear gentle snoring and all falls silent.

We have nine new siblings this year and I have a feeling that watching their curiosity and astonishment at the festivities will make this holiday season Even More Special. As for me, 11 years ago I was dumped under a strange car. Thank you to whoever left me, unbeknown to you, you helped me find the good life.

About the Author

Anna Georghallides, Cyprus
Website: http://annagcyprus.wixsite.com/even-more-special
Facebook: https://www.facebook.com/evenmorespecialpawsup/
Facebook:
https://www.facebook.com/tommyuniquecatwithonlytwolegs/
Twitter: https://twitter.com/evenmspecial

We run a mini home sanctuary caring for 35 senior and disabled animals that were abandoned and waiting to die. We produce our online magazine 'Paws Up' to pay for their medical and comfort needs so we hope you'll subscribe and help us along. Details can be found on our website. We have a lot going on so please join us on our fascinating journey. Life with these precious souls is never boring.

Rocky's Tale
By Alan Parks

Rocky's tale comes from a small farm set in the undulating hills of the Andalucían olive groves. We, Alan and Lorna, are an intrepid couple from the UK, and we left our comfortable lives to start a Spanish adventure in 2008. Leaving behind family and friends, and buying a run-down, ancient olive mill was a chance to get 'back to basics' for us. The olive mill we bought has no mains electricity and no mains water. Our only heating comes from a single log burning stove that we huddle in front of during the colder months. In the summer, the heat is stifling and temperatures can reach over 50 degrees Celsius (over 122 degrees Fahrenheit).

We moved to Spain to start an alpaca breeding business, but sadly, due to the recession around the world, alpacas as a business have never taken off in Spain. Over the years, we have had many wonderful (and not so wonderful) animal experiences. From rescuing abandoned and mistreated dogs, to finding lost donkeys and wandering goats out of nowhere at the farm, hardly a week goes by without some kind of animal tale to tell.

When we moved to The Olive Mill, there was a lone resident farm cat. She didn't belong to the previous owners, she had just moved in and made herself at home. A little black and white thing, she was scared and would run at the first sign of us. "If you don't want her around, don't feed her, she will soon disappear," the previous owner told us as she left on moving day.

We had brought our elderly dog over from England, we were due to have alpacas delivered sometime soon, and we had prepared ourselves that sooner or later we would find some abandoned dogs that would need homes too, so cats had been furthest from our minds. We decided we wouldn't feed the little black and white cat and soon enough she would move on.

When we moved to The Olive Mill, there were building materials and a pile of old firewood that had been left behind. We hadn't yet sold our house in the UK, so the materials stayed in place for months. Occasionally we would see the cat run out from under one of the pallets or the pile of wood and disappear again. We weren't feeding her so I guess she was living on wildlife from around the farm. On one or two occasions, I remember thinking I had seen a tiny kitten, but when I looked again there was nothing there. The following spring, we saw kittens, but we never found out if there had been any the first year. Perhaps there had been and they didn't make it. This time, there were three kittens and we saw them around outside. The mum was skinny, raising three kittens on the thin pickings from the farm, so we started to give her some small portions of food. Although we didn't want to encourage the cats, as we wanted them to hunt, we also did not want them to starve. She seemed to be an amazing mother and the three cats grew big and strong.

The cats hung around throughout the winter, and once again in the springtime, we could see that babies were due. This time, the cat was far braver, even allowing the kittens to play in our garden. There were three new kittens, one of which was a real runt of the litter. There were six cats altogether now, and because they were like a big family, and we were fans of the TV show The Royale Family, we named them after the characters in the show. The mum was Barb, then the largest kittens were Dave and Jim. The three new kittens were Twiggy, Baby David and Our Denise. The runt we named Twiggy because of his little legs.

That winter, every few days we would discover Twiggy was missing. The first time we hadn't realised he'd disappeared, but as we were feeding the alpacas we found him, meowing hard, hiding in a hole on one of the dry-stone walls. We picked him up and returned him to Barb, thinking he may have just got lost. Over the next few days, however, the same thing occurred time and again, and we needed to watch carefully as maybe Barb was trying to ditch the runt. We hadn't had much experience with feral cats, but it was a lesson in their survival instincts.

After a couple of weeks, Twiggy had become strong enough to manage to keep up with the group and we were able to relax a little. And then one day, it happened. When we fed the cats that evening, only

Barb and Our Denise came to eat. All the kittens and the two other big cats were missing. We had a scout around but they were nowhere to be found. For a few days we worried about them, but Barb didn't seem concerned and, after a while, we started to forget about them. We always wondered if they had been eaten by a predator, hit by one of the rare cars that pass The Olive Mill or just wandered off.

In the meantime, Our Denise, who we assumed was a female as she was so beautiful, turned out to be a male. There were two very definite indicators. After the new year, during the period of hibernation for us, Jim, now a fine cat, reappeared. He looked healthy and strong, like he hadn't missed a meal. This allayed our fears about the cats having been hunted and we eventually concluded that the two older cats had taken the little ones off to start a new life for themselves. In our heads, we imagined Barb sitting them all down, and telling them, "Well, it's now time for you to make your own way in the world."

This has been the pattern now for many years. Every year there are kittens, and every year several of the cats go off and find their way in the world. Very often one or two will return after months away and they always look healthy and fit.

One year we had a young cat get pregnant that was no bigger than a kitten herself. We had called her Black Mouth as it looked like she wore black lipstick around her mouth. We could see she was pregnant and we hoped she would be able to handle the stress of the birth. One night, when we were hosting a barbecue with guests, Black Mouth was clearly in distress and we could see blood at her rear end. We had never been close to any of our cats when they have given birth before, as they always go off and find a safe and secure place have their babies, but this time was different.

At first I thought maybe there was a problem, maybe she couldn't manage, but it soon became clear she obviously felt safe near us. There were two children in the family we were hosting and their mother had to give them a short birds and bees lesson as the drama unfolded. The older boy couldn't take his eyes off the action. Each time a new kitten emerged they were hanging from Black Mouth by the umbilical cord, caught up in a little bundle. The boy's excitement couldn't be contained. "Can I touch them?" he kept asking, even as Black Mouth was moving around with them hanging from her.

I found a box, and packed it with hay to make her a comfy bed, and we lifted her in so she could clean up the babies and 'detach' herself.

We watched over the next few days as she seemed to be feeding them, but one morning I came out to find one of the kittens had died in the night. I took the dead kitten away and sought advice online about what to do. Take the kittens away or leave them with Mum? The overwhelming advice was to leave them with their mum, so that was what we did.

The following morning another of the kittens had died, so this time I removed the final two, who were weak and cold. We warmed them both up in our hands. Sadly, another one passed away, but the little grey one was fighting. He was hardly bigger than two of my fingers held together and so fragile. We wrapped him in a fleece and returned every couple of hours to syringe more food into him. The same morning, I visited our vet in the town to ask his advice and came away with a pack containing kitten food, baby cat milk and a tiny bottle. At this stage, the kitten was too small to take a bottle but we persisted with the syringe. Every day he would take a little more and get a little stronger.

Each weekend we had guests and the children would revel in feeding the little kitten. One morning I went out to see the kitten first thing and he had vanished. The door was slightly ajar. Frantically I ran to find Lorna.

"The kitten's not there," I exclaimed.

I could see in her face she didn't quite comprehend what I was saying. "What do you mean he's not there?"

"He's just not there. The door was slightly open, so I don't know if he's wandered off."

We both ran out the kitchen and scoured the big courtyard at the front of our house. He must have climbed out of his bucket, away from the warmth of the fleece and wandered outside. Our only hope was to find him before the cold finished him off. We did a complete circuit of the grounds, and there was no sign of the kitten. As we reached the other side of the house, we noticed Black Mouth jumping out of the box where we had originally placed the four tiny kittens.

"Hang on a minute…" I said.

I slowly approached the cardboard box, and sure enough, there was the little grey bundle of fur, curled up, asleep amongst the hay in the box. Black Mouth must have gone looking for him, maybe hearing his quiet squeaks in the distance, and dragged him all the way back to the box. Although she still looked as though she didn't want much to do

234

with the kitten, the signs seemed to be that she had been feeding him. We decided to leave him with Black Mouth, but to supplement his feeding when she was away from him, which, as it happened, turned out to be 95 per cent of the time.

As days turned into weeks we started to feel confident he was going to make it and he needed a name. We called him Rocky, because he was a little fighter. Rocky made great strides, even becoming a little chubby as children wanted to feed him more and more, as well as Black Mouth still trying to feed him too. We have pictures of Rocky being held like a baby by children as they fed him with a bottle, way past the time he actually needed a bottle and was eating solid food. To date, Rocky hasn't left The Olive Mill, although on a couple of occasions he has disappeared with one or two of the younger kittens and returned a few days later one his own. Personally, I think he likes to keep as much of the attention himself as possible.

About the Author

Alan Parks, Spain
Website: http://whats-an-alpaca.com/ Facebook
https://web.facebook.com/whatsanalpaca/
Instagram @AlpacaWriter
Alan Parks is a nobody turned alpaca breeder and author, based in Andalucia, southern Spain. He divides his time between writing and wrangling the animals who live at his Olive Mill situated amongst the olive groves.

The Story of Charlie
By Karen Thomas

I've always loved cats and, as a rule, have kept two at the same time, as I think they need company while I'm at work. Over the last few years the numbers have increased to four. Here's the story of how that happened.

Alfie is the oldest at nine years old, and I rescued him from an animal hoarder. He came from a house full of children and lots of animals, and was one of three kittens – he had two sisters. I knew the person who owned him and I begged her to let me take Alfie, as he was such a little scrap. She told me he had fallen through the banisters at the top of the stairs. He was a frightened little cat who spent all his time hiding under the bed and creeping out to get his food when he thought it was safe. Finally, she gave in and I took him home.

Thomas, my older cat, adored Alfie. He played with him and cleaned him, it was so lovely to see them bonding. It was a Friday night when I brought Alfie home, he had an upset tummy and was clearly full of fleas. I took him to see the vet and at 12 weeks old he weighed a mere 900 grams, and was full of worms as well. With the correct care he soon gained weight, but even to this day he is still nervous.

Several years later I lost Thomas, also a rescue cat, to a heart complaint at ten years old. It broke my heart as I had fostered his mum and her three-week-old kittens. Then along came Theo from a lovely family in Ringwood. Alfie took over the role of parent and doted on him. Sadly, Theo disappeared aged 18 months and despite advertising, searching for him and him being microchipped, he has never been found. I live in hope that even six years later I still may get a call saying Theo has been found. It would be better than a lottery win.

Freddy joined us when Theo had been missing for a couple of months. He came from a lovely family in Andover and was a confident cat. Freddy also gave us a fright as one Guy Fawkes night he disappeared. I was frantic as I thought he had gone outside whilst the fireworks were going off. We went out in the evening calling him and were so worried. My husband searched the house several times but found nothing.

The next morning there was still no sign of him and we had to go to work. My husband rang to say someone had seen a cat on the verge next to the main road and I was horrified. He rushed to the spot and thankfully it wasn't Freddy. After work, I posted on Facebook that he was lost and we went out looking for him again. Nothing, not a sign. We couldn't eat anything and at 9 pm I decided to have an early night. When I reached the top of the stairs I heard a meow. I shouted to my husband and I'm sure he thought I was hearing things. I followed the meow and opened our huge oak wardrobe and out hopped a chirping Freddy. He'd been in there for 30 hours without a peep. We will never understand how he did that but it gave my friends on Facebook a giggle.

I always said I'd have no more than two cats, as I firmly believe if you can't insure them and give them all they need you then shouldn't have them. It was a long-standing joke with my dad who always said, "I'm going to come back as one of your spoilt cats!" My mum and dad came to visit every Sunday afternoon and my dad would spend all afternoon playing with and making a fuss of Alfie and Freddy. He adored them and I always laughed, saying he came over to see them and not me.

Sadly, three years ago my Dad took a drug which caused Steven Johnson's Syndrome. He was 80 years old and it literally burnt him from the inside out. It was horrific and he spent two weeks in Salisbury Hospital's Burns Unit. Unbelievably, he healed but then caught pneumonia and suffered a heart attack. He was admitted to the Intensive Care Unit and put under sedation. I was due to go on holiday to Scotland a few weeks later and my mum and dad were going to house sit and look after the cats. I knew I had to find a cattery to look after Alfie and Freddy, so I phoned the local vet and they recommended Shangri-La Cattery. I called in and met Ann and Colin who ran a lovely cattery and clearly enjoyed what they did. They had a beautiful cat called Paco who I instantly took too. Ann said he was an Australian Mist and he was bred to be a real people cat.

My poor dad remained under sedation over the next two weeks. I would spend hours chatting to him, hoping for the slightest response but there was nothing. It was becoming more and more obvious he wasn't going to make it. My partner and I decided we would get a special cat and name him Charlie, after Dad. I sat with Dad and told him about the cat we were going to name after him. I told him that an Australian Mist originated from Australia and was a cross between a Burmese, an Abyssinian and a domestic tabby. I really hoped he could hear me as our family had to make the awful decision to turn his life-support machine off.

After a few weeks, we started researching Australian Mists and we read this write up about them:

Once you let an Australian Mist into your heart and your home, you'll be lent a 'helping' paw in every task – whether you need some assistance or not! They want to be involved in everything you do, from sorting the washing to making the bed, from helping to unpack the shopping to sampling what you are cooking. They particularly like helping with anything to do with food and they can be quite greedy if you let them.

We decided this was the breed of cat my dad would have truly loved so we made enquiries with a couple of breeders. We chose a breeder in Taunton and arranged to view the latest litter. We looked at a litter that hadn't come out as typical Mists – they were missing their spots! Of course, we fell in love with them and chose a tiny, chatty grey one. He was only six weeks old so we had to wait till he was 12 to 14 weeks before we could take him home. We took lots of photos of him and kept in touch with the breeder.

Sadly, at his eight-week vet check he was diagnosed with a grade four heart murmur. The breeder said he would need special care and it wasn't advisable for us to have him. We were so disappointed but felt happier when a week later he was given a home with a veterinary nurse. We visited Taunton again to view another litter being fostered by a friend of the breeder. This is when we met our forever Charlie. He was stunning, a brown-spotted and so cute. Again, we took lots of pictures and I counted the weeks until we could bring him home.

Having such a lovely thing to look forward to helped me to deal with the passing of my dad. I used to secretly talk to him and tell him about the beautiful cat we were getting in his memory. Because we had chosen him early we were able to choose his pedigree name. So he was

Rumtumtugger, after the breeder, Charlie after my dad and, for fun, Farley after Charlie Farley in *The Two Ronnies*, my dad's favourite programme. So Rumtumtugger Charlie Farley was christened. I could see my Dad laughing.

In December 2013, three months after losing my dad, we went to collect Charlie. We took my mum with us and brought him home. It was so funny when we got him home, he was 14 weeks old. He came out of his box and turfed Freddy out of his beanbag. That was the start of the antics of Charlie Farley. He very quickly became the one in charge, he was such a little monkey and into everything. Every toilet roll in the house had bite holes in or was completely shredded. He was always getting locked in cupboards because he was just so nosey. He loved to eat melon and had so much love to give he melted my heart. No matter what he did he always got away with it. Whatever we were doing, he had to be in on it. If I went into the garden he chased me and would leap up at my leg and run off, pleased with himself. My dad would have loved him as much as we do.

When we first got Charlie, we agonised over whether to keep him as an indoor cat or to let him out with Alfie and Freddy. They had never wandered far and we made the decision that once he could get over the six-foot fence, he would be allowed to roam. The area we lived in was quiet and we felt he would be safe. He first scaled the fence at about seven months old. Even though we'd made our decision, I used to worry about him while I was out at work. However, he loved his home and was never far away when we called him.

One day he wasn't in for breakfast. We were instantly worried and walked around the neighbourhood calling him. By 4 pm I had started making 'Missing Cat' posters and my husband went out again to call him. I was printing off the first poster when in came my husband with Charlie. He had been locked in a garage up the road and was hungry so he replied with a wail to my husband's call. Goodness me, he was just so nosey.

In October 2014, we were considering getting another Australian Mist as we felt Charlie would benefit from company of a cat like him. Alfie and Freddy didn't want to cuddle up with him. We rang the breeder who explained that due to ill health she was giving up and was looking for homes for Charlie's Mum, Catelyn, and his cousin, Maya. We didn't think it would work bringing an older cat into the house because we weren't sure how Freddy would react. We knew Alfie would be fine as he's a gentleman. We said we'd have Maya and would pick her up in December when she was old enough.

In December 2014 Charlie went out on Sunday morning at about 11 am. We arrived back from shopping and expected to see him asleep on the bed but he wasn't in. Alfie and Freddy ate their food but despite calling Charlie and chinking his dish he didn't appear. Call it intuition but I was immediately worried. I had a feeling of dread that something bad had happened. By the evening, we were frantic and I started putting posts on Facebook. People were so supportive, sharing and bumping the posts. I put him on the lost pet sites and the for sale sites. We continued going out in the evening calling him in case he had got locked in somewhere but it was eerily silent.

I prayed he would appear in the night but there was no sign of him. We hardly slept a wink but had to go to work in the morning. I made posters and put them all around our area. We discovered whose gardens he visited and where he went when he was outside, it really was a small area. One thing that concerned us was the doctor who lived opposite us worked away and he was obviously not at home. We feared Charlie, being so nosey, had sneaked into his house and was now locked in for a week or more, as we had no idea when the doctor would return. It was a wonder no one reported us as we called through the letterbox and looked through the windows to see if we could glimpse him. Worry makes you desperate, and that's what we were.

The days went by with a few possible sightings, which we rushed to investigate, but every time it wasn't him. Someone said he'd been seen at a nursing home a couple of miles away, so we visited the home with pictures of him and a member of staff felt sure it was the same cat. It was a glimmer of hope. I had a day off the next day so I wrapped up warm and walked around the area calling him. It was so hard trying to remain positive. I'd been there for a few hours when I saw a tabby cat in the gardens, I had a sinking feeling that this was the cat who had been visiting the nursing home. I cried all the way home and that night prayed to my Dad to lead us to Charlie.

It was so strange that Charlie seemed to have disappeared into thin air. He always used to show a real interest in our Tesco's supermarket home delivery and he would look up at the baskets when they arrived. I was starting to believe he had got into a delivery van and could be goodness knows anywhere. I always have our cats microchipped so at least that was something. By the end of the first week, my Facebook posts were being followed by many. Unfortunately, there were one or two negative people who would say he'd been stolen as he looked like a Bengal. It was a thoroughly miserable week and we were both exhausted from not eating or sleeping.

By the second week, we were beginning to fear the worst. Then, three people said they'd seen him at the large Asda supermarket. We went there several times and still there was no sign of him. I went in to see the manager and he said he would put a poster in the staff canteen. More people contacted me saying he was there so I spent a whole morning walking around the outskirts of the store on my day off. I received a phone call from one of the staff to say they'd caught him. I couldn't help but get my hopes up and I rushed to the store with the cat box. My world came crashing down when I saw the cat; it was similar looking but it wasn't Charlie. The staff were so heartbroken for me and it turned out the cat they caught was a Bengal that lived nearby.

I returned home deflated and sad. I kept thinking *It's freezing cold, where is he?* The doctor opposite returned home and I rushed over to see him. He was so sorry but Charlie wasn't locked in there. There was a further sighting in Toothill, so we put posters up there and spent several nights walking around when it was quiet. Again, there were no sightings. It was so upsetting.

Towards the end of the second week, we were running out of toilet rolls with bite holes. I sobbed, wishing he'd come home so he could create his loveable havoc once again. It was nearly Christmas and I couldn't imagine it without him. Fortunately, I'm always organised and presents had already been bought, including Charlie's, otherwise no one would have got any and Christmas would have to be cancelled. We couldn't imagine anything more miserable.

On the Friday, 12 days since he had gone missing, we were due to meet friends for a meal out. After all that time, we felt we had to force ourselves to do normal things so off we went. During the drive, I received a phone call from a lovely girl called Natalie. She said she was sure she had seen Charlie over at Taw Hill. That was three miles from home and I couldn't get my hopes up. She said it wasn't a Bengal as she knew her cats. She had tried to get close to him but he'd run off into the bushes and she couldn't find him. The table was booked and we felt we couldn't let our friends down, so we would go and have a look later in the evening.

After dinner, we went to Taw Hill and drove around the neighbourhood. We couldn't see any sign of Charlie so we returned the next day to put up posters. On the Sunday, 14 days since Charlie had gone missing, we were going to the breeder in Taunton to collect Maya. We had considered not giving her a home as we were so worried about Charlie, but we didn't want to let the breeder down. We were a few miles away from Taunton when my phone received lots of notifications from Facebook. Someone had posted a photo and asked if it was of our cat. I opened the picture and held my breath. The body looked like Charlie but I didn't recognise the face as it was scowling. My husband and I just weren't sure if it was him.

We arrived at the breeder and told her the sad news Charlie had been missing for two weeks. We showed her the picture and she too wasn't sure if it was him. She said it wasn't a Bengal and she thought it could be him. I rang Ian, the person who had posted the picture, and explained we would call round as soon as we arrived home. Ian said he couldn't get near the cat and he wasn't happy trying to catch him in case he belonged to someone else.

Then it was time to meet Maya. She was up the Christmas tree, in the tea cups, in everywhere; a real live wire. Maya was stunning and a brown spotted Australian Mist, identical to Charlie. The breeder was concerned about Charlie's mum, Catelyn. She explained Catelyn lacked confidence and was being bullied by one of the other cats. It was so bad that she had to be locked in a bedroom on her own. The breeder had tears in her eyes, the whole situation was clearly upsetting her as she loved Catelyn dearly. We couldn't imagine Catelyn being in a room on her own for hours during the day as an Australian Mist is highly sociable and loves human company. Although we had reservations about what Freddy's reaction would be, we decided to meet Catelyn. We opened the bedroom door and her sad little face stole our hearts. We sat on the bed with her and she purred and purred. She was a blue spotted Australian Mist and stunning. That was it. We both said, "Get the cat box, she's coming home."

A quick cup of tea and we were heading home. It was getting dark when we arrived at our house so my husband stayed home to introduce Catelyn to Alfie and Freddy, while I rushed over to meet up with Ian and Claire, who had found the cat that could be Charlie. When I got there, they explained they hadn't seen him since that morning but he had been around for a few days. They had seen him eating the food they left out for hedgehogs and when they chatted to him he wailed and was clearly distressed. They both thought he seemed lost and, as animal lovers, were concerned about him. We agreed they would call me immediately they saw him and I would rush back over. I returned home still not convinced it was him but hopeful.

We turned on the computer and enlarged Ian's photo alongside one of Charlie. We compared the tail, which had the same stripes, although the face was difficult to tell exactly but the brown nose was the same. My husband noticed a stripe round his leg that didn't join up – it was there on Ian's photo too. Hope surged through me and spookily my phone rang. It was Ian. He'd gone to the local shop and seen Charlie in the Domino's Pizza bin. He called him and Charlie looked around before running into the bushes. I couldn't get there quickly enough. When I arrived, I couldn't see Ian so I rang him.

He whispered, "I'm behind Domino's Pizza because I think Charlie is in the bushes."

I rounded the corner and Ian was sat in the rain, in his best trousers and snowman jumper, stopping Charlie from running away. I called Charlie and he came out of the bushes like a bullet. He pushed past Ian and ran up into my arms. Even though it was very dark I knew it was my precious boy. He screamed and screamed, it was absolutely deafening. I was struggling to hold onto him but didn't want to let him go for the fear he would run away. Ian, the hero, carried him back to the car as Charlie screamed all the way. The car park was busy and everyone looked at us as he sounded like a screaming child. Ian put him safely in his cat box and Charlie screamed and nuzzled my hand through the gaps. I hugged Ian and we both cried – it was a surreal moment. We had put a reward up for £200 and I told Ian I would call round in the morning with his reward. He replied that he wouldn't accept it, reuniting us was reward enough. What a lovely man and a true animal lover.

My husband opened the door to me carrying Charlie and crying. I don't think he could quite believe his eyes. Freddy rushed down the stairs and he and Charlie touched noses. Freddy had really missed him. While Charlie was away Freddy kept going to the patio door and back to me as if to say, *where is he?* Then came the moment when Charlie met our new addition, his mum, Catelyn. He only hissed at her and chased her as if he couldn't believe we'd replaced him already. Incidentally, Freddy, who we were concerned wouldn't take to

Catelyn, was quite happy to ignore her. Alfie, of course, adored her immediately.

After his two weeks scavenging, Charlie was starving and had clearly lost weight. I fed him a little bit and he calmed down. He was so dirty and looked like he had been living rough for a lot longer. As he settled on my lap, I updated my posts on Facebook and comments flooded in, everyone was so happy. It was the best Christmas present I could wish for. My friends wanted him to have his own Facebook page, which made me laugh, so I promised I would create one. Lots of people wanted to meet him, which I had no problem with as in his own environment he loved being the centre of attention. It gave me the idea that it would be a great to raise some money for charity as I wanted to give something back for all the support we had received.

The next day we visited Charlie's rescuers, Ian and Claire. We would never forget what they had done. We took them flowers, champagne and chocolates as they wouldn't accept the cash reward. Charlie settled back at home but he was kept indoors as we never wanted to go through that experience again. For the first few weeks he had nightmares and would wake up howling. My husband researched how we could keep him restricted to the garden and he came across Protectapet fencing. We ordered it online and our friend came round to help us put it up. The cat flap was opened again so they could all go outside. Freddy had not been impressed with being contained in the house but we thought it was a small price to pay to keep them all safe.

After Christmas I organised the first charity coffee morning. Cats Protection would be our chosen charity, and we held one coffee morning in January and one in February and I baked all the cakes myself. The events were great fun and we raised over £330 for less fortunate kitties. Charlie loved walking round chatting to everyone, showing off as he played with his toys and demonstrated how he loved to eat melon. Charlie was the star of the show. Through the events I met lots of new friends and felt they were such worthwhile functions to run.

In March, we decided to move house. Swindon was becoming busier and more houses were being built very close to our home. We put the house on the market and started looking for somewhere to move to. We found our present house with a lovely garden that was more than suitable for cat proof fencing and moved in July. The cats were put in the cattery for a week while the gardeners came in and chopped all the overgrown trees and shrubs down. It was a massive job as the garden is 25 by 15 metres. New fencing was put up and the Protectapet cat proofing was installed.

We collected the cats and brought them to their new home. Charlie and Catelyn immediately investigated the garden and the house, Alfie spent several days hiding under the bed, even having his dinner there and Freddy took a couple of days to feel secure. Now they all love their safe and secure garden. None of them know what's outside the fence so they don't bother to even look. We have outdoor cat trees and tunnels, they can chase after the birds and butterflies and of course catch the odd mouse. The day we discovered Protectapet our lives changed. When we go to work, we know they are safe but can enjoy their outside space.

With outdoor cats, there is always the worry they will upset neighbours by using their garden as a litter tray or will fall victim to the road. The perils are huge and every day there are posts on Facebook about missing cats, sadly some are never found. There is so much to worry about when letting cats out and Protectapet has taken all this away. It's a great invention which will allow our cats to live a safe, yet fulfilling, life.

I'm sure you're wondering about Catelyn who came to us as a shy, nervous cat. She is now full of confidence and takes great delight in chasing the boys. A good decision was made the day we brought her home, she is a wonderful addition to our family.

About the Author

Karen Thomas, UK
Facebook: Rumtumtugger Charlie Farley
I'm just a normal person who loves cats. I work as a self-employed
administrator.

Arpie
By Mike Cavanagh

"Why aren't *you* saying anything?"

Mouth half full of breakfast muesli, I spluttered milky-wet specks of half-chewed oats in response. "Mmmff!" I swallowed as much as I could. "What's it got to do with me?" I managed, aimed at Amanda, who was sitting on my right at the kitchen table and had asked me the question.

Amanda was a slim girl with pale skin and long straight black hair. She had a quiet demeanour, bordering on reserved, so her question had caught me off-guard. Before Amanda could answer, Margaret piped up from my right and I swung my head towards her, still trying to get the dregs of breakfast out of my mouth.

"That's not the point! You're supposed to intervene!" Margaret jiggled her open hands up and down for emphasis. Tall, willowy, long brown hair, aquiline features with piercing green eyes, Margaret came from a well-off background and a family of some standing so she was used to being heard, and obeyed.

"What?" I mustered, as I dropped my hands to the sides of my cereal bowl, the spoon clattering on the wooden table top as it hit.

One eyebrow arched and her brow furrowed, Margaret leaned towards me, about to deliver some 'Margatorial' judgment from on high when Helen, who was sitting opposite me tossed her two cents worth at me.

"Why do you think we got you to move in with us? You're supposed to mediate!"

Et tu, Helen? The wooden chair creaked loudly as I sat back, leaning away from the table, to create some space between me and these three mad, in so many ways, young women. Some half-burbled syllables, half-exasperated breath popped out of my now slack, open mouth as I failed to find any useful words of reply. Eyes wide, I stared at them each in turn, receiving merely some variation on '*What?*' from their gazes. '*What?*' as in '*For Pete's sake, are you really that thick?*' Well, apparently so it now seemed.

We, the four of us, were sharing an old, two-storey tenement house in Surrey Hills, a central suburb in Sydney, Australia. University students sharing accommodation, bills, transport, study woes and now arguments. One young bloke and three young sheilas living together in 1972 wasn't the unacceptable, slightly dubious thing it would have been even ten years earlier. Up to now we'd all got along well, sharing laughs, study tips, house cleaning, the odd joint or glass of wine. Just over the last couple of weeks, however, things had been getting a little fractious. A diggy quip here, a snide remark there. It was Sunday morning, mid-semester assignments were due tomorrow, our various uni scholarships or home allowances (well, only Margaret got that to supplement her scholarship payments) were proving barely adequate to survive on, and completely inadequate in terms of supplying four previously-pampered-at-home students with all they felt they deserved.

This morning, an open argument had finally sparked over breakfast; heaven knows what it was about. I'd listened, mildly interested, as the girls' banter turned to sniping then to arguing, added a few silly remarks at the beginning then opted out of, what to me was, an unintelligible argument between the girls about...whatever it was. Uneven chore allocation or something, I dunno. Nothing to do with me, but now apparently, they thought it was.

I leaned back into the table, raising my hands up like runway semaphores, and frowned at Helen. "What are you talking about? You all 'got' me to move in with you to…what? To be the piggy in the middle or something? You have got to be kidding me?"

Helen's jibe had hit home. She and I had transferred from Wollongong University at the end of 1971 and we were neighbours back in Wollongong. She was a mate; the one I could count on. Or not, apparently.

"Oh, stop being such a Nancy-boy about it!" Margaret rolled her eyes and ever so slightly tossed her long hair back over her right shoulder. Snotty thing, I should have expected this from her, the stuck up…

"Hang on, Margaret!" Ah, finally, Helen to my defence!

"Well, it is true. Margaret's right," Amanda interjected. "What's the point of Mick being with us if he's always on the sidelines?" What the? 'Always' on the sidelines? Oh great, here we go: 'you always' territory. Brilliant.

Thus Amanda-fortified, Margaret turned the full incandescent, copper-flamed blaze of her eyes at me. "Yes, just grow up, Mick. Be a man here!"

The legs of my chair scraped, jagging across the tiled floor, and I leant back to deliver a telling volley of "What the f..." when, in the one second of silence before I launched into my so-bleedin'-well-justified tirade, popped:

"Meow?"

I stopped in mid-back slant, my mouth open but now wordless. The girls' eyes arched, then we all did a quick eyeball to eyeball "Ah...?" across the table to each other.

"Meeeooooow?" again. Barely audible, shaky.

"That's a cat," opined Amanda, rather obviously, but in the bizarreness of the circumstance and complete non sequitur it provided in the midst of our gathering housemates'-tiff storm, not out of place at all.

Clatter-klunk onto the hard floor went the legs of my chair as I leant forward. We turned to look back down the hallway that led to the front door, the source of the sound. Helen was first up, heading through the lounge room to the front hall, as we other three clattered out of our chairs to follow. We paused at the end of the entry hall, before the heavy, double-latched and bolted front door, gathered like children creeping to presents on Christmas morning, and at the same time nervy as rabbits checking a carrot-baited trap. This was the inner city after all, so security was a constant issue.

"Are we sure it's a cat?" Amanda asked at the rear.

As if on cue: "Meoooowwww?" If anything, even fainter, tremulous now.

"Oh, for Pete's sake!" Helen exclaimed and unbolted and double unlatched the door. As it swung open inwards with a heavy creak, we all shuffled back to make way.

Outside it was a bright autumn day. The tenement faced east, into the morning sunlight. While the kitchen had ample window light, it still took a second or two for our eyes to adjust to the brighter outside glare.

"Meoowww?"

Blinking into the light, we stared down at what presented itself on the doormat in front of us. It was…a cat. Probably. It was hard, even now, to describe. A kitten or small juvenile cat, of some sort. Tabby markings and it meowed so… Head squashed to one side, one eye closed, the other slightly bulging. A twisted little body, badly kinked along its back with its skin stretched through malnutrition so its spine looked like a train track laid by a drunken madman. One back leg at a strange angle outwards and its whole body sort of sucked in, as if every breath was a matter of force of will alone, which given the rasping sound it made as it breathed, it might well have been. Cute kitty it was not. Repugnant, unworldly, demon-spawned creature of Doctor Moreau it certainly did appear.

It was lying down, on its side, looking up at us. Well its face was sort of pointed at us, but where its eyes were focussed was hard to determine. Between still adjusting to the bright sunlight, still argument-adrenaline psyched and confronted by this monstrosity in miniature, we didn't move. The crumpled little body shuddered and the little blighter stood up, trembling, swaying, staggering, and tilted its head as best it could to look up at us and, "Meow?" Not pathetically plaintive or demanding or begging, just a very clear 'Please?' It held itself for a second, then collapsed with a soft *purrrumph.* It had expended all its energy and resigned itself to whatever now happened.

"Oh bugger!" Helen's voice quavered as she bent down to touch it.

The sunlight in my eyes was now starting to glisten, so I wiped them.

"It's purring!" Helen exclaimed as she eased the fingers of her left hand under the small, bony bundle, tilted it enough to get her right hand under the other side, then cradled it in her palms and lifted it. We parted to make way for them as she walked past us and carried the bent, broken little thing, surely on its last breaths, into the lounge room.

Helen sat on the two-seater sofa and I eased myself beside her, trying not to disturb the broken kitten now lying purring in her lap. The little mite's lungs shook at each breath and the purring sounded wet, gurgling. Margaret and Amanda sat in the other lounge chairs and it was Margaret who spoke first, voicing what we were all surely thinking.

"He's not going to make it, is he?"

Not quite a rhetorical question, but one we didn't really want to answer. We sat for a minute or so, no further words spoken, just listening to his broken breaths and strangled purrs.

Without looking up, Helen spoke. "We have to take him to a vet."

No-one else said anything. What was the point of taking him to a vet? He was all but dead.

Looking up, turning her tear-filled eyes to each of us, she continued. "We can't just let him die like this. He's asked us for help. We have to try…we have to."

We were broke students, it was a Sunday, and we had no idea about vets anywhere near us.

Margaret got up, went over to the phone table and came back with the Sydney Yellow Pages. "There must be a vet open somewhere," she said, already running her finger down the index page looking for 'Vet'.

"I'll drive there so you can keep hold of him, Helen." said Amanda.

Without agreeing, we'd agreed. Within a few minutes we'd found a vet, confirmed an emergency immediate appointment and were in Helen's car, with Amanda driving while Helen continued to cradle the kitten, who hadn't raised his head since collapsing at the front door. Sitting in the back with Margaret on my left, I could see across to the front passenger seat where the kitten was lying in Helen's lap. He was on his side and twisted in a sort of arch, as if this was the best he could do to curl up like a cat. I knew he wouldn't make it. It was a hard fact, but there it was. We'd take him to the vet, it would cost us a small fortune and tear our hearts out when the vet jabbed him with a needle and he died.

"We should give him a name." I almost didn't recognise it was me who just said that. Nothing like that had been in my head…what the?

"You're right." Margaret looked at me, smiled then added, "What do you think we should call him, Mr Mediator?"

Light chuckles around the car. I felt my own shoulders ease, and took Margaret's gentle comic relief at its face value.

"Come on, Mick, you're good with names." Helen half-turned her head to look at me without disturbing the kitten.

I had no idea. Every 'catty' sort of name just seemed silly. He was a mess, dying, and every part of him was damaged, rearranged. A rearranged cat?

"RP."

Hearing it aloud it sounded stupid, disrespectful, but before I could take it back Amanda asked from the driver's seat, "I like it. But why 'Arpie'?" The way she said it, this is what it sounded like. Even stupider name I thought.

"Well, he's a mess, all rearranged and a cat, so RP for 'rearranged puskin'." Dumbest thing I've ever heard come out of my mouth.

Helen bent down and whispered to the kitten. "Arpie?" She laughed as she sat back up. "He's purring. Arpie it is then!"

The vet, however, was no laughing matter. He was alone as the surgery was closed, but he lived nearby so he'd come over especially in response to Margaret's part-plea part-ultimatum phone call. I think she'd even said at one point, "Well if he dies in horrible pain, just remember you could have done something about that, but chose not to." Ouch – she did have a way with words, but fortunately her immediate follow-up begging plea had soothed whatever feathers she had ruffled. Whichever had worked, she'd pulled it off and now here we were, all five of us, plus vet. After we'd introduced ourselves, the vet laid out a blanket on the cold, stainless steel table in his surgery.

"Just lay him down here if you would."

Helen lowered Arpie onto the blanket and eased her hands out from under him. He was still in his strange side-arched, twisted, lying down shape, eyes closed, breathing shallow and rapid, no more movement now than a fluttering eyelash. The vet ran his fingers along Arpie's spine, then probed his little body, his hands moving fluidly across his torso, then like feathers over his head. Not a sign from Arpie other than his barely audible, gargly noise that I took as purring. The vet stopped, removed his hands and looked up at us, his eyes catching each of ours before he looked back to Helen. Whatever he'd discerned in his quick scanning, his mouth tightened into a half smile and his furrowing brow conveyed he was now intent on getting to the heart of the matter immediately, and it wasn't good news.

"I don't think he'll make it through the rest of today. From his general condition, I'd say he was a feral, a street cat, malnourished and dehydrated. His injuries are consistent with being run over by a vehicle resulting in sprained back ligaments, probably spinal disc trauma, and a dislocated right rear leg. He has a fractured right cheek bone that given its state I suspect runs into his skull and possibly behind his eye socket. I can't ascertain his internal injuries but I don't think he's bleeding internally, and although he obviously has some lung injuries,

I can't diagnose further without sedating him. I doubt very much he would survive that." He paused, looked down at Arpie, then, barely touching him, rubbed his index finger along the back of his neck. "But he's a little fighter." He frowned then looked back up at us. "If I thought he was strong enough, it would take three separate operations to patch him up, and as to any other major treatment, well, that would depend on further investigations. But as I said, he's in no condition to bear that." He paused, drew breath and sighed. "I think the best would be to put him out of his misery now. I understand from speaking with Margaret…" he glanced in her direction with left eyebrow raised "…that you are all students. If you agree, I won't charge you for the procedure."

'Procedure'? Needle of green stuff to put him down I assumed. I could see the tears tracking down Helen's cheeks, and her lips moving, shaking. I put my hand on her shoulder.

"Is there another option?" Amanda spoke from over my left shoulder.

Wow, I thought, quiet, reserved Amanda, always the one to go with the flow, deciding not to. I felt Helen's shoulder's rise under my hand.

"Is there? Isn't there something else we can do, other than just bring him here to die?" she said, no quavering in her voice, just steady determination now.

The vet frowned. He hadn't stopped gently scratching Arpie's neck all this time. We could hear the little cat's wet purring. He'd asked at our door: '*Please?*' To die, or to live? Surely if to die, he'd just have laid down in the gutter?

"If we took him back home, he would at least die at 'home'." Margaret chipping in. Again, seemed we'd agreed without agreeing.

"Is there anything that might help if we take him home? At least give him a chance?" Gee, me again before I even knew what I was going to say.

The vet shook his head, looked down at Arpie and said, "You have to understand I really don't think he'll make it, but I can see you four, and I have a sense this little fellow too, are determined." Looking back up at Helen he continued. "I'll give him a shot for the pain and some intravenous antibiotics in a saline solution so he at least gets a little fluid back into him. It will take a while to allow the saline to drip through. Half an hour. The pain killers should be enough so I can fix his displaced back leg, and I'll give you a course of antibiotics in paste form to administer to him at home. I guess you don't have any cat food so I can give you a tin for today, but he'll sleep most of the time. If he wakes up...", 'if' yes, of course 'if', "...try to get him to drink some water first, then try a little food."

We spent the half hour by Arpie's side. When we left, the vet said he wouldn't charge us, just let us know how he was going. Margaret kissed him, which threw him off. She did have a way with words, as I said.

So, we four and Arpie went home. It was a long day. Each of us went off to do our assignments in turn, leaving at least one person with Arpie throughout the day. He didn't get up, barely moved at all, and his breathing remained shallow and gurgly. But he hung in there. We all came out together at 6.30 pm to get dinner underway. The fractious testiness of this morning was gone, and we all seemed to be taking care to be respectful, understanding, even affectionate to one another. We cobbled together a veggie stir-fry and brown rice and settled down at the kitchen table, accompanying the meal with light and easy banter, comparing statuses on assignments (consensus: woeful) and likelihood of possible extensions and best excuses for getting one.

Margaret was just regaling us with a tale of a past excuse she'd used that involved tying up a late-middle-aged male lecturer in a discussion about 'women's problems' when we were interrupted.

"Meow?"

We turned as one, and there at the top of the two steps up to the lounge was Arpie.

"Arpie!" exclaimed Helen, her chair clattering to the floor as she almost leapt up and strode over to bend down in front of him. Her face in front of his, Arpie leant forward and rubbed his broken, twisted little face onto her nose. We clapped, giggled, cried, and got up and all plopped down on the kitchen floor in front of him.

"Arpie!"

"Meow."

We laughed in response, a world's weight seemingly lifted off us. We gently coaxed him down the steps, and guided him to the water bowl we'd set up. He struggled to get his head down into the bowl, so Amanda upended another small bowl and we placed the water bowl on top of that. Arpie lapped away, flinging off little water drops everywhere as he drank, half side-on to the bowl as he was and his asymmetric head twisting his mouth slightly awry so his tongue flicked at an angle. We laughed and teared up. It was early days, but we knew, each of us with absolute certainty, he was going to make it.

Well, he did. We told the vet and he was genuinely happy to hear Arpie had pulled through, but incredulous that he had.

It was days before Arpie could walk anything like normally. OK, 'normally' for Arpie anyway – a sort of shuffling motion with his body slightly side on. Watching him walk away from you was like driving behind a vehicle that's been twisted in an accident and the rear wheels don't quite line up with the front ones. The swelling in his head went down, but his face remained out of shape and his eyes not quite aligned together. But he began eating, which meant we had to get kitten litter and a tray, and as he always made a mess when he ate or drank and it was a constant mop-up-with-tissues operation after he'd finished. He couldn't jump at all, so we had to pick him up when he asked to get up on the lounge, our laps, a bed.

Arpie loved to talk, about anything and everything, often unnoticed until his quiet "Meow?" interrupted whatever any of us were doing, which, of course, we were always happy for him to do, no matter what occupied us at that moment. Studying, eating, sleeping, sitting on the loo. Anywhere, anytime he was welcome. We had a bent, broken, ugly little cat, but he was loved to bits.

Happy house of five would all have been fine but for one fly in the proverbial. 'No cats'. We'd moved into the tenement with a lease that clearly specified no pets, of any sort. The real estate agent even pointed out that earlier tenants had been turfed out when she discovered they had a cat. None of us had a cat, nor wanted one when we moved in, so that was all sweet. Now, we had Arpie. Our lease conditions for the tenement included three-monthly inspections. We knew when these occurred, and a letter appeared a fortnight beforehand to confirm, but we were pre-occupied students, so tore up the letters without reading them, and forgot about it. At some point, we'd discussed what to do with Arpie if we had an inspection, and decided one of us would take him into Helen's car for a quiet sit. But we forgot.

The front door buzzer yelled down the hallway. Saturday morning, Amanda was off visiting her boyfriend, Margaret had gone back home for the weekend, so just me, Helen and Arpie. I was studying in my ground-level, front bedroom, and was still ruminating on how to fractionate ethers as I wandered out to the front door and opened it.

"Good morning," she said. It was the real estate agent.

257

"Good morning," I said.

"Who is it?" Helen called from the kitchen.

"Meow?" said Arpie, shuffling down the hallway behind me.

"Bugger," was out of my mouth before any semblance of brains were in gear.

The real estate agent leaned in past me, looked at the cat, then straightened to look me squarely in the eye. "Get rid of it, *today!* I'll come back Monday morning and go through this place with a fine-tooth comb. If I find any sign that cat is still here, or has ever been here, you will be served notice." She turned on her sharpish high heels and was gone.

"Bugger," Helen said, having come up behind me. She could say that again.

Helen and I got our heads together, but failed to come up with anything. Neither her family nor mine would take a cat in back home. Amanda's family were out Cowra way or some such, and had three dogs and never owned a cat, so no, not likely. Margaret's parents...yeah, right. I'd been to their house once and left feeling like I'd besmirched the place by entering in non-designer wear. So, no there too.

Margaret and Amanda came back after lunch the next day, Sunday, one day before 'No Arpie' day. They simply confirmed what we suspected. A glum foursome we made, having reached the end of our wits searching for Arpie answers. The front door buzzer yelled, drawing us out of our inward staring melancholic inactivity.

"I'll get it." Amanda got up and went to answer the door. Muffled conversation then footsteps back down the hall. We all looked up as Amanda walked back into the lounge room, a young couple behind her.

"Oh, yes, Terry and Jules, sorry, I forgot you were coming over!" Margaret swept to her feet across the room and embraced and cheek kissed them both. She led them into the lounge and introduced them to us and vice versa, as you do.

Introductions all round, brief small talk. Terry and Jules had come over to pick up Margaret to go to a party at their place that evening. They had offered to also drop her back the next morning, as it was accepted that Margaret would be in no state to drive back either that night or the next morning. I'd seen Margaret drink; this was a wise move on their part. Margaret excused herself to grab some things before they headed off.

I had just asked where Terry and Jules lived, when before either could answer, "Meow?"

Arpie had shuffled in and, now amid everyone, announced himself. The reaction on Terry's and Jules' faces was a story in itself, the script for which clearly went: "Oh a cat, how adorabl... What the...???!!"

"This is Arpie," Helen offered, a firm note in her tone. Don't "What the...??!!" with our Arpie!

Arpie looked at Helen, then at Terry and Jules and went over to do his shuffling, swivelling imitation of rubbing up against someone's legs thing, then sat down in front of them. "Meow?"

There are some moments in life, that wild as they may seem, really do appear to be indelibly etched in some '*And so shall it be!*' tome. Terry and Jules melted. I mean they almost really did. Ooohed and ga-gaahed as if with a baby, picked Arpie up, cuddled him, 'Isn't he adorable?'-ed him...the whole thing.

By the time Margaret came back in, Jules announced to her, "We're taking him home!"

It didn't take long. They took to him, him to them, we looked at each other, agreed without agreeing.

"We can't keep him. Can you take him home with you?" Helen said.

So they did. It broke our hearts and gladdened our lives no end. God, we missed him, but we knew he was loved, well looked after and had a great home. I mean literally a great home. Vaucluse. Terry and Jules lived in Vaucluse in eastern Sydney. Three storey, six bedroom, three bathroom triple garage mini-mansion with harbour views. Think Beverley Hills in the US or Chelsea in the UK or Mayfair in Monopoly. This twisted, battered little street kid ended up living the life of Riley and bling in one of the richest suburbs in Australia.

We kept in touch, they brought him back to visit once, and I went to their place once to visit. The end of the uni year arrived and we all went our separate ways. And here's a thing. We never once even looked like having an argument while we shared that place in Surrey Hills after Arpie showed up. Somehow knowing what he'd been through put lots of things into perspective for all of us. Every now and then I still recall Arpie when I feel like things are getting the better of me.

Thanks, Arpie, you beauty little Vaucluse battler you!

About the Author

Mike Cavanagh, Australia
Website: http://oneofitslegs.org/
Facebook: https://www.facebook.com/One-of-its-Legs-are-Both-the-Same-523298794535102/ Twitter: @MikeJC_99

Mike Cavanagh is now in his sixties and has no idea how that happened. He lives with his wife, Julie, and two black cats in Bateman's Bay, NSW. Three adult children, mostly left home, complete the extended menagerie. Mike writes poetry, plays guitar and composes music, does research on rock-wallabies, and spends far too much time playing computer role playing games. Animals have always been a part of Mike's life and his record for how many at any one time is three dogs, three cats, four kittens, twelve puppies and a duck.

Bramble
By Jacki Lakin

To start at the beginning. Bramble was my adorable cat who I loved dearly. She joined me in my first house in 1999, and after always having cats as a child and moving to my first house, I needed a cat. A house is not a 'home' without a cat. I had two still living with my parents and they were settled, older cats so it seemed unfair to uproot them to move to live with me. Poppi the tortoiseshell (who I rescued, but that's another long story) was devoted to my dad, she was his gardening buddy and lap cat so she had to stay. Muffin, the beautiful but very grumpy long haired tabby I had from 6 weeks old, wouldn't tolerate any undue stress or inconvenience.

It was decided: new home, new cat. And so shortly after moving in, I began the search for a rescue cat to be part of my new home. I thought it would be an easy situation as there always seem to be many needy cats looking for a new home. However, the process took a little while. It wasn't kitten season, we didn't live in an area covered by the rescue centres, we worked full time. There were so many hurdles it seemed impossible and all I wanted to do was provide a loving home to a cat or kitten. Finally, I found a lady who fostered for Cats Protection and asked her to keep me in mind for any new kittens that were brought in, especially tabby girls. I love tabby cats, they remind me of little tigers – independent, strong and beautiful.

A few weeks later a litter came in and I found my companion. Bramble, a long-haired moggie (but surely crossed with a Maine Coon or Norwegian Forest Cat), was tiny, about six weeks old and slightly fluffy. I have always adored long-haired tabbies so she stole my heart. I don't know much about where she came from other than she was from an abandoned litter and I remember her being full of fleas and hating the spray her foster mum administered. Who wouldn't hate that? Now flea-free, my tiny ball of fluff with huge, wide, blue-going-on-green eyes came home with me in September 1999.

We had no idea what to call her, I had no specific names in mind. So for the first week she was just Fluffy Cat. But the cat must have a name. I browsed through various cat magazines for inspiration, looked at people's cat photos and their choice of names and shouted out names and suggestions. My little cat looked very disinterested and a bit bewildered about all the fuss but didn't bat an eyelid. I spotted two cats amongst leaves, partly camouflaged in the surroundings. Bracken and Bramble, they sound nice. "Bramble," I said – a little head looked up at me. I think she likes it. Bramble it is then.

She had such a unique personality like no other cat I have known. She was an unintended house cat. We kept her in while she was tiny, then it was winter and cold, then she was spayed. By the time she ventured into the garden for the first time it was spring time. She had been indoors and safe for well over six months so it was a new experience, a wild world, a new adventure. She loved the fresh air, the sounds of the birds, running water from the pond, but she also just liked to wander in the garden and explore her own territory. She only once tried to climb the fence and got stuck on a neighbour's shed roof. I don't know who was more stressed retrieving her from the dizzy heights, me or her, but she never did it again. She hated to be separated from me and would simply not be locked out, any sign of the door closing she would run like a shot. On the odd occasion the door pushed to, she would scratch it in a mad frenzy – let me in! She loved nothing more than to sit in the garden in the summer with me, rolling in the grass and taking in the air as I long as I was near or close at hand – that was the rule.

Sadly, kittens don't stay kittens very long and soon she was a big fluffy cat. She'd lose her fluffy fur in the summer and develop a huge thick coat in the winter months. The years passed and she was a good companion. People say dogs are loyal and cats aren't but I don't agree. We used to cuddle up together in the winter months and her favourite spots were under blankets. Many a time "Where's Bramble?" was heard, then a sneaky little paw would appear from the corner of the blanket on the sofa. Sometimes an ear or nose would poke out but soon go back under to the warmth. Occasionally she would also be known to sneak upstairs, pull back the corner of a duvet and get into bed, naughty Bramble. "That's my bed not yours," I would tell her.

For 11 years Bramble was my soulmate and *my* cat. She followed me everywhere, never liked strangers, was very loyal to me, always knew when I was sick and needed her attention. She was amazing.

She was a beautiful tiger cat. As a kitten she used to sit on my desk watching me type at the computer and give the printer a helping hand as the paper emerged, before moving to the top of my chair and lie around my neck purring and observing everything I did. As a cat, she was a bit too big to lounge on the chair or desk, so she lay on the landing right on top of where the central heating pipes ran to the edge of my computer room. She guarded that room and me. She liked the simple things in life, always preferring a cardboard box to a fancy cat bed and a scrunched-up piece of paper was the best toy ever. Who needs mice? Although she was always partial to a little bit of fresh catnip.

She was 11 years old and thoughts of not having long left with her never crossed my mind. I had always had cats that had lived to 17 or 18 years old so to me she was still very young. She never had any serious problems, a couple of minor bouts of cystitis and colitis, but generally I thought she was quite fit and healthy. Very suddenly, in June 2010, she got sick.

2010 had been a horrible year for me, right from the start. It was one of those years you want to totally erase from memory or wake up and think it was all a bad dream. Sadly, it wasn't. In the January, my dad had a heart attack completely out of the blue, and tests showed he needed a triple bypass operation. The waiting time for the surgery was 12 weeks, and there were delays, so he was finally scheduled for surgery two days before his birthday in June. It was a long six months, which had been like a waiting game and I often felt anxious and dazed. It was like I was watching someone else's life and not really living in the reality, a horrible picture of life events I didn't want to be happening. The day he was in surgery I kept busy. I love gardening and occupied my body and mind in the garden, Bramble at my side all the time. My constant companion there when things felt bad. She had intuition, I think cats are highly sensitive and often feel things we can't.

My dad's surgery went well but recovery was hard. For a man who was active and hated sitting around, the next few weeks were difficult. One consolation was that he had his companion too – Poppi the tortie cat who was now in her twilight years at 17 years old. Poppi was a little thinner and not as agile on her feet as in her youth. But given her years, not doing too badly and this grand little lady was a good carer too. At the end of June, a hot summer evening, a call came saying my dad had been taken back into hospital for tests as he wasn't feeling well. A blood clot was suspected. Just when things seemed to be picking up, I was back on the treadmill of work, hospital visits, sleep, eat and the pattern all over again. Thankfully, this turned out to be false alarm and his progression was good thereafter.

During the week my dad was back in hospital, Bramble went off her food. We were having a hot spell so I thought it was just the weather. I hadn't been at home very much and came back one lunchtime, she was asleep on the window ledge as she loved to bask in the sun and watch the world go by. I picked her up and she was so hot, I took her outside with a bowl of water which she lapped up in seconds. I felt a sick pain deep in my stomach as I carried her, she felt lighter so much lighter than I remembered. I panicked, how could I not have seen her becoming sick. I know now cats hide their illnesses well and only show it when they are really sick. My mind raced. I had been preoccupied with hospital visits and my beautiful Bramble was sick too. Should I have noticed sooner, she was always there for me, had I not been there for her? An emergency visit to the vets was booked. She was given an injection and antibiotics and came home, but we needed to take her back for more tests the following day. That evening she ate a huge bowl of fresh chicken. I was relieved and hoped it was nothing more than an infection.

However, the bubble soon burst as the following day, after blood tests, the vet said she had a high bilirubin count and liver damage. Everything was a blur. What did this mean? She can be cured, can't she? She had never been sick and had been fine up until a few days ago, how can this happen so quickly? The vet suggested she was kept in and further tests run. This was a difficult decision as I knew she would hate me leaving her, but her eyes told me I had to, and she didn't cry or murmur when I left. That was when I knew it was bad.

A later scan showed an enlarged area on her liver. The vet said a biopsy would confirm the cause of the mass, but there were risks involved in the procedure. So she was treated for an infection and we would wait and see how she responded. From this point, she deteriorated. We visited her several times a day and I knew she would have hated being in a cage, with other cats nearby and not being with people she knew and trusted. I hated being separated from her, and she looked sad and helpless, I felt helpless too. Further blood tests showed the count had increased, she was beginning to become jaundiced and there was kidney deterioration. Her organs were failing. My poor Bramble was slipping away. I couldn't do anything to help, and I couldn't let her suffer. Within two days, on July 3rd 2010, we made the awful decision to have her put to sleep. I was devastated and couldn't believe how this could have happened so quickly. I can't recount the day in words although I remember it as vividly as if it was yesterday. Making that decision and do what I knew was right tore me apart and engulfed me with guilt. I can honestly say it was one of the worst days of my life. Anyone who says you can't feel such pain and grief because it's only 'a cat' has never had a bond with one and never been owned by one.

The next weeks were awful. I couldn't bear to be in the house as it just reminded me she was gone. Anyone who has lost a cat will empathise with the feeling of emptiness, sadness and guilt all rolled into one. Even six years on the tears stream as I write and recall she isn't here anymore and, yes, I still miss her.

Still with a heavy burden from losing her, but knowing life had to go on, several weeks later I decided it was time for another cat or kitten. I could never replace my Bramble but the house was too quiet. I hated not having the patter of paws, a friendly meow and the comforting sound of a purr. Sometimes there were days I caught a shadow in the corner of my eye and was convinced she was still around. A few times I thought I heard a meow, but no one was there. Maybe she was still with me in spirit or maybe my mind was playing tricks.

With some thought I decided that as I was at out at work, two cats would be better as company for each other. But having failed to find two together I decided to adopt an eight-week-old tabby girl kitten, from a cat rescue charity. Sadly, this is not where the happy ending is and my story gets worse before it gets better. I didn't entirely feel ready and I thought the lady was coming to check our house and chat with us in preparation for adopting a cat in the coming weeks. But she arrived with a kitten. Note to self: check facts in the future and don't get caught up in the moment. So, when faced with a kitten who made herself quickly at home, how can you say no? Cleo was a funny little kitten, bright as a button and playful. She filled the quietness and helped heal my mind, although the pain and loss was still strong. I felt some comfort in the fact I had helped her and given her a safe home, and I thought Bramble would be happy with this too.

Unfortunately, the day after she arrived she had awful flu symptoms: runny nose, eyes and sneezing. It got worse and a trip to the vet was needed. This was hard, I now associated vets with bad things and could only visualise going there with my Bramble and coming out lost and empty handed. I couldn't even face using the same vets, even though they were wonderful with Bramble, it was too much. Poor little Cleo had cat flu. I didn't worry too much, it can happen to kittens when they are rehomed and have come from multi cat households or shelters. Antibiotics should clear it up and they did, but it came back a week or so later, this time with an eye infection. More antibiotics and eye drops. She seemed better, so I took a much needed few days away with my parents on cat sitting duty. Upon return, her eyes were cloudy and she was acting strangely. She was normally responsive and came to her name and she just didn't seem as responsive or sprightly as she was.

The vets said they needed to rule out underlying causes. What did this mean? The abbreviated and long names of various illnesses such as FIV, Toxoplasmosis and FIP (Feline Infectious Peritonitis) became a bit of a blur. Blood tests showed that after two months and one illness after another, she had the fatal FIP. I had never heard of FIP and it wasn't until I came home and researched on the internet that I learned there is no cure and only barely do kittens reach adulthood with this horrible disease. There is much more awareness of FIP now and some trials and research, which I hope will lead to a vaccination or cure in the future. I could write more about Cleo and the few short months with us, as well as FIP and what it means, however, this is Bramble's tale and Cleo's story is for another time.

How could this happen, losing two cats in the space of a few months? Heart-rending, I found myself a few months after losing one cat suddenly having a poor little kitten put to sleep as well. She was constantly sick and as the prognosis was so poor, with the ultimate outcome being death, I was again making the decision that leaves you with such guilt in the pit of your stomach. What was worse was the fact she was so tiny and helpless, she'd had no life, but if I prolonged her time with me she would probably still have no life, not a quality one at least.

What made the decision even more difficult was we had found another rescue kitten who had joined us in the last few weeks Cleo was still with us. I had never introduced them as Cleo had been sick; I kept them totally apart as we didn't know what was happening. I was terrified I would not accept my new kitten, Kassie, as I had lost Bramble and Cleo and now I was back to square one – one kitten, no pair as playmates. There had been so much heartache and grief in the space of a few months. I was worried, since cats are sensitive souls, that she would pick up on my anxieties. However, Kassie became a rock to me, a pretty little silver grey girl with a ginger paw, heart shaped pink nose and the highest pitched meow I ever heard. The purring in the morning helped me to want to get up and face the day. I had to care for her, she needed me, so I had to put the bad things to the back of my mind and keep going.

She settled in well and became part of the family, never seeming to pick up on the past events of the previous months. She had been living in my bedroom and so, a couple of weeks after losing Cleo and completely cleaning the house and replacing bowls, trays etc. to prevent any cross contamination, she was introduced to the downstairs quarters of the house. It was like a whole new playground, she discovered curtains and cupboards. Kassie is an explorer and a climber, sleek and agile, curtains are no mean task – bottom to top in seconds. Oh, what fun she was having in her new playground.

The story isn't quite over. I was happy with my solo cat, growing well, healthy and settling in, loving her fusses and evening lap cuddles. Finally, things were settling down. I was destined to be a single cat household. Kassie was wonderful, completely different to any other cat I have had, but aren't they all? Just like humans, cats are unique, each one with their own personality and little quirks.

It was our annual trip to the Supreme Cat Show and this is where fate took a funny turn. There were hundreds of stalls, hundreds of breeders, and after a busy morning viewing the cats on show, I decided to look back again at the long-haired cats. I would never normally consider a cat from a breeder, not because I have anything against them as such, but my philosophy is that there are so many unwanted cats in the world and they take priority. These should be the ones you rehome first.

However, walking up and down the aisle of Norwegian Forest Cats I noticed a beautiful black and white boy. He was huge, you could not pass by and not look. We commented that you would certainly know if he was asleep on your lap! I stopped for a closer look and saw on the top of his cage a notice 'kittens for sale'. The breeder came over and spoke to me. I had picked up an album of photographs from the top of the cage and was browsing through. I asked if she had any pictures of the kittens from the recent litter and what colours they were, not intending to buy. She told me the litter was mostly tortoiseshell girls with one tortie/silver and one mostly tabby with a little tortie.

"Oh, the tabby sounds nice," I asked. "Do you have a photo?"

"Yes," she replied, "that's Bramble!"

I burst into tears and in between sobs tried to explain the coincidence. She told me she called her Bramble because she sat in the sun light and her coat looked like leaves. The breeder said she was keeping one of the litter, likely to be Bramble, but I was welcome to have a look at the others. I never have to be invited to someone's house twice when there are cats involved! And, so two weeks later, there I was viewing kittens, still not really intending to buy one, but maybe Kassie did need a friend.

Guess where Bramble now lives? Bramble was never for sale but the breeder agreed if I was to have one of the kittens, it was just meant to be. We decided it was too much of a coincidence to be brought together like this, it wasn't chance, it must have been fate or destiny.

I called Bramble Two her pet name of Bella. She needed her own identity and she is her own unique self, although her pedigree name and what brought us together was Bramble. I have noticed a few uncanny similarities in both of their mannerisms, the way she lies fully stretched on her back, her chirp-like greeting and the way she brings mice to me, and brings papers back when I throw them.

One can never replace a beloved pet and Bramble One is always in my thoughts. But I often wonder what strange coincidence brought my new Bramble (Bella) and me together. Was Bramble watching over and guiding me to my new friend? Was there a reason my sweet little kitten tragically left me so early? I guess I will never know until one day we all meet again at the Rainbow Bridge.

In the meantime, Bella and Kassie live happily together. Well, sometimes they do! I'm not sure whether they are companions or just tolerate each other, it's hard to tell sometimes. But, one thing is for sure, they are both meant to be with me and I hope they will be for many years to come. After all, a house is not a home without a cat or two.

In Memory of Bramble (July 1999 – July 2010)

About the Author

Jacki Lakin, UK
Facebook: www.facebook.com/jacki.lakin
Twitter: @jackilakin Instagram: jacki_lakin

I am a mad cat lady and think that's 'purrfectly' fine! I'm currently owned by two cats: Kassie, the athletic moggy who climbs anything, and Bella, the slightly over-weight (she says it's all fur!) Norwegian Forest Cat, whom I adore. I love travelling, photography, music, concerts and writing, and if I can combine three or more that's even better. I enjoy writing short stories, travel accounts and letters. I still have over 50 pen-pals worldwide – that's an achievement in the modern age of social media! I am an amateur photographer with published work.

Let the Animals Live, Israel
By Riva Mayer

This is a story that will touch the heart of any cat lover. It concerns an incredibly high feral cat population in Israel and a charity called Let the Animals Live (LAL) that is seeking to help solve what seems to be an insurmountable issue. The hard work and efforts of this amazing organisation are the reason why so many cats like Yisrael have lived. Here's his tale.

Yisrael's Story – as told by Michal Lee (a volunteer)

It was a typical Jerusalem morning. It was still dark outside, and we made our way to another TNR campaign (Trap, Neuter, Return). As all cat lovers know, the only way to alleviate the suffering of community cats (cats that live on the streets) and give them quality of life is by performing high quality, high volume spay or neuter operations. A project exists in Israel called Trap, Neuter, Return (TNR) to do just this. While we were in the middle of trapping, I felt a cat rubbing against my legs. I looked down and saw Yisrael.

He meowed in a heart-breaking way and looked up at me. He had a cold and a runny nose, and he couldn't smell or eat anything. His eyes were almost completely shut. It looked like something was hurting him – he was suffering pains around his mouth, and he was thin and weak. He came to ask for help. At the time, it was thought his condition was so bad we might need to take him out of his misery. If only he could speak he would probably tell us about his tough life in the Jerusalem streets, about the battles he had with other males, about his desperate search for food, about his hunger and thirst that accompanied him from the moment he woke up until he went to sleep.

If only he could speak. But if we think about it, he does speak, cats speak to us all the time. We are the ones who don't always listen. If only we would listen more, and if only there were more people sensitive to their suffering, to the pain they endure every day, to their rough lives in the streets, to their battles, to their asking for help. For Yisrael, there was someone who listened.

The professional cat trapper at the TNR campaign put him in a cage, sadly thinking it was the end. But Yisrael wanted to live, and he came at exactly the right time to be saved. He was checked by a vet; a big ulcer was found on his tongue and he had several rotten teeth. Moreover, he was dehydrated, frail and had a cold. During his check-up and treatment, he was neutered so he wouldn't need another anaesthetic, and because neutering male cats is a simpler procedure than spaying females.

Yisrael went through a recovery and rehabilitation process, with devoted care, antibiotics and nutritious food. After several weeks of treatment and lots of love, Yisrael was released back to his 'natural' surroundings. He is happy and healthy, and obviously very thankful for the help he received.

For Yisrael there was someone who heard him. Unfortunately, there are many, many cases of cats like him who need help. To prevent situations like this in the first place a spaying and neutering clinic was recently established in Ashkelon, which is in the southern part of Israel, as a first step. The clinic operates with the highest professional standards, at low cost, while listening to and caring for the cats themselves and considering their quality of life. (Yisrael lives in Jerusalem where there is only a small and rather old spay/neuter clinic.)

* * *

The reasons behind the high numbers of feral cats are unusual. It is thought that it began in the 1930s when the British imported boatloads of cats to the country to combat a major rat epidemic. Whilst the pest control idea might have been sensible, they failed to factor in the potential for the cats to do what came naturally. The result was a rapid population explosion. Aided by the mild Mediterranean climate and irresponsible people who dump cats with their kittens, nature inevitably took its course. Reproduction continued unchecked and gradually numbers ballooned to an estimated two million plus feral cats who roamed the streets.

Ironically, the pest controllers became the pests.

They were not treated properly at the beginning and therefore became a kind of a nuisance and lived miserable, short lives.

The cats lived off garbage scraps, vermin if they could find them, and the food provided by a few kind people. The males fought, the females had multiple litters and disease was rife – these animals endured a harsh life.

According to the newspaper *Haaretz*, until 1994, to control numbers and in response to complaints about the noise and nuisance the cats created, the government acted. The Municipalities' vets 'dealt' with this issue by scattering poison in the streets. Their aim: to kill feral cats. Understandably this harsh approach created a serious backlash from the many people who had tried their best to help feed and care for the colonies of cats. One of these people was Riva Mayer.

In 1986, Riva, one of those caregivers, found her own cats dead. They had been accidental victims of the poisoning programme. Distraught and appalled by what had happened, she decided to try and stop the awfully cruel process. She learned how to deal with feral cat problems from Professor Peter Neville, a leading expert on the subject from the UK, and specifically the work of TNR. On her return from the UK, Riva founded The Cat Welfare Society of Israel (CWS) in 1990. The charity took the Government's veterinarian to court and won an historic ruling stating the cats' right to live. The High Court of Justice agreed with the CWS petition and passed a decision that year known as the First High Court Cat Decision of 1994. This meant that the Agriculture Ministry's veterinary service was ordered to refrain as much as possible from killing strays for nuisance reasons, and to revise its procedures. The CWS established that the only way to deal with the feral cat overpopulation crisis was to undertake TNR projects all over the country.

This was a fantastic victory for cat lovers, led by the CWS, who had fought so hard on behalf of the animals. But their fight was by no means over. In reality, it seemed the situation on the ground remained largely the same. Claims were soon rife that the veterinary service still allowed the killing of cats for reasons that did not present any real risk to humans.

Further lobbying from a joint petition of the Cat Welfare Society and LAL (Let the Animals Live), a non-profit organization founded in 1986, resulted in The Second High Court Cat Decision of 2004. The courts were once again sympathetic to their arguments and finally outlawed the poisoning of cats altogether. Whilst this was a resounding victory for the cat welfare organisations it did not solve the problem. The country still had a major feral population and something had to be done to check the reproduction rates.

LAL has sought to meet this challenge. One of its key visions is to achieve a situation where:

The State of Israel is a nation where animal cruelty has ended and all animals live peaceful, full lives of quality.

With this mission clearly in mind, and existing solely on donations, they, along with others, set about tackling the issues in the most humane way possible.

Throughout its existence, LAL has brought the importance of protecting animal life and preventing animal cruelty to the attention of the public by expanding the Animal Welfare Act and enforcing it. The association, does not (unless on veterinary advice due to physical reasons) put animals to sleep, and works to reduce the performance of euthanasia. In other words, they fight for every single life.

The charity is active in the following areas:

Emergency hotline – answering calls from the public regarding distressed animals, as well as giving telephone information.

Search and rescue – picking up distressed animals and transfering them to the charity's clinics in Ramat Gan, Jerusalem and Ashkelon, (described below) for veterinary care and rehabilitation.

Animal shelter – housing around 300 dogs and 100 cats who receive dedicated care until a warm home is found for them.

Veterinary clinic services – providing veterinary treatment, including spaying/neutering, at reduced cost or free for those animals with no caretaker. The clinic is open to the public and provides low-cost treatments for those who are unable to afford private veterinary care.

Legal department – undertaking inquiries into animal abuse and maintenance; taking care of farm animals; understanding and interpretating legislation; operating a legal clinic; and public campaigns. A recent example of the department's activities was the "From Violence to Compassion" project – an activity to educate about compassion towards animals.

Today the situation is much more positive with many TNR projects active in Israel. Even the municipality vets, who used to poison cats, are involved. They now understand the only legal and professional way to deal with the issue of overpopulation is through massive TNR projects.

Tel Aviv Municipality was the first to do it using their own budget and as part of their veterinary department's work. In addition to the municipality vets, they now employ LAL and other animal charities to spay/neuter more cats. The goal is to perform at least 100 spaying and neutering procedures a day in high quality, high volume clinics; to perform successful targeted TNR; and to keep up with the rate of cats giving birth at the moment. This is the only professional way to control the over-population of community cats in towns. The aim is to have such clinics in every town all over Israel. However, at the time of writing, the clinics are unable to perform the procedures in such quality and numbers.

Following the example of Tel Aviv, many more municipalities are starting their own TNR programmes. But whilst the government authorities agree about the effectiveness of the programmes, and the need to keep TNR initiatives running, there is a huge problem. Lack of funds. Israel is in a constant state of war and therefore most of the government's budget goes to support the military. Very little remains for TNR. LAL solely relies on donations to perform free TNR. Each spay (plus trapping) costs NIS 120 (USD 30). But the treatment doesn't stop there. All the cats get pain medications, antibiotics and a general check-up – of course many of them are being treated for other problems they have.

* * *

Riva Mayer, who joined LAL in 2012, is now part of the LAL staff and is one of the key activists helping these animals. One of the first messages she gives is to stress that these cats are not meant to live indoors.

"For those of them who were born on the streets, this is their home. What we caring people need to do is get them spayed/neutered and give them food and water on regular basis. In cold areas, a shelter is a must. There are also those cats that have been abandoned or lost and they need a foster home until they find their forever loving home.

"The feral cats were born on the streets and that's where they're comfortable. They don't know anything else. And they don't want to be inside, because feral cats cannot live inside. Closed areas make them frightened. That said, if someone wants to adopt a feral kitten, it is possible, but a correct socialization needs to be done in a very early age (earlier than two months)."

The facts are stark and not just confined to Israel. If *not* spayed/neutered and fed, community cats anywhere only live to a few years old. Nevertheless, during their short lives, they often still manage to reproduce at amazing speed. The rate of birth is very high. They give birth up to three times a year and when their kittens are about five to six months old, they can give birth themselves.

The evidence shows that spaying/neutering changes animals' lives. It hugely improves their quality of life – just like cats that live indoors. It stops the horrible, endless deaths of kittens born to suffer and die at a very young age. TNR has a positive effect on the human population too. The feral cat nuisance factors are stopped and thus make the community cats a wonderful part of our human lives.

Partly in response to their ongoing research, and due to the wider feral cat problem in Israel, LAL has launched the first of its kind veterinary centre in the country. A decade of studies conducted all over the world resulted in a model closely based on a similar American model (please see the link below).

The project, exclusively funded by donations, has been built in Ashkelon in the southern part of the country, and was opened on January 1st, 2017. It lies in a war-torn area of Israel, which has endured bombing, and the overall situation is very poor. The citizens of this area have already suffered terribly, and the cats have had no welfare facilities like this.

The model is based on efficiency, professionalism, focus, service and quality without compromise. The programme allows for neutering and spaying of up to 40 cats per day in the first stage and 80 per day after a year, or when donations are available.

This unique centre promotes the goals at the core of the LAL mission values:

High quality of life for cats wherever they live (at home or on the streets), for their benefit, for the benefit of those who love them, and for everybody's quality of life and the environment.

Their aim is simple. The centre is organised to conduct high quality, high volume, low-cost/free neutering and spaying operations in order to help bring an end to the critical situation of over-population in the region.

A separate wing at the centre has been set up to treat rescued sick or injured cats and dogs. This veterinary aid is available free of charge. The facility is intended to be a place where low-income animal lovers can find the help and support they require for their loved ones. It is hoped the veterinary social venture will set an example to all those caring for homeless animals throughout the entire country.

LAL's desire is to reach the day when every cat will be wanted, either at their home or on the streets, where they will enjoy a high quality of life. As Riva says, "In many areas where TNR has been performed, you can already see lots of differences. TNR works and eventually will restore the feral cat population to a balanced situation.

"With our facility and help we aim to enable every cat and dog-lover, regardless of financial ability, to receive basic care for their pet at an affordable price. This will be achieved by conducting neutering and spaying in large numbers. There will be no compromising of the highest and most cutting edge global standards in the field, all at low prices that cannot be found elsewhere or free of charge."

LAL helps cat lovers to help cats in need in Israel.

Here is another story of a cat, again told by volunteer, Michal Lee. It's about Gingoni, who, without the help of his dedicated caretakers, would almost certainly have perished.

Gingoni's Story

Gingoni was a young, ginger cat living in the streets of Jerusalem. Since the day he appeared at our feed distribution times, he gave the impression he would like to become friends with us. As time passed he became friendlier and friendlier, and even let us pat him on the top of his head while he stood on two legs, closing his eyes with pleasure.

Gingoni used to come to the feeding corner at the same time every day but one day he disappeared. We were worried. We searched for him in the entire neighbourhood, to no avail. One early morning, three weeks later, he appeared, dragging his hind leg. He looked as if he was starving.

We immediately rushed him to an emergency veterinary hospital. The vets said he had been seriously hit, probably by a car, and he was lucky to have survived. They said Gingoni's tail had to be removed, but the injured hind leg could be operated on and there was a chance to save it, after a long rehabilitation process. However, we were warned that since Gingoni was not a house cat, it might not be easy for him to stay in a hospital cage for several months, which was necessary for his full recovery. The doctor added that it was a very complex operation, there was a chance it would not succeed and Gingoni's leg would have to be amputated after all. We took the chance.

Gingoni went through the operation. Luckily, it was successful and he began a long and what seemed like an endless rehabilitation process. For about twelve weeks, Gingoni was hospitalised in a special cage at the home of two volunteers, Rivi and Rini, who decided to adopt him. He had to stay in this cage to let the surgery heal.

He was given his medication under Rivi's close supervision, to ensure the wound would not become infected. He behaved like a real hero, it seemed he really appreciated all that was done for him, and he felt all the love and care that surrounded him.

The rehabilitation was amazingly successful. After three months, Gingoni was released to wander around a larger space, to strengthen his leg and remind him how to walk all over again. Gingoni is a very brave cat. We discovered he is also a very smart cat.

Gingoni taught himself how to open doors. Doors that many other cats couldn't open. And these days he has new friends, he roams around the house and the garden, he jumps and plays, he opens doors and knows to come back by himself. A new door, a new chapter, a new life was opened for this special and beloved cat.

Thanks to a generous donation it was possible to pay for Gingoni's medical treatment, which included the surgery, X-rays, medication and long rehabilitation process. It is only with such donations that it will be possible to help the many community cats in Israel and to enable them to survive and to open new chapters in their life, like Gingoni did.

* * *

Since its establishment, LAL, a non-profit organisation, dependent on donations, has continued to grow. Properly regulated, LAL operates under the scrutiny of the Official Registrar of Associations in Israel and its accounts, signed by an accountant, are inspected every year. In addition to the hundreds of wonderful volunteers, the charity employs highly dedicated professional animal lovers who are committed to improving the lives of feral cats in Israel.

About the Author

Riva Mayer, Israel
My Facebook page: www.facebook.com/two4cats
Email: catsexperts@gmail.com
Website: http://www.letlive.org.il/eng/donate/
Riva is a cat welfare specialist and founder of The Cat Welfare Society of Israel. She has made it her life's work for the past 30 years to fight for the plight of Israel's homeless cats.

Mr Frog
By Charlotte Smith

Two ladies peered at me through the bars of my cage. The younger of the two women waggled a feather on a stick in front of my nose, but I was too sad to play.

"Laura, I can't bear to see him like this," whispered the older lady. "I think I'll have to take him home."

"Oh yes, please do take him. He'll be so happy in your lovely house with so many things to do there!"

"My husband won't be happy though. How many times has Nick pleaded with me not to bring any more animals home?"

"Nick will love him, this little fellow is such a character," laughed Laura. "I'll go and sort him out a collar and shiny new name tag."

"Now then, Mr Frog," said Laura solemnly, as she fitted a smart new collar and name tag around my scrawny ginger neck, "you're a very lucky kitten to have Charlotte as your new mum, so behave yourself, OK?"

My life up until this point had been perilous to say the least. I came into the world as one of the thousands of stray kittens born every year in Muscat, Sultanate of Oman. Actually, I was luckier than most, as my 'home' was a grand estate belonging to an important Omani family. Stray dogs and cats have a tough life in Muscat, living in small colonies around every city refuse bin, eating scraps that fall from rubbish bags. My cat family was slightly more fortunate in that the estate workers would give us a little of their food, and if any of us looked really poorly they would try to take us to the clinic for treatment.

I was a sickly kitten. There was never enough food to go around and I suffered from a lot of respiratory problems. One of the estate workers saw me struggling for breath one day, and decided to take me to the veterinary clinic.

The doctors were very kind to me, and although I didn't much like all the needles they kept sticking in me, I soon began to feel a lot better. I tried to meow my thanks, but the sound that emerged from my mouth was a low-pitched, gribbity sort of noise. It was decided at that point my name would be Mr Frog.

Once I was feeling well, I could share a cage with another kitten of a similar age. Choo Choo was in the clinic because he couldn't move his back legs. A nasty big tomcat had pushed him off a wall, and his spine had been damaged. Choo Choo and I were soon firm friends, enjoying good food, riotous games and plenty of attention from the people who worked in the clinic. They loved to watch us playing.

I grew bigger and stronger every day, but poor Choo Choo developed complications because of his spinal injury. He was no longer well enough to play with me and had to be moved to a special care cage next to mine. The doctors did their best, but my best friend died soon after, and I was sad and lonely.

But now I was to have a proper family. I was carefully stowed in a cat carrier and my new mum picked it up, put it in her car, and drove me to my new home.

I'd never been inside a house before. As soon as I was carried through the door, a grey and white face with a black button nose started snuffling at the door of my cat carrier. It was a little overwhelming so I gave a half-hearted hiss and threw in a spit for good measure. The grey and white face backed off, just as a man walked through another door.

"What have you got in there?" he asked. His voice sounded very suspicious.

"Oh, this is Mr Frog," my new mum replied, plucking me out of the carrier. "His friend died and he was so miserable I thought I would bring him home for the weekend."

"Hmmmph, I hope you're not thinking of keeping him, we have quite enough animals, thank you."

My mum busied herself getting me settled, but I was keen to explore and make new friends. Another family cat walked into the room, looked at me in a rather unwelcoming way, and flounced out again.

"That's Frodo," my mum told me as she filled a little dish with delicious biscuits, "she's a bit of a princess, but I'm sure you'll soon be friends."

I decided making friends with the man was an easier option, so jumped onto his desk and started playing a complicated game involving rearranging pens, pencils and paperclips with my paws.

"What an odd-looking creature you are." The man at least softened these harsh words with some lovely tickling under my chin. It wasn't the first time someone had called me odd. I was a skinny ginger boy with long, long legs, huge paws and rather misshapen ears. Spying my shiny new tag swinging from my collar, the man demanded to know why it had my mum's telephone number engraved on it.

"One paw in the door," she said sweetly and rushed off to pour my new dad a large glass of wine.

I celebrated becoming an official family member by sending a pencil sharpener skidding off the desk, and pouncing on it until I was quite sure it was dead.

Another two-legged family person arrived home. "What on earth is that?" giggled the girl when she spotted me. "Oh Mum, you are hopeless. How many more waifs and strays are you going to bring home?"

Deciding to be friendly, I launched myself at the girl's leg, digging my needle-sharp claws into her thigh.

"Ouch!" she cried. "Get off me, you naughty kitty."

"I think he likes you," said Mum, unpinning me from the girl's jeans and setting me down on the floor. I didn't want to be down there, so jumped onto a handy table and shoved a bunch of keys onto the tiled floor, where they landed with a most pleasing clatter. Satisfied with myself, I settled down to a good wash.

Pushing things off high surfaces was one of my favourite games, but did not always make me popular with my two-legged family. Mum was not happy when I sent her mobile phone flying off a shelf. I didn't break it, but the speaker was a bit damaged and could only manage a rather sad croak, a quieter version of my own language.

One morning I was sitting on the arm of a chair, quietly contemplating life, when I noticed dozens of pretty rainbows appearing from all directions when the sunshine landed on a crystal jug containing flowers. I was quite mesmerised by all the patterns and decided further investigation was needed.

I was in perfect pouncing position when my mum walked into the room. I was too late to stop myself, and flew in the direction of the table on which the pretty rainbow jug sat.

"Noooooooo, Mr Frog!" cried my mum, as I landed close to my prey, which skidded off the table and smashed on the floor. Tiny fragments of crystal flew in all directions and settled in the pool of flower-strewn water, still sparkling but now without the rainbows. "You wretched cat!"

My mum was clearly upset, so I pretended I'd done absolutely nothing wrong, and settled down for a wash. I would have quite liked to have a paddle in the pretty puddle, but sensed maybe that wasn't such a good idea.

I tried to make friends with the other four-paws in the house. The grey and white face with the black button nose belonged to Billy the dog. He was quite interested in playing with me at first, but for some reason he didn't like me ambushing him from behind doors or sofas, so preferred to stay as far away from me as possible. I didn't fare any better in the friendship stakes with Frodo, who was indeed a princess and treated me with complete distain. I told her if you kissed a (Mr)Frog, he might turn into a prince, but was rewarded with a hiss and a flick of her tail for my trouble. The other family cat was a big boy called Goji who liked to patrol the outside neighbourhood, and was far too busy to be bothered with a little squirt like me.

I grew fast, and became a rather handsome, leonine-looking cat. My health still gave everyone cause for concern, and if I was really poorly I had to go back to the clinic so the doctors could look after me. After a particularly bad episode, when I couldn't eat anything and had to spend a long time in hospital and didn't even have any energy to be naughty, I heard my mum talking to my dad.

"I can't wait to get these animals out of Oman," she said. "I'm sure they'll be healthier away from all this heat and dust."

A few weeks later, mysterious crates appeared in the house. They were like the carrier I went to the vets in, but bigger. They had some of our favourite blankets inside and I rather liked having a nap in them, but neither Billy nor Frodo wanted to go near them.

One day, Mum didn't let us out into the garden after breakfast like she usually did. Instead, I was put into one of the mysterious crates, and the door was shut firmly. Frodo was also made to suffer this indignity, and was so cross that she bit mum before the door of her crate was closed. Billy was next, and he just looked plain miserable. What on earth was going on?

A short car journey later we arrived at a huge, noisy building. Strange faces peered into our crates and lots of pieces of paper were stuck onto the outside. Mum had put a few biscuits in the crates but we were much too bewildered to even think about eating them. Water bowls were attached to the wire doors, and I did manage a little drink. I was glad Mum had put a T-shirt that smelled of her for me to lie on, but was worried I would never see her again.

A little later, we were loaded onto a pallet and a funny vehicle called a forklift drove us outside to an enormous vehicle with wings. The pallet was hoisted up to a vast black hole, and once inside, our crates were secured against the wall. The light was very dim and we were too frightened to make a noise. After what seemed like a very long time, there were different sounds, and we started moving, slowly at first, then very, very fast until it seemed like the ground would disappear from under us. I didn't know that was exactly what was happening, not being a frequent flier. Actually, once we were in the air it felt quite nice. The constant hum from the engines made us feel a little sleepy, so we could escape our worries about what was happening to us and take a nice long nap.

Many hours later, we were woken by more strange noises and I felt as if we were dropping out of the sky. There was a bump, and then a feeling like we were driving very, very fast again before slowing down and finally stopping. Light flooded into my crate when the door of the strange, winged vehicle was opened, and before too long we were on the move again.

I felt a bit chilly when our crates were taken out of the black hole and loaded into a van. Everything smelled different, and I was stiff and hungry. After a short drive, we arrived at a building. There was no sign of Mum, but there were lots of cages with other animals in them. I hoped this wasn't going to be our new home. The people were kind to us and moved us from our crates to the cages, and gave us some food. Billy and Frodo wouldn't eat theirs, but I was starving and managed to force down a few mouthfuls.

At last I heard my mum's voice. Billy could walk to the reception area on his lead, but Frodo and I had to go back in our crates in case we ran away. I was so relieved to see Mum, and I think she was pleased to see us too, even though she was crying. We had one more journey, this time in a car. Frodo and I sang loudly the whole way, while Billy sat with Mum and licked her nose a lot.

Finally, we reached our destination, and were carefully carried into the house where at last the door to my crate was opened. After seventeen hours of travelling, my legs were not working so well, but I was keen to explore. I was very happy to see one of Mum's two-legged girls in the house. She used to visit our other home in Oman quite often, and I know she really liked me because I made her laugh when I did naughty things.

Frodo and I were not allowed to go outside for a few weeks. We were very jealous of Billy who was always being taken for walks, and came home with tales of new smells and green grass. We had to be content with sitting on the windowsills, watching people, cars and other cats and dogs pass by.

At last the day came when the door of the house was not shut in our faces and we could venture out into the back garden. We were very cautious at first, everything smelled strange and walking on grass was a very odd feeling indeed. It took no time at all before we were feeling braver, jumping up onto the garden wall and eventually disappearing over onto the other side. Mum would worry about us at first, calling our names a lot, but she soon trusted us to come back when we were good and ready.

An old lady lived just up the street, and she often left her back door wide open. Having watched her house from the safety of the garden wall, I decided the time had come to make friends with the old dear, so, without waiting for an invitation, I marched into her kitchen.

"Shoo, off you go now," scolded the old lady, brandishing her broom. "Go on, I don't want you here."

Unused to such rejection, I decided to give her several more chances at making friends with me. I thought she must like me, because one day she came up our garden path and rang the doorbell.

"Good morning!" she boomed. "Does that rather exotic-looking cat belong to you?"

Mum was in no position to deny my parentage, given I was sitting on the windowsill, enjoying a good wash in the sunshine.

"Er, yes," she admitted, "I do hope he's not causing any trouble."

"Well," the old lady drew herself up to her full height of four foot, eleven inches, "I'm afraid he is being rather a nuisance, he keeps barging into my house. Yesterday he opened all my kitchen cupboards, and ripped open several packets of food. There were pasta shapes all over the floor when I came downstairs."

"Oh dear, I am so sorry," said Mum. "Please, you must let me replace anything you've lost. Perhaps you could spray Mr Frog with some water when he comes over the wall?"

"I've tried that, my dear, he seemed to love it! Well, I must get on, good day to you."

Poor Mum dreaded walking past the old lady's house in case I had been in there again (generally I had). It cost her a fortune in replacement food and gifts to placate the old dear. She was right in that I did indeed love water. Nobody in our house could pour themselves a glassful without me sticking my face in it for a good drink. Frodo and I both liked drinking straight from the tap best of all, it must be because we are desert animals, and never know when the next opportunity to quench our thirst might come.

The old lady did get some respite, as once again I was poorly and had to stay at the vet for a few days, and I was kept inside for two weeks until I was better. It was a good summer in England that year, but we had our first taste of proper winter, and this one happened to be the wettest one on record. Unaccustomed to cold weather, Frodo and I spent most of the time huddled as close to the warm radiators as possible.

Our stay in England was always going to be a temporary one. Spain was our destiny, and plans were being made for our big move soon after Christmas. I don't think any of us were sorry to be leaving this soggy British winter behind, but Frodo and I were going to have to endure one more trip in an aeroplane before we could get to Spain.

This was a much shorter flight, and although we were both very cross, Frodo and I recovered from our journey quickly. Of course, we had to stay inside again until we got settled. This house was near a golf course, and I managed to escape one day. I had a wonderful game chasing some people who were carrying some funny sticks on the eighteenth green before being escorted home. Before too long I was exploring all over the great outdoors once again. What a relief it was to get away from all that English rain. I had a good snoop around all the neighbours' gardens and found a few exciting trees to climb. I was feeling well and life was good.

Mum went along to the Residents' Association meeting and came back looking hot and bothered.

"It was awful," she moaned to Dad, "a German man was complaining about a ginger cat digging up all his plants."

"No prizes for guessing who that cat might be I suppose?"

"Don't laugh! Honestly, I wanted to slide under the table. I was so embarrassed. Wherever we go that cat finds people to annoy, thank goodness we're moving to the countryside soon."

And move to the countryside we did. I thought we were in heaven when I saw the thousands of olive trees that surrounded our new house. Determined to climb as many as possible, I spent a great deal of time outdoors. There were geckos to chase too, but Mum got very cross with me if I caught them. Usually they ran off, leaving their tails behind.

We didn't have anyone living very close to us, but one day we did have some visitors.

"Hello," called a friendly voice, "anyone at home?"

"Just coming." Mum was busy in the garden as usual, but hurried down to the house to see who was there.

Tilly and Mark had a holiday home up the hill from us, and had dropped by to introduce themselves. I wandered onto the terrace when Mum was making coffee.

"Oh, what a beautiful cat!" exclaimed Tilly.

I wasn't often called beautiful, so decided I liked these people very much indeed. They told Mum they had two ginger cats back in London, who would be coming to Spain for several weeks in the summer.

Mark and Tilly invited Mum and Dad to their house for a paella one evening. Deciding to walk up the hill so they could enjoy a couple of glasses of wine by not taking the car, they were unaware I was following a safe distance behind.

"I hope you're hungry," I heard Tilly say, "there's loads to eat."

The paella was brought to the table with a flourish, and just as it was placed on the table I made my appearance.

Of course, Tilly and Mark were delighted to see me, but for once I wasn't all that interested in them. No, my nose had picked up the delicious smell of prawns. I loved prawns more than anything in the world.

I did try jumping onto the table, but was told that was bad manners. I had to be content to sit on the floor and have several juicy prawns passed down to me. What a great evening we all had.

Now I knew where Tilly and Mark's house was, I would walk up the hill often. I was sad to find the place empty most of the time, but one day to my utter delight, they returned. But wait a minute, why did they have two cats with them? To say that I was a little jealous of Dylan and Thomas would be an understatement.

Of course, because Dylan and Thomas were only in Spain for their holidays, they were not allowed to roam free outside like I could. They had to suffer the indignity of wearing harnesses with leads attached, and being taken for walks like dogs. I found this very amusing, and after my breakfast, I took great pleasure in skipping up the hill to sit outside Tilly and Mark's glass doors and annoy the two ginger imposters.

Tilly took videos of my bad behaviour and sent them to Mum. She was worried Dylan and Thomas were becoming upset with my constant presence outside their door.

"Oh, for goodness' sake, Mr Frog," Mum berated me. "Congratulations, you've managed to upset the neighbours even when they're so far away that we don't really have any!"

Luckily, because Tilly loved me, she was quite patient about my antisocial baiting of her precious cats. However, she and Mum did come up with a plan so that Dylan and Thomas could at least go for their evening stroll in peace. I would be kept indoors for an hour after my supper. I wasn't happy about this enforced curfew, but apparently it was non-negotiable.

It was an idyllic summer. I loved the freedom, the warmth, climbing trees and the abundance of prawns in Spain. The searing heat of an Andalucían summer gradually gave way to the freezing temperatures of winter. It was during this period that my health began to fail, and I spent a lot of time at the vets. My kidneys weren't working very well, my heart was giving cause for concern and I needed several injections and pills every day to keep me alive.

There were days that winter when Mum and Dad were worried they were going to lose me, but spring arrived and I was still around. There were trees that still needed climbing, and with the warmth my energy levels rose. I was still very poorly, thirsty all the time and as skinny as a rake despite eating twice as much as any other cat.

Walking up the hill to see Tilly and Mark was too much effort for me that summer, much to the relief of Dylan and Thomas. I slept a lot and saved my energy for climbing the trees closest to our house.

By autumn, I had very little strength. My organs were failing, and I was tired of the constant injections and horrid pills and medicines.

Mum asked the vet whether there was anything else to be done, but I think we all knew I was not going to live much longer. I was only four years old, but with all the problems I had been born with, I was probably lucky to have reached that age. I had done a lot of things in my short life too.

My final weekend on Earth was made special for me. The family played Monopoly (my favourite game, even though this time I was too weak to push all the pieces off the board, although I did manage a few). I had a special bed right next to the sink so I didn't have to jump up to get to the tap, and I was allowed to eat as many fresh prawns as I could manage.

On Monday morning, Mum loaded me gently into my carrier and took me on my last journey. I was ready to say goodbye and was glad Mum was with me until the very end, even if she did make my fur wet with all her tears. I'm in heaven now, strong and healthy and so happy that all the people on Earth who loved me still talk of 'The legendary Mr Frog'.

About the Author

Charlotte Smith, Oman, UK and Spain
Website: www.billypaws.com
Facebook: Paw Prints in Oman
Twitter: @billypaws
Paw Prints in Oman, the full-length story of Mr Frog and his friends, is available from Amazon.

A Veterinary Tail
By Victoria Veterinary Practice

Working in a veterinary practice we have seen some challenging cases, to say the least, and none more so following a frantic phone call from a concerned member of the public one morning in June 2016. Clearly distressed, they explained that a feral cat, who sometimes slept in their shed, had given birth to a litter of four kittens. Mum was nowhere to be seen and now, who knows how, the kittens were entwined in a mixture of wire and twigs and rotten placenta cord. All stuck together in a ball, unable to move and entirely alone. Obviously, they would have no chance of survival if left alone so we asked the lady to bring them to us at Victoria Veterinary Practice, in Merthyr Tydfil, immediately.

Upon arrival, we were amazed at what we saw. How on earth had these little kits got into such a predicament? They were literally bound tightly together, the wire wrapped around them over and over. Could someone have done this purposely? That we will never know, but now we had to concentrate on treating these poor little things as a matter of urgency. Carefully we cut through the wire and untangled them, removed all the spiky twigs and started to try and warm them up. It was at this point that we sadly realised one of the litter had died. As upsetting as it was, it made the team even more determined that his litter mates would not suffer the same fate.

All hands on deck! One nurse was frantically making up supplement kitten milk, while another was warming up heat pads.

Others were quickly creating a warm padded kennel for them and the rest rubbing their little bodies vigorously. As we felt them slowly warming up we tried to move on to getting them to feed. No need to worry there! They quickly latched on to the tiny feeding bottles and eagerly drank the warm kitten milk. Now warm and fed, our vets checked them over and thankfully they all seemed healthy despite their shaky start. Now it was just a matter of trying our best – all fingers crossed. As they were not yet a day old they were going to take a lot of care if they had any chance of making it. Seeing them snuggled together in their warm and comfy kennel, the staff quickly became attached, preparing the milk, feeding every two hours even stimulating them to make sure they toileted. That night they went home with one of our caring nurses, Faye, who did just that.

Our thoughts returned to their mum. She must have found the whole experience traumatic, to say the least, and we didn't want her to have to go through it again. What could be done for her? How were we going to catch her? It was reported that at the first sign of any human she was off like a shot. However, working closely with our local cat rescue, we laid a trap containing some tempting cat food in the shed she sometimes sheltered in. Bingo! We had a call from the owners of the property who had been keeping a close eye on the situation. They told us the cat, who was definitely the mum, was in the trap. She was quickly transported to us as we knew she would be very afraid at this point, and wanted to make the experience as quick and painless for her as possible.

When presented at the practice, it became clear Mum was extremely feral – hissing and spitting, clearly terrified. The vets, using gauntlet gloves, managed to examine her. This beautiful tortoiseshell was thankfully fit and well – and spirited to say the least! Trying to introduce her to her kittens was not going to work. She wanted nothing to do with them. To save her from going through the same thing again we admitted her to be spayed and she went to the local cat rescue the next day.

As the kittens grew, we established we had one ginger boy, a ginger and white girl and an all-white girl, all with totally different characters. The little lad was nervous and very shy. Faye, the nurse who was looking after them, named him Doc Brown after a character in her favourite film *Back to The Future*. The ginger and white girl was feisty and very protective of her litter mates. She even tried to take on Faye's huge chocolate Labrador, much to his amazement, hence she was named Hissy Spit. The all-white little girl, appropriately named Whitey, was an odd mix. She didn't act like other cats and was almost unsure of herself. We were quite concerned about her behaviour. Appearing constantly anxious and worried, our hearts went out to her. The only thing that seemed to ease her stress was to hold her close and gently smooth away her concerns. When we did this, we could visibly see her start to relax.

As time went on, the trio began to thrive physically and we started to think about finding them their forever homes. Animal-mad Faye already had dogs, cats and numerous chickens, including a blind silky chicken, called Cilla, who slept in her bedroom. However, we would need to be very choosy regarding who would have the pleasure of making each of the kittens an addition to their family.

When the kittens were eight weeks old, a lovely family expressed interest in Hissy Spit, the ginger and white little girl. It was arranged for them to go to Faye's home to visit her and see how they got on. Much to our delight they fell in love with her and, it seemed, her with them. She confidently strode up to them, rubbing up against their legs and purring loudly. This lady knew how to sell herself! Happy in the knowledge that this lucky girl would clearly be loved and cared for, she went home with her new family that same day.

The visit from the family had alerted Faye to another issue. Whilst in her home, despite being calm and speaking softly, the visitors' appearance had clearly distressed Doc Brown, the little ginger lad. He ran and hid at the mere sight of them. Despite trying to be gently coaxed to come and say hello, he didn't want to join in. Originally, we thought this was a one off but it soon became apparent that new people were not his thing. The thought of him going to a new home and being so scared was awful. Everyone was very protective of him, especially given his start in life. In familiar surroundings, he was calm and happy. He also had become very attached to Marty, Faye's older cat. There seemed to be only one solution. Faye had gained a new family member.

That left little Whitey, the puss so unsure of herself. Why was she so worried all the time? She didn't develop natural cat behaviour and, although she wasn't scared or aggressive towards the other animals, she didn't to want to interact with them. A loner. What she really craved was human cuddles, as she had from day one. The kittens had spent a huge amount of time at Victoria Veterinary Practice, being

293

Faye's place of work, and the fact that they needed such close care. During one of their frequent visits, Whitey was being examined by one of our vets to check all was well. During the examination one of our nurses accidentally dropped a metal kidney dish which went clattering to the floor. Everyone jumped out of their skin, apart from Whitey who didn't flinch. She sat calmly on the table, not even turning around to see what had caused the commotion.

The stark realisation hit us all. Whitey was stone deaf! It explained a lot. Now we were even more worried about her finding a new home with an owner who would be committed to her needs. As she curled up contentedly in Faye's arms I said, "Oh Whitey, you're such a worry. What are we going to do with you?"

To which Faye replied, "I know exactly what we are going to do with you. We're going to take you home."

With shrieks of joy from all the staff, we were thrilled that Whitey was going to join Faye's family too. She would have the highest level of love and care alongside her brother.

We can say that both Whitey and Doc Brown are loving life in their forever home. Doc Brown is no longer as shy as he was but we think will always be slightly reserved. His favourite pastime is eating chicken and following Marty everywhere. Whitey is a proper lap cat and loves nothing more than being held and stroked. We are also still in touch with the family that rehomed Hissy Spit. Amazingly they kept her name as they said it suited her. She loves people but is quite the cat boss of the neighbourhood and rules the roost.

Such a happy ending for the trio who had a wobbly start in life. All the staff here at Victoria Vets are thrilled that they will live their lives with the love and care that they all truly deserve.

About the Author

Mrs Marsha Kear, UK
Reception Manager at Victoria Veterinary Practice Ltd, Wales.
Email: marketing.victoriavets@mail.com

Luca's Story
By International Cat Care Patrons,
Mark Bolland and Lord Guy Black

Cats have been part of our lives for 20 years: pedigree cats, moggies, even cats we've inherited. At one point, we had five of them, spread over different locations in different countries: two beloved Russian Blues in London, Alexandra and Victoria; two country moggies at our house in Umbria in Italy, the aptly named Romulus and Remus; and an old faithful Burman, Toby, whom we took in after Guy's mother died and cared for during the rest of his life. That's a whole other story.

But, sadly, with the passage of time, the five dwindled one by one until our last cat, the adorable *grand dame* Victoria, died at the stately age of very nearly 20 (not bad for a pedigree) in the summer of 2015. It was the first time since August 1996 we had been alone – and it felt dreadful.

We talked about whether and when we would get another cat to share their lives with us, but reached no firm conclusion. We couldn't do it too soon, that would have seemed wrong and we didn't know *where* to do it – in London or in Italy, where we want to spend more time and where cats can roam freely in the way they can't in central London. We'd had Russian Blues specifically because they are happy living in apartments, and they have the most perfect nature for "flat cats".

So, we lived in a state of indecision, desperate to have another cat, or even several, in our lives, but unclear on the way forward. But, as you may already have guessed, Fate intervened to make our minds up for us. And, as Fate often does, did so in a spectacular and very unexpected fashion.

It was early August in 2016, just 13 months since Victoria had died, and we were staying at our house near Perugia in the Umbrian hills. It is an old farmhouse set in some lovely gardens and Remus had lived happily there for many years (Romulus having died quite young), helping keep down the rodent population, often bringing them back as presents, of course, terrorising the lizards, entertaining our friends who visited in the summer, and in the winter hogging the bed. An old sign next to our door says "These buildings and grounds are preserved solely for the enjoyment of the cat." Quite so.

Those of you who have travelled to central Italy in August will realise that it can be punishingly hot, and the weather is broken sometimes in the most dramatic fashion possible with a huge thunderstorm. One such storm happened on the late evening of Friday 6th August, Guy's birthday. The heavens opened, the noise of thunder filled the air and lightning moved back and forth across the valley for over two hours. We pitied anyone who was out in it, including the animals.

If you like storms, this was a cracker. We had five friends staying and we did the only thing we could – take shelter to watch it, put some Wagner on very loudly in the background, and open a few more bottles. By about 2 am on 7th August, the storm had blown itself out and the next morning the sun returned to azure blue skies, so had the heat. The mercury hit 35 degrees by lunchtime. Time for siesta.

It was then, perhaps fittingly after so epic a storm, that Fate intervened in our idyllic little Umbrian world, and turned it upside down.

Just after breakfast, we were pottering around the place – clearing up, putting some cushions out, preparing for another day of doing absolutely nothing – when we heard the unmistakeable sound of squeaking coming from the courtyard. We went there straightway to find Fabio – a wonderful local man who, with his family, looks after the house for us, and was devoted to Remus. He was holding in his hands a tiny ball of very, very dark brown fluff. It was, of course, a kitten.

Fabio had found it at the bottom of the drive, by a pile of wood, when he arrived that morning. He got out of his car, heard the noise and investigated, finding this tiny object alone, and clearly very frightened.

The kitten cannot have been more than ten days or so old, as his eyes were still shut. He (or she? – we didn't know) must have been born around 26th July. He was in quite a state, particularly with what looked like conjunctivitis round his eyes, and was obviously very dehydrated.

We don't know, and can never know, how he got there or why he was alone. We are too far from a road for him to have been dumped deliberately, and in any case, why would anyone just get rid one kitten? The Italians tend to have more brutal ways of getting shot of unwanted litters. But because of our gardens, we do have several feral cats nearby. So our best guess is that one of these, his mother (of whom more anon), had been moving some new born kittens to shelter and safety the night of the Great Storm, 36 hours earlier, and had become separated from him. Perhaps she had left him there to pick him up later and couldn't find him? Unless we teach him to talk, that will remain an unsolved mystery.

All that speculation was quite unimportant at the time because we had a bigger problem on our hands: what on earth were we going to do with this kitten? Neither of us had ever looked after anything so tiny before – all our previous cats were five to six months old when they arrived – and we were completely unprepared. And, given the distressed state of this little creature, so small he would fit in the palm of one hand, we knew we didn't have long to do something.

While Guy made a few phone calls to Cats Protection in the UK, and to our own vet in London, the amazing Mark Lindfield at Clerkenwell Animal Hospital, Mark, Fabio and our friends started trying to give the poor little thing some liquid. After all, he had probably been out in the sun all the day before, with none of his mother's milk and no water to sustain him.

Guy was given hard, but correct, advice, which was we should take him back to where Fabio found him and leave him there as long as possible in case his mother came back for him. After all, it would be infinitely better for him to be weaned by her, than hand-reared by two hopeless novices! So, intensely painful though it was, we returned him to his woodpile, and waited in complete agony for the next few hours. While that was going on we made more calls, including to International Cat Care who pointed us in the direction of their excellent website, which was packed full of advice for such eventualities. We were so grateful to everyone who helped give us information and guidance.

By three in the afternoon, it seemed clear to us that Mama was not returning, and we either had to take the kitten in or he would die. Italy doesn't have the luxury, either, of services like Cats Protection who would take in an unwanted or abandoned kitten. This was going to be down to us. The next two weeks of our holiday were taking on a wholly different complexion.

The first thing we did was to rush him to the local vet. Because Perguia is a University town, it has a big veterinary teaching hospital, where Remus has been well cared for, and Fabio took him straight there. They were exceptionally efficient and gave him a thorough examination. Our kitten was, they said, a girl who – though dehydrated and with bad conjunctivitis – appeared mostly healthy. They gave us a powder mixture for kitten milk, along with a tiny bottle, and showed us how to feed her and help her go to the toilet. She would have to have be bottle fed every three hours, they explained, for two weeks – after which she could begin drinking milk on her own. For the next few months she'd have to be totally isolated because of the very severe risk of infection. Our poor little girl, deprived of her mother's milk, would have no immune system to speak of for some time and the risks to her health were very grave. A friend from International Cat Care had already warned us that anyone who weans a kitten must have a heart of steel, because so many do not survive.

With that reality check ringing in our ears, we took the little girl home where she took up residence as our newest, and most vulnerable, cat. We installed her in a nice, cool room off our bedroom, safe from the perils of the outside world and from where it would be easy to feed her in the middle of the night. A robust cardboard box, that earlier had contained bottles of local red wine, with a soft towel in it provided a little bed and as Mark gave her the first bottle, she began to open her eyes. Big blue eyes, it was a wonderful sight. This kitten was *gorgeous*.

Fate had delivered her to us. Fate, of course, did not decide on a name, and once we had settled her down after her first feed, and left her in peace for the first time, we had to christen her. Our friends provided a large variety of wholly unsuitable names, including Mrs Slocombe, but we knew this was an Italian cat and had to have an Italian name. We found her on a Monday (*Lunedi* in Italian) and she arrived the night after an incredible, almost red full moon – the result of the storm – so we decided to call her Luna. It's a lovely name, and Fabio and his family thoroughly approved.

Luna spent her first night well – better than we did as we fretted over her constantly and struggled to find a feeding regime that worked. (How on earth do new mums with babies manage?!) Next morning, however, things did not look so good. She was very quiet and not taking the milk as voraciously as she had the day before. We fretted. We were supposed to be going out with our friends to visit nearby Montefalco. Fabio was going to feed her, but that didn't feel right. Mark decided Guy should go, and he would stay at home to sit with Luna. One piece of advice we had from International Cat Care and Cats Protection was to try to simulate the feeling a kitten would have from a mother by holding her close to the heart. So that's what Mark did the entire day, until late in the afternoon when suddenly she perked up, started eating again and for the first time doing what kittens do best, darting about the place and finding deeply inaccessible places to go. There is no doubt he saved her life.

Our lives began to settle into some sort of pattern. We worked out that to ensure we both got about six hours' sleep, Mark would go to bed around 11 pm after mixing the powder and feeding Luna, and Guy would stay up to 2 am and do the next feed before retiring. Mark would then get up at 5 am before we were both up at 8 am. It was a good system. When we had to go out for a time, Fabio, or Joseph, a friend of ours who lives nearby and is brilliant with animals, would come and feed her. Within days she had learned the sound of the bottle and couldn't get the milk down quickly enough. She was learning how to use the toilet, we got her a tray within the first ten days, and her eyes were improving as we bathed them with warm water. And we were learning all the time, not least with some of the excellent advice from the International Cat Care website (http://icatcare.org/advice/hand-rearing-kittens). The lovely vet paid a house call after another week and pronounced herself pleased. We were doing well but there was, she said again, a long way still to go. The first eight weeks were critical.

Things are of course never that straightforward. It was after about ten days that we thought disaster had struck. Luna was becoming more and more greedy in drinking down her milk – she couldn't get it down fast enough – and starting to bite at the end of the teat. We managed to move it away in time each time, but she went through an increasing number of teats as her sharp little teeth were constantly puncturing them. Then during the 8 am feed one morning, Guy took the teat out of her mouth to find that she had bitten the end off it…and swallowed it.

Pandemonium and panic ensued. Guy thought he had killed her and neither of us knew what to do. But again, the experts calmed us down: keep an eye on her for 48 hours and look out for any vomiting they said, but the chances are that it will pass through. Incredibly anxious two days passed by, we were checking on her the entire time, fretting and fussing (to which she was oblivious), but the advice was right. Nature took its course and the drama subsided. We know not whether that was one of the nine lives. One thing was clear from this: it was time to move on from a bottle to the bowl. After a few false starts, little Luna started taking her milk from a tiny saucer. As she became better at it, we increased the bowls in size and, towards the end of August, started adding in a little mashed up solid food, which she really enjoyed.

After two weeks, the vet came around again to see her. As before, she said she was very pleased – but there was one thing we ought to know. Our little girl was…a little boy. It is an easy mistake to make when they are so young but two weeks in it was now obvious. So, a name change was in order! (Luna is a feminine word in Italian.) Rather than go back to the drawing board, and given that he was already getting used to his name, we decided just to change one letter. Luna became Luca.

Of course, the days were passing by quickly as we cared for the tiny addition to our family, and getting closer and closer to when we had to return to London. Luca had made wonderful progress. He was eating properly. He was litter trained. His big blue eyes were much brighter. His coat – healthy and gleaming – seemed to be getting darker. And he was immensely playful. But the time had come to leave him.

We knew it had to happen as there was no way to take him back to London. He couldn't travel without a rabies injection, and little kittens can't have that until they are six months old. We also knew Fabio and his family, who had looked after Remus so brilliantly, would come to the house every day and care for him wonderfully. So, with a heavy heart – he was, after all, still less than two months old so at some risk – we took our leave of him for a bit.

It had been an extraordinary three weeks. We had not really expected to get another cat for some time, and certainly never imagined we would be presented with the Herculean task of hand-rearing a tiny kitten, something neither of us knew anything about. It had not been easy, but it was worth every ounce of effort and anxiety because Luca had pulled through, against the odds. Already he looked entirely different from the tiny, scared bundle of fluff who had turned up on 8th August. And of course, we had fallen in love with him.

We arranged to return to Italy at the end of September, at the close of the crucial eight-week period, to see him. He was on cracking form. He'd grown so much bigger, was playing with his toys and even using his scratching post, his very dark brown coat had turned jet black with just a tiny bit of white fur under his chin, and the blue eyes had turned green. He recognised us immediately. Another visit from the vet confirmed his excellent progress and for the first time we could believe he would make it.

As we write this, we have just been with Luca over Christmas. He's now five months old and his Italian carers say that he is turning into a 'panther' because he's grown so big and so black. He's developed a lovable personality, enjoys being around people (and following them around), and his health is (touch wood) great. We wouldn't have dared hope at the start of August he would make it this far, and be in such great shape. In another few months, we will have another hurdle to cross – letting him out into the outside world, once he has been neutered and completed his vaccinations – but we'll cross that one when we come to it!

We promised at the start of this tale we would return to the mystery of his mother. As we mentioned, there are feral cats in our gardens and without doubt Luca belongs to one of them, because a few days after he came to live with us we spotted a big cat wandering round with four tiny little babies – Luca's brothers and sisters. We asked advice on what to do about them and the vet said first and foremost the adult cats must be spayed, otherwise we would end up with a colony. She captured them humanely and did just that before returning them. And although they won't come near the house – and certainly couldn't come in while Luca is in isolation – we have been feeding the kittens and providing them with shelter in the colder weather. One day we hope Luca will be reunited with them, and that they will all come and live with us. But that'll be another story.

We've learned a huge amount from Luca's tale – and not just now to wean a kitten from birth, how to care for them, how to toilet train them and how to stimulate them in the absence of other kittens.

We've been reminded of how lucky we are in the United Kingdom to have such a fantastic and diverse range of domestic animal charities who care for abandoned or lost animals. Organisations like Cats Protection, the Dogs Trust and Blue Cross don't exist in Italy or much of Europe, so too many animals still die.

We've been reminded, too, of the importance of the basics – of ensuring that cats are spayed, and that you deal humanely where you can with feral cats. This is where the work of International Cat Care is so important and needs to be supported.

And we are enormously grateful to all those originations and individuals, including the teams at International Cat Care and Cats Protection, who helped us through those early days.

At the centre of it all is little Luca, the new feline love of our life, so different in many ways to those who went before him – whose memory we cherish – but so like them in many other respects. He already has the big tummy of Victoria; like Alexandra he leaps on the computer when you are working on it; like Remus, he lies purring on the bed in the sunshine; and like stately Toby, he has a bearing and a poise which set him out as very special. People say he was incredibly lucky the day he walked into the lives of two people who love cats as much as we do. We think it is the other way around – we are the lucky ones. Now we must all do more to make sure other cats throughout the world who are abandoned or strayed have the same chance he does.

About the Authors

Lord (Guy) Black and Mark Bolland, Italy
Website: www.guyblack.org.uk
Guy and Mark are communications professionals, who have spent their working lives in the media, public relations and reputation management. They work with a number of animal welfare charities, including Cats Protection and the Dogs Trust in the UK, and are honoured to be Patrons of International Cat Care. They have been married for eleven years, and over time they have been joined by eight cats – the latest arrival being Luca, whose story this is. Mark is a former Private Secretary to HRH The Prince of Wales. Guy sits in the House of Lords and speaks frequently there on animal welfare issues.

Afterword

Before we close we want to say a big thank you to our pals at Katzenworld, who have been incredibly supportive during the compilation of our book. Here's some background about their amazing work.

Katzenworld was founded in 2014 by Marc-André Runcie-Unger and his close friends, Yuki Chung and Laura Haile. Their combined love of cats led them to develop a community-focused online publication dedicated to our furry friends.

Katzenworld is all about being a fun, informative place that promotes all things related tocats. Their focus points are:

- Advice on cat care
- Cat welfare
- Informing about top cat events
- Promoting cat cafés – venues where cats are watched and played with for a cover fee and some even offer cats to new homes
- Online shop exclusively selling cat products

Katzenworld enjoyed instant success. From the beginning, it was recognised as a high quality, inclusive organisation that welcomes its cat-loving community with open arms, providing a forum where stories, hints and tips are shared.

Kazenworld is also an incredibly dynamic publication. Through listening to their followers, fun posts such as the Friday Art Cat, Tummy Rub Tuesday and Purrsday Poetry have been introduced. Many are commonly recognised by hashtags on Twitter, and they have now become popular, permanent additions to the regular schedule.

As with many great ideas, Katzenworld has quickly grown into an international community project with thousands of followers. In addition to the core Katzenworld team, there are currently approx. 100 active contributors around the world. Using both Twitter and Facebook, they post fresh content on a regular basis. There is also a growing army of guest bloggers who also submit stories.

Because of its focus on feline care, Katzenworld has forged a close relationship with International Cat Care, who ensure posts containing technical information and advice are accurate. Both organisations work closely to promote one another's cat welfare campaigns.

Katzenworld's help and encouragement in our work to promote International Cat Care is ongoing. They are strong supporters of our aims to help cats in need, and are doing everything they can to spread the word about our project to raise awareness and funds for International Cat Care. We will always be incredibly grateful to them for that.

With millions of cat lovers around the world, unsurprisingly Katzenworld is still thriving. And why not? Its messages are always accurate, positive and feline-driven, we think it's a wonderful on-line publication.

https://katzenworld.co.uk/

Acknowledgements

Our aim in producing this book is to raise as much awareness and funds for the fantastic work of International Cat Care as we can. The moment we made our intentions clear, we were overwhelmed with support and help. For example, the Twitter and Facebook cat-loving communities have been amazing in their support, but many individuals too. We'd like to specifically thank some of those who have been instrumental in helping us achieve our aim.

Katzenworld
Marc-André Runcie-Unger, founder of the superb Katzenworld blog, has been incredibly supportive and helpful throughout. A major advocate of cat welfare, he's always there for us with ideas and support, we just couldn't have managed without him.

International Cat Care
Working with Shelley Gregory-Jones, Development Director at International Cat Care, has been nothing short of wonderful. Always full of enthusiasm and ideas for our project, she's been a joy to work with.

Johanna Tarkela
When we explained to Johanna what we wanted to accomplish, she immediately joined the team. Her art is here for all to see, we love it and we're so grateful for all the selfless time and energy she has given in helping make our project a success.

Our book contributors
It's not easy to write a story for the first time, even harder when it includes heartache or trauma – that goes for seasoned authors too. But it's exactly what our contributors have done. We honestly can't thank them enough. Without their generous time and efforts this book would not have been produced, and we would not have been able to help International Cat Care in the same way. We thank you *all* from the bottom of our hearts – this has been a fantastic team effort.

Other books by Ant Press

If you enjoyed *Completely Cats – Stories with Cattitude*, you may also enjoy these Ant Press titles:

MEMOIRS

Chickens, Mules and Two Old Fools by Victoria Twead (Wall Street Journal Top 10 bestseller)

Two Old Fools ~ Olé! by Victoria Twead

Two Old Fools on a Camel by Victoria Twead (thrice New York Times bestseller)

Two Old Fools in Spain Again by Victoria Twead

One Young Fool in Dorset (The Prequel) by Victoria Twead

One Young Fool in South Africa (The Prequel) by Joe and Victoria Twead

Midwife - A Calling by Peggy Vincent

Midwife - A Journey by Peggy Vincent

Into Africa with 3 Kids, 13 Crates and a Husband by Ann Patras

More Into Africa with 3 Kids, some Dogs and a Husband by Ann Patras

Fat Dogs and French Estates ~ Part I by Beth Haslam

Fat Dogs and French Estates ~ Part II by Beth Haslam

Fat Dogs and French Estates ~Part III by Beth Haslam

Simon Ships Out: How One Brave, Stray Cat Became a Worldwide Hero by Jacky Donovan

Smoky: How a Tiny Yorkshire Terrier Became a World War II American Army Hero, Therapy Dog and Hollywood Star by Jacky Donovan

Smart as a Whip: A Madcap Journey of Laughter, Love, Disasters and Triumphs by Jacky Donovan

Heartprints of Africa: A Family's Story of Faith, Love, Adventure, and Turmoil by Cinda Adams Brooks

How not to be a Soldier: My Antics in the British Army by Lorna McCann

Moment of Surrender: My Journey Through Prescription Drug Addiction to Hope and Renewal by Pj Laube

Serving is a Pilgrimage by John Basham

One of its Legs are Both the Same by Mike Cavanagh

Horizon Fever by A E Filby

Cane Confessions: The Lighter Side to Mobility by Amy L. Bovaird

FICTION
Parched by Andrew C Branham
A is for Abigail by Victoria Twead (Sixpenny Cross 1)
B is for Bella by Victoria Twead (Sixpenny Cross 2)

NON FICTION
How to Write a Bestselling Memoir by Victoria Twead

CHILDREN'S BOOKS
Seacat Simon: The Little Cat Who Became a Big Hero by Jacky Donovan
The Rise of Agnil by Susan Navas (Agnil's World 1)
Agnil and the Wizard's Orb by Susan Navas (Agnil's World 2)
Agnil and the Tree Spirits by Susan Navas (Agnil's World 3)
Agnil and the Centaur's Secret by Susan Navas (Agnil's World 4)
Morgan and the Martians by Victoria Twead

Chat with the author and other memoir authors and readers at
We Love Memoirs:
https://www.facebook.com/groups/welovememoirs/

19950031R00186

Printed in Poland
by Amazon Fulfillment
Poland Sp. z o.o., Wrocław